PHILIP ZIMBARDO is professor emeritus of psychology at Stanford University and has taught at Yale, New York University and Columbia. He has been president of the American Psychological Association (2002), president of the Western Psychological Association (twice) and chair of the Council of Scientific Society Presidents (CSSP); he is currently chair of the Western Psychological Foundation. He narrated the award-winning PBS series *Discovering Psychology* and has received numerous awards and honours for his work, including the 2015 Kurt Lewin Award for Distinguished Research on Social Issues. His many publications include *The Lucifer Effect*, *The Time Paradox* and the classic textbooks *Psychology and Life* and *Psychology: Core Concepts*. His current passion is the Heroic Imagination Project, exploring and encouraging the psychology of everyday heroes. See www.zimbardo.com for information.

NIKITA D. COULOMBE graduated from the University of Colorado with a Bachelor of Arts in fine art and psychology. After university, she worked with Philip Zimbardo as his personal and executive assistant for several years, collaborating with him on the early development of the Heroic Imagination Project, and co-writing *The Demise of Guys*. She created the surveys and conducted many of the interviews featured in this book. These conversations, in part, inspired her to co-found the sex education blog BetterSexEd.org. She is passionate about understanding human nature. Visit her website nikitacolumbe.com

Man (Dis)connected

How the digital age is changing
young men forever

Philip Zimbardo
and
Nikita D. Coulombe

RIDER

LONDON · SYDNEY · AUCKLAND · JOHANNESBURG

1 3 5 7 9 10 8 6 4 2

Rider, an imprint of Ebury Publishing,
20 Vauxhall Bridge Road,
London SW1V 2SA

Rider is part of the Penguin Random House group of companies
whose addresses can be found at global.penguinrandomhouse.com

Penguin
Random House
UK

First published in Great Britain by Rider in 2015. This edition
published in 2016

www.penguin.co.uk

A CIP catalogue record for this book is
available from the British Library

ISBN 9781846044854

Printed and bound in Great Britain by Clays Ltd, St Ives PLC.

To my grandchildren, Philip (Panda) and Victoria Leigh (Bunny)

– Philip Zimbardo

To my husband, Chris, and three brothers: thank you for your support

– Nikita D. Coulombe

Contents

Part III: Solutions

Preface:

Note to Readers

Many trends are born and magnified in the tech-heavy San Francisco Bay area, which is where we both lived when we started writing this book. There wasn't one event that inspired the book's creation; rather it resembled a light rain that slowly turned into a torrential downpour. While one of us had started clipping articles out of the newspaper about boys' poor academic performance and noticing the dwindling number of male graduate students in his class, the other had started to notice her male peers crowding around computers and video games at parties, rather than having conversations. We began to wonder why more young men didn't care about getting their driving licences, or moving out of their parents' homes, and why they preferred to masturbate to porn than be with a real woman. Down the rabbit hole we went.

Around the same time, I (Phil) was asked by the TED organization to give a five-minute talk on a topic of my choosing. I wanted to discuss what we were observing. At the end of my short but provocative TED Talk in 2011, I made clear that my primary goal at the conference was to raise awareness and even alarm people into action about an impending disaster. After the talk was greeted with much enthusiasm, Nikita, already familiar with the issues as my assistant, came on board and together we wrote a short TED eBook inspired by that talk in 2012 called *The Demise of Guys: Why Boys Are Struggling and What We Can Do About It*. *Demise* was a polemic meant to stimulate controversy and conversation around these topics and encourage others to do research on the different dimensions of these challenges.

Man (Dis)connected is an elaboration of *Demise* that delves much deeper into this important discussion about young men and the complex issues and challenges they face. *Man (Dis)connected* has also been restructured by symptoms, causes and solutions, making the issues easier for readers to understand and navigate.

We felt it was important to approach the topics from multiple angles. This book weaves together the perspectives of a young female, Nikita, who, as a millennial, has grown up in the thick of changing technologies, and an older male, Phil, who has an abundance of life experience, along with the views of many young men and women, making it a unique collaboration. In order to challenge our personal views, we developed a detailed online survey with a host of questions that touched on different aspects of *Demise*. We created a survey related to this topic and posted it alongside the TED Talk, asking questions such as, 'How would you change the school environment to engage young men?' and 'How can we empower men in safe, pro-social ways?'

Remarkably, in barely two months, 20,000 people took the short survey referred to throughout this book. About three-quarters (76 per cent) of the participants were men; more than half were between 18 and 34 years old. But people of all ages and backgrounds and both sexes shared their thoughts and feelings about these issues and their subplots. In addition, thousands of respondents were sufficiently motivated to go further by adding personal comments, from a sentence to a page long. We also conducted an additional smaller survey with 67 high school students from across the UK to get a better feel for their concerns (which we'll refer to as our 'student survey' throughout to distinguish it from the larger study). After reading all of the replies, we followed up with some of the respondents for personal interviews, and their opinions and experiences will be shared later on. You can find more highlights of the survey in Appendix I of this book. Additional supportive statistics can be found in the endnotes.

Our book is presented with the intention of finding solutions to the problems we highlight, and also inspiring men, and those who love them, to find their voice and create positive social change in their lives and the new world that surrounds them.

Introduction:
Just Drifting

Why do you sit there looking like an envelope without any
address on it?

    – Mark Twain, nineteenth-century American novelist

It's a new world out there for everybody, but amid the shifting
economic, social and technological climates, young men are
getting left behind. Unlike the women's movement, there has
been no cohesive men's movement to give a much-needed update
to men's roles in society. Instead there are a record number of
young men who are flaming out academically, wiping out socially
with girls, and failing sexually with women. You don't have to look
too far to see what we're talking about; everyone knows a young
man who is struggling. Maybe he's under-motivated in school, has
emotional disturbances, doesn't get along with others, has few real
friends or no female friends, or is in a gang. He may even be in
prison. Maybe he's your son or relative. Maybe he's you.

Asking what's wrong with them or why they aren't motivated
the same way young men used to be isn't the right question. Young
men are motivated, just not the way other people want them to
be. Western societies want men to be upstanding, proactive
citizens who take responsibility for themselves, who work with
others to improve their communities and nation as a whole. The

irony is that society is not giving the support, guidance, means or places for these young men even to be motivated or interested in aspiring to these goals. In fact, society – from politics to the media to the classroom to our very own families – is a major contributor to this demise because it is inhibiting young men's intellectual, creative and social abilities right from the start. And the irony is only compounded by the fact that men play such a powerful part in society, which means they are effectively denying their younger counterparts the opportunity to thrive.

Whenever we want to understand and explain complex human behaviour, it is essential to resort to a three-part analysis: first, what the *individual* brings into the behavioural context – his or her dispositional traits; next, what the *situation* brings out of the person who is behaving in a particular social or physical setting; and finally, how the underlying *system* of power creates, maintains or modifies those situations. That sort of analysis, which was featured in Phil's book *The Lucifer Effect*, helped to explain the abusive behaviour of guards in the Stanford Prison Experiment, and also the brutalizing behaviour of US guards in Iraq's Abu Ghraib prison.

In applying that reasoning to understanding why today's young men are failing academically, socially and sexually we first highlight aspects of their dispositions, such as shyness, impulsiveness and a lack of conscientiousness. Next, we take into account situational factors, such as widespread fatherlessness, the availability of exciting video games, and free access to online pornography. Finally, systemic factors enter in to add another layer of complexity, including the political and economic consequences of legislation that recognizes women's needs but not men's, environmentally generated physiological changes that decrease testosterone and increase oestrogen, media influences, the resulting lack of jobs from the recent economic downturn, and the widespread failure of school systems in many nations to create stimulating environments that challenge the curiosity of boys.

This three-pronged attack has resulted in many young men lacking purposeful direction and basic social skills. Today, many live off, and often with, their parents well into their twenties and even thirties, expanding their adolescence into an age once reserved for making a career and starting a family. Many would rather live at home under the security blanket of their parents than head out on their own into a world of uncertainty.

In the United States, only one in three millennials headed up their own household in 2013, and half of 18- to 24-year-olds who are not enrolled in university lived at home with their parents.[1] It is true that since the economic downturn, across the globe, young people have fewer opportunities for employment, to demonstrate their abilities and professional attributes. The diminished opportunities are a problem for men and women, but young women under 30 years old are surpassing their male counterparts academically and financially for the first time. Young men are also 25 per cent more likely than young women to be living at home with their parents.[2] Relating it to gender role expectations, since women are better able to take care of themselves financially than men their age, they are less likely to find a male partner of similar status, which consequently creates new challenges for men. Society has a hegemonic view of masculinity, and for men, there are no socially acceptable alternatives to being a warrior or a breadwinner. All the possible new roles threaten the traditional concept of masculinity and any male who embraces them gets less respect from his male peers and fewer social and romantic opportunities with the opposite sex.

A couple of the most common examples are the ways in which stay-at-home dads are seen as losers, and 'nice guys' don't get dates. One father, commenting in a *New York Times* article about the stigma of paternity leave, said he would almost prefer to tell future employers that he had been in prison than admit he had taken time off to be a stay-at-home dad.[3] Across the blogosphere countless posts are written by women claiming there is a lack of nice and respectful men to date, while there are about as many posts written by 'nice and respectful' men asking for dating advice because women have told them they come across as *too* nice, passive or desperate. This gridlock of men's roles makes it difficult for young men to want to change, and for young men and young women to relate to each other as equals.

Because of the new difficulties facing young men in this changing, uncertain world, many are choosing to isolate themselves in a safer place, a place where they have control over outcomes, where there is no fear of rejection and they are praised for their abilities. Video games and porn are this safer place for many young men. They become increasingly adept and skilled at gaming, refining their skills, and they can achieve high status and respect within the game. This is not something you see women doing, because they often don't find those kinds of competitions meaningful, nor do they receive respect for developing their gaming skills. Generally, chat rooms have low expectations of female gamers. Additionally, men may become more easily hooked on games. When Russian researcher Mikhail Budnikov broke down the propensity to become addicted to computer games into low, medium and high levels of risk, he found that women slightly outnumbered men in medium-level risk while men were more than three times likelier than women (26 per cent versus 8 per cent, respectively) to have a high level of risk.[4]

We have nothing against playing video games; they have many good features and benefits. However, when they are played to excess, especially in social isolation, they can hinder a young man's ability and interest in developing his face-to-face social skills. In addition, the variety and intensity of video game action makes other parts of life, like school, seem comparatively boring, and that creates a problem with their academic performance, which in turn might require medication to deal with attention deficit hyperactivity disorder (ADHD), which then leads to other problems down the road in a disastrous negative cycle, as we will see.

Porn adds to the confusion. Porn itself is not as great a problem for casual viewers, or for those with some personal sexual experience to juxtapose it against what they see. But for young men that have had no sex education or real-life sexual experiences, it can be very problematic. Many, we have learned, are developing their sense of sexuality around hard-core porn, not around real people. During our research, a lot of young men told us about how porn has given them a 'twisted' or unrealistic view of what sex and intimacy are supposed to be, and how they then found it difficult to get aroused by a real-life partner. For many of them, a real-life sexual encounter can be a foreign and anxiety-provoking experience because communication skills are required, their body needs to be engaged, and they must interact with another flesh-and-blood person who has their own sexual and romantic needs. Other young men told us about how other areas of their life are affected, such as concentration and emotional well-being, by watching excessive amounts of porn because they noticed massive positive shifts in their personal lives and outlooks once they stopped masturbating to it. Other experts noticed this same phenomenon. Physiology teacher Gary Wilson, creator of YourBrainOnPorn.com and author of *Your Brain On Porn: Internet Pornography and the Emerging Science of Addiction*, has collected hundreds of self-reports from online forums where young men have been experimenting with giving up online porn. They recount how social anxiety improved drastically – including increased confidence, eye contact, and comfort interacting with women. The young men also often reported more energy to get through their daily lives, concentration became easier, depression was alleviated, and erections and sexual responsiveness were stronger after voluntarily engaging in a 'no fap' challenge (no masturbating to online porn).[5]

Like video games, we emphasize the overuse of porn as a problem. Overuse is difficult to define however. Though there are more and more studies being done on porn's physiological and psychological effects on adults, most studies do not control for personality or other extraneous factors, and there are no similar studies done on children below 18 years old, only the occasional survey. It is also difficult to find a control group of young people that has not watched porn online. One University of Montreal study that initially sought to compare the behaviour of men who used porn versus those who didn't could not even find a single 20-something male participant who had not seen porn.[6]

Plus, most health and psychology communities do not officially recognize porn as something a person can get addicted to. In some circles it is thrown in with Internet addiction disorder (IAD), which has only recently been acknowledged as a legitimate problem. Despite this, many young people, mostly young men, are beginning to speak up about how porn is affecting their motivation, ability to focus, social and sexual abilities, and perceptions of the world,[7] and their testimonies should not be ignored. Their symptoms are real, and shouldn't be brushed aside as merely a phase or 'all in their heads'.

Again, we're not saying women don't play video games and watch porn, they do. But they don't do it nearly as much as men do. And the concept of watching porn is definitely a male thing. For their book, *A Billion Wicked Thoughts: What the World's Largest Experiment Reveals About Human Desire*, researchers Ogi Ogas and Sai Gaddam sifted through over 400 million Internet searches and found that 55 million of them (about 13 per cent) were for erotic content. Who is doing these searches? You guessed it: guys (mostly). Though more women seek out erotic stories than men, Ogas and Gaddam determined that men preferred viewing erotic images and movies more than women six times to one. Indeed, on popular pay sites like Brazzers and Bang Bros, the audience is about 75 per cent male, but when it comes to actually paying for porn, only 2 per cent of all the subscriptions are made on credit cards in women's names. Even CCBill, the popular billing service used by adult sites, flags female names as possible fraud.[8]

Why the differences? Certainly there are many female porn connoisseurs and men who enjoy erotic literature. Ogas and Gaddam explore this by delving into men's ability to be aroused by 'or' and women's need to be aroused by 'and'. They explain that men have single-cue arousability: nice breasts *or* a round butt *or* a hot MILF [mother-I'd-like-to-fuck] will do; whereas women need multiple cues: attractive *and* nice to children *and* self-confident. Though most women are actually physically turned on by just about any kind of porn, they only become psychologically aroused when the 'and' threshold is met. The woman herself must also feel safe *and* irresistible *and* physically healthy. The 'Power of Or' exists to help men exploit opportunities for sex. Women do not work the same way. In stressful environments, for example, a man's libido goes up while a woman's libido goes down. Male brains separate sex and romance, neural systems that are united in female brains, while female brains separate mental arousal from physical arousal, which are united in male brains.[9] Men and women just pick up on different erotic cues, have different ways of processing those cues, and behave differently in response to those cues.

If you look at why young men are gaming and using porn you'll find that those factors are both symptoms and causes of their overall decline. There is reciprocal causality where a person may watch a lot of porn or play video games to excess and develop social, sexual and motivational problems, and vice versa. This perpetuates a cycle of social isolation. We are concerned that the more provocative and lifelike video games and porn become, the more reality will mesh with virtual reality, and the more egocentric young men will become – living entirely in their own media-centric world.

Overuse of either outlet can result in real-life problems, but it's the combination of excessive video game playing and porn use that creates a deadly duo, leading to ever more withdrawal from usual activities, social alienation and inability to relate to anybody, especially girls and women. Porn and video games have addictive qualities, but it's not the same as other addictions. With alcohol, drugs or gambling you want more of the same, but with porn and video games you want the same ... but different; you need novelty in order to achieve the same high. The enemy is habituation to a regularly experienced stimulus. We call this *arousal addiction*; in order to get the same amount of stimulation, you need new material, seeing the same images over and over again becomes uninteresting after a short time. The key is novelty of visual experience. Both these industries are poised to give users that endless variety, so it's up to each individual to find what the best balance is for engaging in these digital outlets along with other activities in their lives – especially with constructive and creative ones, not just consumer ones.

Diversion is a double-edged sword. We have more information at our fingertips than ever before, but we can lose ourselves in alternative worlds. These alternative worlds are not even necessarily more efficient, as many of them purport themselves to be. They are just more distracting. For example, a busy New York restaurant was perplexed as to why the number of customers they served hadn't changed in the last ten years, despite adding more staff and reducing the number of items on the menu. When they watched a surveillance tape from 2004 and compared it with a tape from the same time in 2014, they found out it was not such a mystery. Between customers taking pictures of the food, pictures of themselves, asking waiters to take photos of themselves and their friends, and then sending their food back to be reheated, customers took twice as long to dine.[10]

One of our strengths and weaknesses as humans is our natural inclination to shift our attention from one thing to another. We do this so we can be aware of what's happening all around us in our environment. Having nearly everything available instantly at any time on the Internet exacerbates this impulse. 'Clouds' – virtual storage spaces accessed through the web – act as a second brain where we can put our memories and tasks, allowing us to focus on the present instead of the past or future. They are an incredible technology that goes wherever we go, provided we have the means to access them. The flip side is that this makes us more focused on ourselves and less conscious of the world around us and other people, because we don't have to remember as many details about them, nor do they seem as relevant to fulfilling our immediate needs.

In 2007 neuropsychologist Ian Robertson took a poll of 3,000 people and found that while almost everyone over 50 years old could remember a relative's birthday off the top of their head, less than half of people under 30 years old could do the same. The rest had to reach for their mobile phones to find out. Clive Thompson, a writer for *Wired*, says the reflexive gesture of reaching into one's pocket to find the answer epitomizes the problem. By offloading data onto computer memory, we're remembering fewer basic facts. Thinking about the future, Thompson wonders whether our growing dependence on machine memory will disrupt other ways of understanding the world, eventually causing people to be mentally impaired when they're not plugged in.[11] Whether he's right or wrong, the externalization of our thoughts and memories to technology and the Internet is only going to become more pronounced, especially as younger and younger children access them regularly.

Writing and reading enlivens people's experiences of life and nature through thoughtful consideration, reflection and imagination. Yet writing anything by hand is going extinct, and books and newspapers in their current form are becoming obsolete. Many newspapers and magazines have either gone out of business or now focus on the web as their main way to distribute content. It's great for the forests, which, paradoxically, don't get visited by many young people. Instead, the web has become our loyal companion and our preferred place to find, process and share information. It's clear that companies pay a price if they don't have a presence on the Internet, losing readership, sales and business from advertisers. Western schools too have 'lost' students' interest with static and under-stimulating lesson plans and outdated technologies.

In 2013 the American Academy of Pediatrics (AAP) published a report saying children now spend more time engrossed in media than they do in school: 'it is the leading activity for children and teenagers other than sleeping'. The imbalances were even greater if an adolescent had a television in their bedroom, which the majority of teens do. Though the AAP believes that media can be pro-social and teach children ethnic tolerance, and a variety of interpersonal skills, they recommend children have no more than one to two hours of screen time per day.[12] But as they pointed out, many youths are spending five to ten times that amount of time in front of a screen, and their brains are becoming accustomed to it.

Sherry Turkle, cultural analyst and founder of the MIT Initiative on Technology and Self, says that all the tweets, texts and 'sips' of online communication don't add up to one big gulp of conversation because we learn how to have productive inner dialogue through our conversations with others. Thus, limiting in-person communication with others can limit one's own ability for self-reflection and deep thinking. Turkle observed that people were becoming so used to functioning with fewer real conversations that many almost felt they could get through life without having *any* direct conversations with other people.[13]

Our ability to engage in the deep thinking required to understand printed material and engage in lengthy conversations is slipping away as the physical make-up of our brains adapts to short spurts of information. The more we are required to shift our attention from moment to moment, the less able we are to experience the more profound forms of emotions, including empathy and compassion. Underdeveloped emotions combined with a lack of engagement with others can stunt future social and romantic relationships, which require going beyond superficial considerations.

Over the past decade, this pattern has escalated into adulthood where many grown men remain like little boys, having difficulty relating to women as equals, friends, partners, intimates, or even as cherished wives. Some have come to prefer the company of men over that of women. Through our survey, we discovered that many young men aren't interested in maintaining long-term romantic relationships, marriage, fatherhood and being the head of their own family – which is, in part, due to the high percentage of young men who are growing up with physically or emotionally absent fathers. Others, who are either sheltered by their parents or are working on becoming 'the next big thing' or simply becoming financially stable, are reluctant to move out of their parents' houses.

Today many of the young men who do manage to find a partner feel entitled to do nothing to add substance to that relationship beyond just showing up. New emasculating terms such as 'man-child' and 'moodle' (man-poodle) have emerged to describe men who haven't matured emotionally or are otherwise incapable of taking care of themselves. Hollywood has caught on, too, to this awkward bunch of males, who appear to be comically hopeless. Recent films such as *Knocked Up*, *Failure to Launch*, the *Jackass* series, *The Hangover* series and *Hall Pass* present men as expendable commodities, living only for mindless fun, 'bromances', and intricate but never-realized plans to get laid. Their female co-stars, meanwhile, are often attractive, focused and mature, with success-oriented agendas guiding their lives. The sense of being entitled to have things without having to work hard for them – attributed to one's male nature – runs counter to the Protestant work ethic, as well as to the US football coach Vince Lombardi's victory creed: 'Winning isn't everything. It's the only thing.' Feeling entitled to have things done for you or to you, without having to work for it, just because you are a male, is a dead-end in any relationship with women, except those who are desperate to have any guy, even a loser, rather than being alone.

Through illuminating the symptoms and causes of these gloomy trends, we hope to shed more light on how we arrived at this state of affairs as well as provide context for the solutions we will present to you in Part III.

Part 1

Symptoms

Disenchantment with Education

New York Times columnist David Brooks wrote that the information age is liberating because it allows us to offload mundane mental chores to 'cognitive servants'. [1] At some point in the future Mr Brooks may be right. But for now, as liberating as this ability to externalize is in many ways, it is making the world – as spoken-word artist Gary Turk succinctly put it – full of 'smart phones and dumb people'. [2] The problem with this notion, explains Nicholas Carr, author of *The Shallows: What the Internet Is Doing to Our Brains*, is 'the proponents of the outsourcing idea confuse working memory with long-term memory. When a person fails to consolidate a fact, an idea, or an experience in long-term memory, he's not "freeing up" space in his brain for other functions.'[3] Carr argues that storing long-term memories does not bog down our mental powers, rather it increases our level of intelligence because it makes it easier to learn new ideas and skills in the future. In other words, we think we're smarter than we actually are.

As a culture, we are losing our ability for sustained attention. The more we 'outsource' the less we retain, and in turn, the less we know. While 76 per cent of Americans said they watched, read or heard the news on a daily basis, only 41 per cent said they went beyond the headlines.[4] So there's this potential illusion of knowing. It is the danger of having a superficial level of knowledge about anything, but believing you know everything. A retired English professor mentioned to us that towards the end of his career he noticed that although his students thought they understood something, when they were asked to describe the topic they stumbled over their words. One student even dropped the class after refusing to do revisions on his work. This example is a microcosm of the 'giving up before you try' attitude that has permeated the minds of young men en masse.

Some people think it's been a case of boys not doing well in school and giving their teachers hell since the beginning of recorded history. A recent large-scale meta analysis of over 300 studies that reflected the grades of more than 500,000 boys and nearly 600,000 girls revealed that, for many decades, girls all over the world have been making higher grades than boys in all subjects.[5] The authors suggested that this data undermines the 'boy crisis', but we have to disagree. Good grades have become crucial to earning a living wage – and it is all the more reason for society to show boys the importance of doing well in school. Boys also used to have far more motivation to compete and succeed in every other aspect of life – moving out of their parents' house, getting a girlfriend or wife, setting long-term goals and embarking on a career – which they are sorely lacking now.

For the first time in US history, boys are having less education than their fathers.[6] Moreover, academics are now more of a girl's pursuit. Girls are outperforming boys at every level, from primary school through university. In the US, by 13 or 14 years old, not even a quarter of boys are proficient in either writing or reading, versus 41 per cent of girls who are proficient in writing and 34 per cent who are proficient in reading.[7] Young men's SAT (a standardized test that measures scholastic aptitude) scores, meanwhile, in 2011 were the worst they've been in forty years.[8] Boys also account for 70 per cent of all the lowest grades given out at school.[9] Similar achievement gaps between the genders have been documented worldwide. The Organisation for Economic Co-operation and Development (OECD) found that boys are more likely to repeat school years than girls, had poorer grades and got lower pass rates on school leaving examinations. In some countries, such as Sweden, Italy, New Zealand and Poland, the girls scored so much higher than the boys on reading in the PISA Assessment (a global measure of skills and knowledge) that they were essentially a year to a year and a half ahead in school.[10] Internationally, in just over half of the countries that participated in the 2009 PISA Assessment, boys outperformed girls only in mathematics, but the mathematics gap was only one-third the size of the reading gap.[11] In the UK, girls and boys performed more equally on all PISA Assessment subjects.[12]

In her book, *The War Against Boys: How Misguided Policies Are Harming Our Young Men*, Christina Hoff Sommers, a resident scholar at the American Enterprise Institute for Public Policy Research, described even more imbalances. She said that girls not only outnumber boys in student government, honour societies and after school clubs, they also do more homework, read more books and outperform boys in the arts and in musical abilities. Meanwhile, more boys are suspended from school and more are held back from advancing to the next grade level. Simply put, girls are more 'engaged' academically.[13]

In a 2002 National Center for Education Statistics (NCES) survey asking students how often they came to school unprepared – without books, paper and pencil, or their homework – three out of ten boys answered 'usually' or 'often' compared with one out of five girls. Predictably, students with the lowest test scores who came to school unprepared outnumbered the unprepared high-scoring students more than two to one.[14]

Rates of ADHD diagnoses increased 5 per cent every year between 2003 and 2011; boys are between two to three times more likely than girls to have ever been diagnosed in their lifetime,[15] and therefore are more likely to be prescribed stimulants, such as Ritalin, even in primary school.

On top of this, boys are far more likely to drop out of school.[16] NCES notes the ripple effects of this trend:

dropouts ages 25 and older reported being in worse health than adults who are not dropouts, regardless of income...Dropouts also make up disproportionately higher percentages of the nation's prison and death row inmates. Comparing those who drop out of high school with those who complete high school, the average high school dropout is associated with costs to the economy of approximately $240,000 over his or her lifetime in terms of lower tax contributions...higher rates of criminal activity, and higher reliance on welfare.[17]

The National Longitudinal Survey of Youth, a study that began in 1997 and ended in 2012, found that by 27 years old a third of women had received bachelor's degrees compared with one out of four men.[18] By 2021, in the US it is estimated that women will get 58 per cent of bachelor's degrees, 62 per cent of master's degrees and 54 per cent of PhDs.[19] Abroad there are similar trends. In Canada and Australia, 60 per cent of university graduates are women.[20] Fewer than three boys apply to university in England for every four girls who do, and in Wales and Scotland, 40 per cent more girls apply than boys,[21] a gap that widens among those from disadvantaged backgrounds.[22]

Two-thirds of students in special education remedial programmes are boys. It's not a question of IQ – young men are just not putting in the effort, and it translates into a lack of career options. These gaps are much greater for males from minority backgrounds: only 34 per cent of college bachelor's degrees awarded to black students go to black men, and 39 per cent of bachelor's degrees awarded to Hispanic students go to Hispanic men.[23]

It is obvious to us that it is time for a loud wake-up call, to be sounded in every nation around the world where young males are failing to perform adequately in academic domains. The consequences for them, their families, their communities and even national destinies could be catastrophic unless dramatic corrective actions are taken soon.

2

Men Opting Out of the Workforce

Where has the Protestant work ethic gone these days in the minds of young men? Between 2000 and 2010 the percentage of American teens participating in the workforce fell 42 per cent and the number of employed 20- to 24-year-olds dropped 17 per cent.[1] In the UK, the unemployment rate for 15- to 24-year-olds is 21 per cent, nearly 5 percentage points higher than the Organisation for Economic Co-operation and Development (OECD) average.[2] Male unemployment between the ages of 25 and 34 in the US is more than double what it was in 1970. Other countries, such as Italy, France, Spain, Sweden and Japan, have all seen more than a five-fold increase in young men not employed. The OECD records show that the global average unemployment rate for men in their late 20s and early 30s has jumped from 2 per cent in 1970 to 9 per cent in 2012.[3] That is an enormous increase, and means millions of young men are not working.

The growing interconnectedness of the world's economies means that modern boom and bust cycles have further and deeper reaching consequences for all nations. The global recession of 2009 was the worst recession since the Second World War, causing unemployment to skyrocket. On a personal level, job losses hit men harder than women. In the US, the male unemployment rate doubled between January 2008 and June 2009. Manufacturing industries that de-emphasize manual and technical skills in favour of technological advances – such as the car industry – mean that many developed countries no longer make things, creating an atmosphere of uncertainty for many men. Even having a higher degree is no guarantee of employment.

Health care – a major female-dominated industry – was relatively insulated, while industries such as manufacturing and construction, where most employees are men, accounted for about half of the 6.5 million US jobs lost since the most recent recession started.[4] At the same time, personal care and home health aides are projected to be the fastest-growing occupations, and women are predicted to fill a large portion of these new jobs.[5] Yet this new landscape of opportunities offers rather a grim harvest for bright young men, compared to what would have been available to them only a generation or two ago.

But there's more – an entitlement curse. Although the adverse state of the Western economy has contributed to fewer men in the workforce, a highly educated female colleague alerted us to a new phenomenon. Some males now feel a sense of total entitlement simply because they exist as males. And they do not have to do anything to earn that special privilege. Many now seek long-term shelter either with Mum and Dad or within their marriages or relationships with a live-in partner. A surprising amount of men don't seem to want to work at jobs that will bring in money or even help out with household chores that will keep their living space tidy. These guys are content just to hang around doing 'their thing' but perform nothing that traditionally resembles 'work'.

Some of these men have even reframed dependency to make it look like an accomplishment and not a social failure, and they feel it is their right to absent themselves from having to make money or do drudgery around the house. In a sense, they are like old-fashioned gigolos, attractive men who were taken care of by older women in return for being charming dates or sexual adventurers, except this new breed of males want it all while giving little in return. Consider a couple of the vignettes that our colleague shared with us:

A physical therapist I know married a guy who basically quit his job once they got married. She did all the work and all the housework. She would come home after a long day at work, schlepping her heavy equipment through the rain, and he would not even come out to help her carry anything. When she got in, he would ask her what was for dinner, and she would have to go back out to the store and come home and cook. He sat on his ass all day and did nothing. Nice guy, handsome, but did not work or want to work. She divorced him after four years of marriage.

Another academic I know gets together with this guy who quits his job to go back to graduate school. He incurs a $100,000 debt and is not able to get a steady job. She supports him although he is not willing to get married nor willing to help with any house chores.

Why do women stick it out with such guys? Even their mothers might call them losers. As we'll explore in more depth in Chapter 20, the depressing alternative for these well-educated women appears to be no man at all, so they stick with their bad decision until it gets so unbearable that they decide to dump the deadbeat.

Aside from not understanding that all relationships involve a negotiation of rights and obligations, what this entitlement suggests to us is the abandonment of a sense of having to work for anything. The stigma of unemployment still exists, but isn't even close to what it used to be. These men don't make the connection between responsibility, paying dues and success. Some of them don't care. Others are acting as if one gets what one wants just by being at the head of the queue when the doors open or the party starts.

A young man told us this in his survey comments:

> It is my belief that entitlement can help shape men. What they
> are entitled to is responsibility. The achievement is fulfilment
> of responsibility that will let the world trust them to shape the
> future. Yes, men can be strong if they care about others.
> Responsibilities – such as being gentle and a gentleman,
> manners to others to show courtesy, to take on duties to
> reassure others, being selfless – will help a young man find
> himself . . . The key to being a man lies in responsibility. The
> responsibility to care about oneself and not ruin or abuse
> oneself, to care about others and not ruin or abuse them.

We could not agree more. But it seems to us that this new sense of
male entitlement is different from what it may have been in the past.
It is more generalized, spreading to more settings and activities that
tend to undermine any meaningful social or romantic relationships.
These men seem to be emulating successful media celebrities and
personalities such as David Beckham, the swimmer Michael Phelps,
and entrepreneur Mark Zuckerberg, who appear to have it all; but
they only see and admire the desirable outcomes and products.
What is missing from the analysis is any appreciation of what goes
into any kind of success: a lot of hard work, trial and tribulation,
practice and failures that are part of the process of trying to attain
a goal. The good things in life usually take a commitment to success,
to delaying gratification, to putting work before play, and to
understanding the importance and vitality of the social contract –
not expecting more than what is being put in.

3

Excessive Maleness:
Social Intensity Syndrome (SIS)

S hyness plays a key role in the complex causal cycle between the self-imposed social isolation of many young men and their excessive time spent on watching porn and gaming. Traditionally shyness implied a fear of rejection by being socially unacceptable to certain social groups or individuals, such as authorities, or those a person wished to impress, such as members of the opposite sex. In the 1970s and 1980s when I (Phil) pioneered the scientific study of shyness among adolescents and adults, about 40 per cent of the US population rated themselves as currently shy people, or dispositionally shy. An equal percentage reported that they had been shy in the past but had overcome its negative impact. Fifteen per cent more said that their shyness was situationally induced, such as on blind dates or having to perform in public. So only 5 per cent or so were true-blue never-ever shy.

Over the past thirty years, however, that percentage has steadily increased. In a 2007 survey of students by the Shyness Research Institute at Indiana University Southeast, 84 per cent of participants said they were shy at some point in their life, 43 per cent said they were presently shy, and just 1 per cent said they had never been shy. Two-thirds of those who were currently shy said that their shyness was a personal problem.[1] The deep fear of social rejection has risen in part as a result of technology, which minimizes direct, face-to-face social interaction such as conversing with other people, seeking information, shopping, going to the bank, getting library books, and much more. The net does it all for us faster, more accurately and without any need for making social connections. In one sense, online communication enables the very shy to make easier contact with others in the realm of asynchronistic communication. However, we believe it then makes it more difficult to make real-life connections. As one of the researchers, Bernardo Carducci, noted:

> ... changes in technology are affecting the nature of interpersonal communication so that we are experiencing more structured electronic interactions and less spontaneous social interactions where there is the opportunity to develop and practise interpersonal skills, such as negotiating, making conversation, reading body language and facial cues, which are important for making new friends and fostering more intimate relationships.[2]

The new breed of shyness then arises not from wanting to reach out but fearing social rejection from making a poor impression, but, rather, *not* wanting to make social contact because of not knowing how to, and then further distancing themselves from others the more out of practice a person gets. Thus, this new shyness gets continually reinforced, internalized, and, worse, not even recognized when it leads to the absence of contact with most other people. Thus, many shy people behave awkwardly or inappropriately with peers, superiors, in unfamiliar situations, and in one-on-one opposite-sex interactions.

Aside from the steady increase in shyness, what is different today is that shyness among young men is less about a fear of rejection and more about fundamental social awkwardness – not knowing what to do, when, where or how. Most young men used to know how to dance. Now they don't even know where to look for common ground, and they wander about the social landscape like tourists in a foreign land unable and unwilling to ask for directions. Many of them don't know the language of face contact, the non-verbal and verbal set of rules that enable a person to comfortably talk with and listen to somebody else and get them to respond back in kind. This lack of social skills surfaces most especially when around desirable females.

The absence of such critical social skills, essential to navigating intimate social situations, encourages a strategy of retreat, going fail-safe. Girls and women equal likely failure; safe equals the retreat into online and fantasy worlds that, with regular practice, become ever more familiar, predictable and, in the case of video games, more controllable. A twisted sort of shyness has evolved as the digital self becomes less and less like the real-life operator. The ego is the playmaker; the character is the observer, as the external world shrinks to the size of a young man's bedroom. In this way, we can say that shyness is both a cause of the problem as well as one of the consequences of excessive gaming and porn use. As one young man from our survey commented:

> I play video games and watch pornography on a regular basis ... but I've always been average looking and I've hated the tiresome aspect of having to make the effort to appease the opposite sex. It's expensive, confusing and rarely successful. I feel like the personal relationships with any girl/woman I've known have meant nothing to me and can be easily substituted with male company whilst pornography fills the rest.

Bros before hoes: Social Intensity Syndrome (SIS)

In the film *My Fair Lady* (based on George Bernard Shaw's play *Pygmalion*), lead actor Rex Harrison has just achieved his successful transformation of a poor flower-shop girl into a stunningly beautiful and sophisticated woman, played by Audrey Hepburn. When she becomes distressed that he fails to show her any affection or even recognition for all she has done to modify her entire being so dramatically, and hints that she would perhaps like a bit of romance as well, he rudely dismisses her. Harrison then sings a song of lament to his friend, Pickering: 'Why can't a woman be more like a man?'[3]

In doing so, he reveals what we believe is actually a common set of attitudes and values held by a good portion of men: a deep preference for male company and bonding over association or partnership with women.

A more modern-day example of this attitude can be seen in the 1999 romantic comedy, *She's All That*, starring Freddie Prinze, Jr, and Rachael Leigh Cook. After Zack's (Prinze) popular but self-absorbed girlfriend dumps him for a reality television star, Zack finds comfort in convincing himself she can be replaced by any girl in his high school. One of his jock friends disagrees and makes him a bet that he can't turn the unpopular art nerd girl Laney (Cook) into Prom Queen within six weeks. After repeated attempts to charm her and convince her that his efforts are not part of some 'dork outreach programme', Laney steps into Zack's world and allows his sister to give her a makeover, revealing her hidden beauty. Only after her outward transformation does he become attracted to her and develop genuine feelings.

Along with co-researchers Sarah Brunskill and Anthony Ferreras, Phil has labelled this phenomenon Social Intensity Syndrome (SIS). Similar to 'laddism', the key dimensions of this 'excessive maleness' are outlined as follows: having a strong preference for social settings that involve the ubiquitous presence of other men. The attraction to this social setting is greater the more intense the nature of the relationship, the more exclusive it is towards tolerating 'outsiders' or those who have not qualified for that group membership, and the more embedded each man is perceived to be within that group. Examples of such social groups include the military – especially during boot camp and deployment – gangs, physical contact sports (i.e. American football, rugby), 'gym rats' and fraternities. Men experience a positive arousal – such as cortisol, adrenergic system activation or an increase in testosterone – when they feel they are part of such all-male social groups. Men gradually adapt to that level of social intensity as the preferred form of social contact.

On the positive side, many of these organizations teach men how to work together with other men, which is crucial to the fabric of society. Yet over time, that degree of social intensity becomes a set point of desirable functioning, operating at an unconscious level of awareness. Men experience a sense of social isolation and then boredom immediately following their separation from such socially intense male group settings, such as having to participate in groups of men and women or family settings. Men may experience withdrawal symptoms when removed from such socially intense group settings; symptoms are greater the longer and more intense the prior duration of their all-male group participation has been.

This phenomenon peaks on days with important sport matches, such as the World Cup Final or Super Bowl Sunday, when many males would rather be in a bar with strangers, watching a totally overdressed Tom Brady, the New England Patriots' star quarterback, than with a totally naked Jennifer Lopez in their bedroom. The popular porn site PornHub recently released a report confirming this occurrence. During Superbowl XLVIII, traffic to their site dramatically decreased while the event was taking place, especially in Denver and Seattle, the two cities whose teams were competing for the championship. After the game there was a noticeable spike in traffic across the US and Canada, and a smaller spike in worldwide traffic.[4]

This hidden desire to be an alpha male or part of the 'guy thing' is double-edged, however. For young, straight men, it must not become too intimate and personal for fear of seeming feminine or gay, or throwing off the cohesion or morale of the group. So that enforces a rule of superficiality and of physical distance with other guys, except for high-fives, chest bumping and slaps across the back. As one infantryman told us:

> The emotional distance between guys is one that resides in the context of warrior societies or the fighting classes. Men will communicate to other men that they care but that there is a fine line that emotions cannot cross. This is anchored in several concepts: among peers, men are their own individual being, and are not to be influenced by anything but their own logic. Men don't go to war because someone convinced them to; they go to war because they know it is right. Men's friendships among peers in competitive atmospheres are based on what abilities they bring to the group; remembering that their life is devalued but their skillsets are not. Showing concern means that you question their ability in that competition and have compromised the dynamic of the group, or fear for their performance level, which pits them against the team as a whole. Lastly, it strikes too similarly to the concerns of a woman's nagging.

It is possible to generate some interesting predictions of potential behavioural consequences for men with high SIS levels. They might respond to the negative effect of disengagement from such groups by partaking in arousing activities, such as high-risk hobbies or behaviours, arguments and fights, drinking to excess, developing strange or rigid eating habits, gambling and speeding. They may also develop unfavourable comparisons between men and women. They will spend more time in symbolic male groups, such as watching sports in a sports bar or even engaging in fantasy football or baseball competitions, and are unable to find common ground with women. They do not have many, if any, female friends.

Texting is often an exclusive form of communication of this crowd. Not only is it convenient, it allows them to passively communicate on their terms. New apps like BroApp – which sends pre-scheduled texts to a girlfriend or partner – take the trend to a whole new level. The creators offered this explanation on their site: 'BroApp is a tool to help Bros out. We know that people are busy and sometimes forget to send enough love to their partners. We invented BroApp so that even if you forget to manually write a message, your love is still communicated. BroApp provides seamless relationship outsourcing.'[5] If Easy Cheese – or cheese in a can – were an app, it might look like BroApp – it vaguely resembles the real thing, but there's something a bit … off. Actually, a lot off. Why have a relationship at all if you can't even bring yourself to text a simple 'I love you' or 'Thinking of you'?

For some, there is even memory distortion with greater recall of positive aspects and poorer recall of negative aspects of their time in those previous male-bonding groups.

Members of the military sometimes deal with the arousal deficit by seeking redeployment or hanging around settings where there are likely to be other men who also belong to such high-intensity groupings, such as soldiers hanging around VA hospital lobbies. Non-military men who are sports fans may become team 'fanatics'.

Poor bonding with family and spouse also characterize SIS. These men are more likely to abuse their spouse, especially when drinking, and more likely to become divorced or separated from partners with whom they had a positive relationship prior to deployment or team membership. They are also likely to develop generally negative attitudes towards women as 'the other' who do not understand them, and prefer porn, sex with prostitutes, or erotic massage parlours to consensual sexual relationships with equal-status female partners.

Paradoxically, then, males can get generalized arousal merely from being in the presence of other men in group settings yet they must avoid showing or even experiencing feelings of intimacy in those associations. Then, when they are presented with the prospect of intimacy with a woman, the opposite response occurs: they may fail to get sexually aroused or they develop social anxiety.

Social intensity syndrome is prevalent worldwide. In Japan, young men are increasingly apathetic to sex. Even married couples have less sex. The Japan Family Planning Association recently reported that the number of young men aged 16 to 19 who have no interest in sex is now more than one in three, double the estimate from 2008, and four out of ten marriages have been sexless for a month or more.[6] The phenomenon is so common that these men have been given a name: *soshoku danshi*, or 'herbivorous men', in contrast to carnivorous men, who are still interested in sex.

One particularly poignant response to our survey came from a young male student at Bard College in New York:

> I must admit that I haven't had one real physical relationship in my entire life. I'm a complete extrovert who has a core group of [male] friends along with a whole bunch of other friends [including some women] but has always been rather unsure when it comes to women. I feel like I can't really interact with them, and end up treating them like men, which makes them my friend but not someone who is a romantic interest...I would definitely rather hang out with my friends and enjoy the company of a small group of guy friends where we hang out and relax.

Another young man commented on our forum after reading *The Demise of Guys*:

> It hits close to me because I grew up without a father, spent a lot of time playing video games as a teenager, and was addicted to porn. When I turned 18, I joined the Army and became an infantryman. The infantry is a very tight-knit brotherhood. I deployed to Afghanistan in 09–[2010]. Now that I'm out of the

Army, I find myself missing the camaraderie a lot, even hoping for another war to break out so I have an excuse to re-enlist. I have trouble in school and find it hard to focus. I'm socially awkward, shy, and not very successful with women. I don't live at home anymore though, I have two female roommates but I still feel isolated, lonely, and depressed even to the point of suicide sometimes. I am 22 years old and trying to change my life. I see the effects that these things have had on my life . . . I feel as men, our environment is changing and we're in this transition phase but the old rules still apply. Therefore those of us stuck in the middle are just screwed over.

We wish his story wasn't as common as it is, but many of the veterans that Phil and Sarah Brunskill interviewed shared similar experiences. You can learn more about the scale that measures the different aspects of SIS in Appendix I.

4

Excessive Gaming:
Mastering the Universe from
Your Bedroom

I n the late 1960s, if you wanted to connect a computer up to a video screen, you could only do it at a handful of places, and you had to be one of only a few people that had access to this sort of technology. Things have changed quite a bit in the last fifty years. There is an assumption that the more time we devote to the Internet the less time we spend watching television, but statistics reveal the opposite. Europeans are spending just as much time in front of a TV as they ever have, and Americans now spend sixty hours a week across an average of four digital devices, the majority owning high-definition televisions (HDTVs), computers, tablets and smartphones. Complementing these devices are more choices for how and when people access content.[1] In addition, Jane McGonigal, director of game research and development at the Institute for the Future in Palo Alto, California, estimates people spend a collective 3 billion hours playing video games each *week*! She predicts that the average young person will spend 10,000 hours gaming by the time they reach age 21.[2] To put this figure in context, it takes the average university student half that time – 4,800 hours – to earn a bachelor's degree.[3]

Some gamers are females, there is no doubt; and video game companies are very aware of this. (*FarmVille*, *Moshi Monsters*, *World of Warcraft* or *Mario Kart*, anyone?) Still, young women don't play nearly to the extent that young men do – only 5 hours per week compared to guys' 13.[4] For many young men, 13 hours *a day* can also become habitual, as we will see.

One month after its release in 2010, *Call of Duty: Black Ops* had been collectively played for 68,000 years.[5] In 2012 *Call of Duty: Black Ops 2* made $500 million in sales in its first twenty-four hours, and in 2013 more than 8,300 stores in North America had midnight openings to help *Grand Theft Auto 5* – one of the most controversial game series of all time – rack up $800 million in its first day.[6] *Grand Theft Auto 5* surpassed the $1 billion mark after only three days, faster than any movie in history, including any of the *Harry Potter* films and *Avatar*.[7] In 2013 the worldwide revenue of the gaming industry, including mobile games played on smartphones and tablets, was $66 billion, a $3 billion increase from 2012.[8] Compare these numbers with the US Department of Education's annual discretionary appropriations budget of $68.8 billion in 2013[9] or the size of the entire US publishing industry, which in 2010 had net sales revenue of $27.9 billion.[10] *Game Informer*, a monthly magazine featuring news, strategies and reviews on video games, was ranked the third-largest magazine in the United States by circulation in 2013. The only two above it were *AARP The Magazine* and *AARP Bulletin*,[11] which are usually free for older and retired Americans. In the UK, gaming sites such as Twitch.tv, IGN, Steampowered and Battle.net all had more web traffic than the BBC.[12]

When 15-year-old Steve Juraszek of Illinois set the world record for the arcade game *Defender* in 1981, he became an instant celebrity and had his picture taken for *Time* magazine. He played for sixteen hours straight.[13] Today games not only test a player's skill, they test the player's bodily limits for intense duration. There are gamers like George Yao, who play online games like *Clash of Clans* for forty-eight hours straight. Yao even took iPads covered in plastic into the shower in order to continue playing and stay ranked number one.[14] There are many other (mostly young) people who log thousands of hours in a single game just for the chance to pursue a 'gaming career' and compete fiercely in televised tournaments for million dollar-plus prizes.[15] Marathon gaming has become so common there is even a term for the hazy, sleep-deprived state a gamer must endure on their third night of uninterrupted play: Valley of Death.[16] For the ordinary gamer a sixteen-hour stretch would be just another typical weekend, and few parents would even bat an eyelid. Two-thirds of children and teens report that their parents have 'no rules' regarding their media consumption, and the majority continue to play games and use other electronic devices after the lights are out.[17] In the UK, six in ten parents surveyed say their child is more knowledgeable about the Internet than them.[18]

According to the Sleep Center at the University of California in Los Angeles (UCLA), teens need an average of nine hours of sleep each night to be alert and well rested the next day.[19] Most teens don't get even close to this much. In the National Sleep Foundation's 2014 Sleep in America Poll, parents estimated their 13- and 14-year-olds got 7.7 hours of sleep each night while their 15- to 17-year-olds got just 7.1 hours;[20] these estimates are probably high considering that kids themselves report staying up past their bedtime. Interestingly, because they share similar symptoms, a lack of sleep is often confused with having ADHD, and some teens are thought to have ADHD when instead they actually have a sleep problem.[21] Kids who have at least one electronic device in their room also get one less hour of sleep per night than kids who don't.[22] The number of 5- to 15-year-olds in the UK who own a tablet computer has doubled since 2013.[23]

Colin Kinney, a teacher from Ireland, observed some students would spend nights gaming and come to class with such limited attention spans that 'they may as well not be there'. He added, 'I have spoken to a number of nursery teachers who have concerns over the increasing numbers of pupils who can swipe a screen but have little to no manipulative skills to play with building blocks or the like, or the pupils who cannot socialize with other pupils but whose parents talk proudly of their ability to use a tablet or smartphone.'[24] We are talking about *nursery*-age children – 3 to 5 years old!

These problems continue beyond adolescence. A study published in the *Journal of Leisure Research* found that in 349 marriages where just one partner was a gamer, it was the husband 84 per cent of the time. In the other couples where both spouses played but one person played more than the other, it was the husband 73 per cent of the time.[25] In 1982 Duke University researchers started following several men who had become obsessed with gaming just before their respective marriages. After watching the men's game time quadruple – one man taking his fiancée on dates to watch him play, and another putting off leaving for his honeymoon to play just a few more games – the researchers made the assertion that marriage was both the cause and cure for the 'Space Invaders Obsession'. They wrote that 'the disintegration of invading aliens who were trying to overrun "home base" took on symbolic significance'.[26] Today, there are support groups online for 'gamer widows', where the partners of gamers can share their frustrations. Massive multiplayer online games (MMOs) are especially absorbing because a player can become anybody in the virtual world, attaining looks, acceptance, wealth and status that are elusive in real life for most people without hard work, education and social connections. 'They aren't just better looking,' said one gamer widow, 'they are "better" people.'[27]

Even if games were originally designed to inspire players and make a better reality, they are now being used to replace reality, and many young men are losing themselves in increasingly sophisticated virtual worlds that are totally enchanting. As one decade-long gamer from our survey said, 'I can't emphasize enough the predictability and control that a virtual world offers. In a world growing ever more complex, the simplicity of the virtual life is a very welcome distraction.'

5

Becoming Obese

Today, roughly 70 per cent of adult males in the US are overweight,[1] and a third are obese.[2] Though some countries are less flabby than others, obesity is a worldwide problem. As of 2008, roughly a quarter of Australian, British, Canadian, German, Polish and Spanish men were obese.[3] 'It's going up everywhere,' says Christopher Murray, director of the Institute for Health Metrics and Evaluation at the University of Washington-Seattle. He said he used to be optimistic that there would be some success stories that would serve as models, but found that there was not a single country that has seen a decrease in obesity in the past three decades.[4] So we are dealing with a worldwide epidemic.

Americans, perhaps the most vocal in their anti-obesity crusade, sabotage their own efforts by taking two steps back for every step forward. Ridiculous portion sizes, 'all you can eat' buffets at family restaurants, fast food drive-thrus on nearly every busy street corner, the sedentary nature of many jobs, changing modes of transportation and increasing urbanization combine to create a 'fat ass' nation. In addition, American schools are currently selling 400 billion calories of junk food every year – the equivalent of nearly 2 billion chocolate bars.[5] Twenty-one per cent of elementary schools, 62 per cent of middle schools and 86 per cent of high schools have vending machines, while just 20 per cent of middle schools and 9 per cent of high schools offer healthy snacks only.[6]

The government in the UK has done a better job of cracking down on unhealthy foods and beverages sold at schools, but that doesn't stop fast food chains from opening drive-thrus right outside school property.[7] Many UK schools have also sold off their playing fields where children used to be free to roam and exercise.[8]

While adult obesity rates have doubled over the past thirty years, adolescent obesity rates have tripled.[9] It is also evident from much research that obesity is a killer – shortening lifespans by triggering a range of autoimmune diseases, like 'adult' type II diabetes. Young children have a one-in-three chance of developing type II diabetes – with a 50 per cent chance if they are Hispanic – as well as a greater likelihood of developing heart disease, hypertension and certain kinds of cancer.[10] The Centres for Disease Control and Prevention (CDC) noted that the trend was especially pronounced in boys, where the heaviest are getting progressively heavier.[11]

In America, this is creating a national emergency. The *Army Times* reported that military-age youth are 'increasingly unfit to serve – mostly because they're in such lousy shape'.[12] Recent statistics from the Pentagon showed that over a third of Americans aged 17 to 24 would not qualify for military service just because of medical or physical problems. Curt Gilroy, the Pentagon's director of accessions, said that obesity was the main culprit: 'There's no question about it . . . Kids are just not able to do push-ups . . . they can't do pull-ups. And they can't run.'[13]

Obesity is just one side of it, however. When men gain weight – the bad kind, as opposed to bulking up muscles – a metabolic change happens that drops the hormone levels in the body, making them surprisingly less effective socially and sexually. The more dominant a man becomes, the more testosterone he produces, which in turn increases his libido.[14] Researchers from the University of Buffalo recently determined that obese men have lower levels of testosterone, and when that male hormone drops, one of the biggest victims, aside from male fertility, is his bedroom performance. The study shows that 40 per cent of obese men have abnormally low levels of testosterone.[15] Obesity can also trigger type II diabetes, one effect of which is restricted blood flow to veins, especially the small blood vessels in the penis and testicles. That surge of blood is essential for male erections. A curious corollary of this combination of obesity and testosterone decline in males is the unhealthy rise in their bodies of the female hormone oestrogen, which is naturally present in small amounts, but excessive levels of which can in turn lead to erectile dysfunction and infertility.[16] Talk about a double punch below the belt!

Over the last few decades, physical activity among youth has decreased while screen time has increased. Sedentary behaviour fills time that children could be spending on physical activities or even sleeping, contributing to excessive snacking and eating meals in front of the television or computer screen. Young men and boys who spend their evenings gaming instead of getting a good night's rest are putting themselves at a much greater risk of becoming overweight.[17]

Childhood habits tend to stick with people for the rest of their lives, and an obese child often becomes an obese adult, the likelihood becoming stronger the older the child.[18] Thus kids who watch television and play video games instead of being active are setting themselves up for a sedentary future, noted a recent Harvard University Medical School Special Health Report.[19] Not surprisingly, several studies have found a positive association between screen time and prevalence of excess weight in children.[20] In sum, a sedentary lifestyle is not only unhealthy for males; it can lead to other wide-ranging problems and shorten their lifespans.

6

Excessive Porn Use:

Orgasms on Demand

I have the same problem third-world refugees who relocate to suburban America report after visiting their first supermarket. They are paralyzed by the overwhelming options, unable to choose from so many nearly identical but clearly different brands of pasta sauce. They are stuck in a permanent, unpleasant state of browsing, fearful of making the wrong choice. Now imagine how much more difficult that decision would be if pasta sauce gave you an erection.

– Joel Stein, contributor for *Playboy*[1]

Parents used to worry about their teenagers having sex. Now they have started to worry that they are not.

– Helen Rumbelow, *The Times*[2]

Back in 1996, Peter Morley-Souter drew a comic scene that depicted his initial shock at seeing a couple of his favourite cartoon characters, Calvin and Hobbes, having sex with Calvin's mother. He figured if there was porn of Calvin and Hobbes, everything could be made into porn, which resulted in the caption 'Internet Rule #34: there is porn of it'.[3] It is safe to say online porn is the marketplace of virtual pleasures. Although the top 5 per cent of descriptive tags are associated with 90 per cent of the videos, the popular site XNXX has compiled over 70,000 different tags to help users find the specific and less common content they're looking for.[4] The notion that somewhere on the web anything you can imagine exists as porn has become difficult to disprove as the Internet becomes more saturated with X-rated images and videos. In fact, we are sure that there are porn categories that are beyond what most people could ever have imagined existed.

In 1997, just six years after the World Wide Web went live, there were approximately 900 online porn sites.[5] Later, in 2005, approximately 13,500 full-length commercially available pornographic films were released, compared with the 600 or so films released in Hollywood.[6] Today millions of companies and outlets are generating porn clips directly online in quantities impossible to calculate accurately. In 2013 alone, PornHub had nearly 15 billion views, or 1.68 million visits every hour for the entire year.[7] The US is the top producer of pornographic web pages, with 244.6 million, or 89 per cent, of all porn web pages worldwide.[8] Just type 'porn' into Google and you'll get hundreds of millions of results, with the entire first page of hits offering free instant streaming videos. We have been told by reliable sources that Russia is developing a prolific amount of porn videos, taking over the industry in Europe from Hungary to Czech Republic.

By offering unlimited visual stimuli in a wide variety of categories and compilations, which can be paused or fast-forwarded at any time, tube sites like PornHub, Youporn and Redtube are catering to the male sexual brain. Using a tool called PornIQ, PornHub will even generate a playlist for the user based on their specific desires.[9]

In 2013 PornHub was the thirty-fifth most visited website for children aged 6 to 14 in the UK.[10] One in three boys is now considered a 'heavy' porn user, watching more times than they can count.[11] A survey in the UK found that the average boy watches nearly two hours of porn every week. One in three of the young men categorized as 'light' users spent less than an hour a week viewing porn, while four out of five who were categorized as heavy users (only a small percentage of those surveyed) watched more than ten hours a week. A third of the light users said they had missed an important deadline or appointment because they could not break away from their pornographic adventures.[12] There's actually a word for it – 'procrasturbation' – which means procrastinating through porn. Add to the mix older guys, married men and businessmen watching adult videos online, at work, at home and in hotels across the country and around the world. Through their adult television or 'late night' channels, hotels typically offer porn specials of unlimited viewing around the clock – before and after meals and appointments.

Can these guys make up for the lost time? That depends on how susceptible an individual is to media effects and how much porn they watch. A 2014 Belgian study of 325 adolescent boys found that frequent use of online porn lowered academic performance. The researchers found that boys who went through puberty earlier and boys who scored high in sensation-seeking watched more porn than other boys their age. It was not just the time devoted to porn that displaced engagement with other activities, there was a cognitive absorption effect where the complete involvement in a highly pleasurable activity – porn – excited cognitive, sensory and imaginative curiosity to the point where a boy lost track of time and other attentional demands became inferior. Using the excitation transfer model and sexual behaviour sequence of psychologists Dolf Zillmann and Donn Byrne, respectively, the researchers also suggested that the high states of arousal achieved in porn stimulated impulsive and 'restless' behaviour that may impair behaviour that requires long periods of constant focus and attention. More research is needed to explore this intriguing theory.[13]

Another consequence of teenage boys watching many hours of online porn, says Penny Marshall, columnist for the UK's Mail Online, is they are beginning to treat their girlfriends like sex objects. According to a 16-year-old girl, 'Boys just want us to do all the stuff that they see porn stars do.'[14] As a result, says Cindy Gallop, a dynamic TED speaker and author of *Make Love Not Porn: Technology's Hardcore Impact on Human Behaviour*, young men don't know the difference between making love and re-enacting porn.[15] In an online survey conducted by the University of East London, a fifth of boys between 16 and 20 years old said they 'relied on porn as a stimulant for real life sex'.[16]

Of the 500 teens polled in a 2014 survey by the Institute for Public Policy Research (IPPR), two out of three boys and three out of four girls say they believe that porn causes unrealistic attitudes about sex. Two-thirds of boys and girls believe porn can become addictive, and 62 per cent of boys and 78 per cent of girls believe that porn may have a negative impact on young people's views of sex and relationships. Perhaps most revealingly, 77 per cent of boys and 83 per cent of girls believe 'it's too easy for young people to accidentally see pornography online' and for teens who thought accessing porn was seen as typical for their peer group, approximately two-thirds said viewing porn became common by age 15.[17]

We think the negative effects of excessive, socially isolated porn use are worse for young people who have never had real-life sexual encounters. Why? They see sex as only physical performance, mechanical arrangements of body parts, without romance, emotion, intimacy, communication, negotiating, sharing, and even touching and kissing. Sex becomes an impersonal 'thing', and for men, a desirable sex partner becomes an object that they have no connection to after they 'finish' on her or inside her. Whereas adults may understand that the idea of porn is to turn real life into fantasy, some young people view what they see in porn as the opposite, or even something to strive for. As one UK teen told us, 'the idea of porn is to make fantasies into real life'.

Then there are the other dimensions of unreality and inevitable negative social comparisons: the actors are generally good-looking, in great shape, with endless stamina to continue all-out sexual acts for long periods before orgasm. The effects of viewing film after film with male stars showing off huge penises that are instantly erect and stay that way even after the big O cannot be positive for young men.

Finally, it becomes the norm to have unprotected sex, from oral to anal, and to promote every possible arrangement of penises, vaginas, breasts and mouths. Porn is a world of fantasy, not education. But without a decent real-world sex education, the high risks of certain sexual behaviours that are performed so casually in porn go unchecked. A 2014 study on sexuality by the Burnet Institute's Centre for Population Health in Australia found that weekly use of porn was significantly associated with early sexual behaviour, inconsistent condom use, sexting and anal sex.[18] In the US, just 16 per cent of women aged 18 to 24 said they'd tried anal sex in 1992. Today, at least one in five women aged 18 to 19, and two in five women aged 20 to 24 have tried it.[19] Many times, because pregnancy is far less likely to occur because of anal sex, young people think they don't need to use protection.[20] What they are unaware of is how much easier it is to acquire a sexually transmitted infection through anal sex. Not incidentally, half of young people in the 15- to 24-year-old age group will get a sexually transmitted infection by 25 years old.[21]

7

High on Life, or High on Anything: Over-reliance on Medications and Illegal Drugs

In 2006 Massachusetts Institute of Technology (MIT) professor John Gabrieli and his research team found that medication for ADHD improves the focus and academic performance of normal kids by the same degree that it improves the focus and performance of kids with ADHD.[1] So when someone responds well to the medication – better behaviour, focus and grades – it doesn't necessarily mean they have ADHD, yet many parents and doctors are using these improvements to confirm the disorder exists.

What's the harm if the medications help the kid do better in class? While kids generally do perform better and become more manageable, being on these medications for even just a year can lead to changes in personality. Friendly, outgoing, adventurous boys become lazy and irritable. Children also learn that taking a pill can make their problems go away.

Professor William Carlezon and colleagues at Harvard University Medical School recently reported that giving stimulant medications – such as those used to treat boys with ADHD – to juvenile laboratory animals resulted in those animals displaying loss of drive when they grew up. These animals looked normal but were lazy. They didn't want to work hard, not even to escape a bad situation. The researchers suggested that similar effects could be seen in children. Children might look fine during and after taking these medications, but when they become adults they won't have as much motivation or drive as they would have had if they had not been reliant on those medications. So the apathy we noted in Chapter 2 may continue to worsen as these heavily medicated new generations get older.

The psychologist and family physician Leonard Sax wrote in *Boys Adrift* that stimulant medications appear to harm the brain by damaging an area called the nucleus accumbens, where inner motivation is turned into behavioural action. If a boy's nucleus accumbens is damaged, he may still be hungry or sexually aroused, but will lack the drive to do anything about it. Independent groups of researchers at universities in the US and Europe have found that even when young laboratory animals were exposed to low dosages of these medications for short periods of time, permanent damage to the nucleus accumbens can happen. Sax writes:

> One particularly disturbing study – conducted jointly by researchers at Tufts, UCLA, and Brown University – documented a nearly linear correlation between the nucleus accumbens and individual motivation. The smaller the nucleus accumbens, the more likely that person was to be apathetic, lacking in drive. These investigators emphasized that apathy was quite independent of depression. A young man can be completely unmotivated – and still be perfectly happy and content.[2]

He just won't do much or want to do much, but be a smiling couch potato. This is especially relevant to young men in the US, since nearly 85 per cent of all stimulant medications are prescribed to them.[3]

One of the side effects of taking stimulants is nervousness and anxiety. What's a great way to reduce these side effects? Smoking a joint and getting high. Many young men, both those taking and not taking medication, smoke marijuana. And marijuana is not the same drug it used to be. The average potency of weed has risen steadily for the last three decades. The average THC content (the psychoactive constituent of marijuana) in 1983 was less than 4 per cent, but in 2008 the THC content was more than 10 per cent, and it is expected to rise to 15 per cent or 16 per cent in the next ten years.[4] In 2011 the Dutch government announced that high-potency weed (with a THC content of 15 per cent and higher) would now be classified in the hard drugs category along with cocaine and ecstasy.[5] One reason for the reclassification may be that high-potency weed significantly impairs executive function and motor control,[6] processes that are involved in planning, memory, attention, problem-solving, verbal reasoning and resisting temptation. From one generation to the next, marijuana has become an entirely different drug that can potentially do more harm than good.

Let's revisit that temptation vulnerability. Life is filled with temptations that are dangerous pleasures. 'Lead us not into temptation,' is a common prayer for Christians. What makes people less able to resist temptation drives them to be more present-hedonistic than future-oriented. My (Phil's) research on the psychology of time perspective reveals that being present-hedonistic is being vulnerable to all addictive substances and behaviours.[7] This is because being dominated by present-hedonism means you are constantly seeking out novelty and intense sensations.*

Your decisions are always limited to the immediate situation, what you are feeling, what others are doing and saying, what the tempting thing looks like, smells or tastes like. You never imagine

---

* Not to be confused with the Buddhist practice of being in the present moment, which emphasizes mindfulness and a non-judgemental focus on one's emotions, thoughts and sensations.

the future risks and costs, as future-oriented people do. Meaning, when you see something you like, you 'go for it', enjoy it, derive pleasure from it – and then you are dependent on it. That is addiction in action.

One male college freshman told us a story that is becoming more and more common:

> In the first grade, I was diagnosed with ADHD. I began taking Ritalin soon after. That diagnosis has complemented the trajectory of my social and academic life up to this very day. My teachers and parents always told me I was smart, but I had a hard time believing them, as I always found myself in trouble or with a tutor. Middle school was particularly turbulent for me, as I moved to an elite private school in the seventh grade. My grades were abysmal, and from the start, up until I transferred after the end of my freshman year of high school there, there was not a semester where I was not on some form of probation, be it academic or social. Furthermore, trouble, in school and out, has never failed to find me.

He added that he smoked a fair amount of marijuana, which was a common practice across campus.

In Part I, we briefly examined the 'tip of the iceberg', exploring a set of symptoms that we believe young men are manifesting in various ways to their detriment, including the overuse of video games and online porn, over-reliance on prescribed medication and illegal drugs, lack of motivation and drive, social and sexual difficulties, and poor health choices. We believe these symptoms have resulted from a complex combination of interconnected causes, which we will now consider in Part II.

Part II

Causes

8

Rudderless Families, Absent Dads

> Whatever landscape a child is exposed to early on, that will be
> the sort of gauze through which he or she will see all the
> world afterwards.
>
> — Wallace Stegner, historian and novelist

Young men haven't changed a whole lot in recent years, but
the environments and social conditions in which they hang
out, go to school, woo girls and mature have. If we take a
closer look at their worlds we can better understand the meaning
behind the data that we just reviewed in Part I. In this section we'll
briefly examine the main situational and systemic factors that
influence young men's thoughts and behaviours, including cultural
changes, social expectations and what's happening in schools,
within families and among peers.

Throughout history the vast majority of humans lived in
multi-generational, often multi-family groups, so whether or not
they wanted to be, kids were surrounded by adults. Essentially
there would have been two parents as well as other caregivers in
the picture: siblings, grandparents, uncles, aunts and cousins.
Today, however, with classroom ratios at about one teacher per
twenty students,[1] with only one or two adults living at home, and
with great distances between extended family members, children
have far fewer quality relationships with any adults. Today the
average household size in America is three or fewer.[2] In the UK,

it's 2.4.[3] Furthermore, these ever shrinking family units spend less time together, especially quality time like sharing a sit-down meal. Maia Szalavitz and Bruce D. Perry, authors of *Born for Love: Why Empathy Is Essential – and Endangered*, suggest this lack of relational richness is having a negative effect on our culture's capacity to care for others.

As infants we depend on our primary caregivers – first Mum and then Dad – to feed us when we're hungry and protect us when we're threatened. In other words, our parents regulate our level of stress until we are able to self-regulate, and how they respond to stress affects the way our stress response develops. Our earliest interactions with our mothers will serve as a kind of template for how we react to future human contact. But lately there has been a problem: because of modern demands, mothers are under constant pressure and stress. And if a mother is under stress, if she's not being nurtured, it's far less likely she's going to be able to provide consistent nurturing for her young children.

Furthermore, stress is regulated by social systems; the brain regions involved in social relationships are the same ones that control stress response. They develop together, and therefore development problems in the stress response can interfere with the development of social and emotional functioning and vice versa.[4]

Over the last few decades, the birth rate for unmarried women in the US has risen steadily from 18 per cent in 1980 to 41 per cent in 2012.[5] For women under 30 years old, who bear two-thirds of all children, the rate is 53 per cent. Many of the unmarried women are cohabiting with a partner at the outset of their child's birth, but those couplings disintegrate at twice the rate of marriages – two-thirds of them will break up before their child turns 10 years old.[6] In total, about a third of boys are raised in father-absent homes.[7] In the UK, single mothers account for approximately a quarter of families with dependent children[8] – triple what it was in 1971.[9]

With such high percentages of children born to single mothers today, who is nurturing these young, new mothers who raise these children? How will these children deal with stress when they have their own children? Moreover, as human lifespan increases, there is an ever larger number of older relatives in elderly care facilities. Who is responsible for visiting them regularly and dealing with their survival issues, even their basic legal and accounting problems? Usually, it's their daughters – the same overstressed mothers – who must deal with this new stress of caring for beloved parents who are feeble, suffering memory losses and are able to give back little affection to their now grown girls.

One place where families used to talk, exchanging experiences, ideas, values and more, was around the dinner table. That is now an ancient tradition, honoured more in the breach than in practice. *USA Today* newspaper did a survey twenty-five years ago on the 'time crunch' that people increasingly felt. One alarming statistic uncovered was that 60 per cent – three in five – of families said life was more hectic than five years ago and they were not able to do things like have regular sit-down family dinners.[10]

Today, about half of teens report having frequent dinners at home with their parents.[11] According to the National Center on Addiction and Substance Abuse, compared with teens who have five to seven family dinners a week, teens who have infrequent family dinners (fewer than three times a week) are almost four times more likely to use tobacco, more than twice as likely to use alcohol, two and a half times likelier to use marijuana, and nearly four times likelier to engage in future drug use.[12]

Unstable role models, tarnished trust

Although it was far from routine, in the early twentieth century Americans had enough trust in each other that some actually affixed stamps to their children and 'mailed' them to another destination, often to a relative's, via the US Postal Service.[13] Contrast that to today where we don't even trust the babysitter; people buy small 'nanny cams' that can easily be hidden in stuffed animals or alarm clocks to monitor what goes on in their own homes while their children are being 'looked after'.[14]

The percentage of Americans who believe 'most people can be trusted' plummeted from 55 per cent in 1960 to 32 per cent in 2009, meaning the majority of Americans now view other citizens as untrustworthy.[15] Although numbers have increased since for the general population, in a 2012 Pew Social Trends survey, only 19 per cent of millennials felt others were trustworthy.[16] In the UK, those numbers similarly dropped from 56 per cent in 1959 to 30 per cent in 2008.[17] So most people in the UK also feel they can no longer trust others. Sources of this downsizing of trust is the media highlighting instances of corruption, deception and deceit by politicians, unreliable eye-witness accounts, shifting perceptions of the lower class, celebrity scandals and the collapse of reputations of other public figures.

Other causes that merit further exploration are actual events people observe or experience first-hand. In his book *Bowling Alone: The Collapse and Revival of American Community*, Robert Putnam, Malkin Professor of Public Policy at Harvard, explained:

> In virtually all societies 'have-nots' are less trusting than 'haves,' probably because haves are treated by others with more honesty and respect. In America blacks express less social trust than whites, the financially distressed less than the financially comfortable, people in big cities less than small-town dwellers, and people who have been victims of a crime or been through a divorce less than those who haven't had those experiences.[18]

We think that the high divorce rates of many nations are of particular concern, because the destructive effects of divorce are never isolated, even in subtle ways that we may not connect right away. For example, when psychologist and marriage expert John Gottman studied blood samples of divorced people and those in unhappy marriages, he found their immune systems were depressed and contained fewer white blood cells, making them less effective at fighting infectious diseases. When he examined samples from pre-schoolers being raised in various home environments, he found chronically elevated levels of stress hormones in the children from homes with hostile parental environments.[19]

In 1969 Governor Reagan of California enacted the nation's first no-fault divorce bill, eliminating the need for spouses to state a reason why they wished to end their marriage. Other states followed over the next decade and by 1980 the divorce rate more than doubled from what it had been in 1960.[20] Today, more than half of first marriages in the US will split up before 'death do us part'; about half of them will occur in the first seven years.[21]

Around the world there are similar trends. In the UK, which also allows for no-fault divorce, 48 per cent of children will see their parents divorce by the time they are 16 years old.[22] In China, more people are filing for divorce than are tying the knot. The country's overall divorce rate is low, but it has been rising every year, with the most divorces occurring in larger cities.[23] Even traditionally Catholic European countries like Poland, which have lower divorce rates than the less religious surrounding countries, have seen a spike in recent years – one marriage in three now ends in divorce there.[24]

One Polish mother wrote in saying that divorce was the result of many contemporary social phenomena:

The 'dissolution' of the family and the instability of human relations are just some of them. Feminism, overprotectiveness of single mothers coping with raising a boy without any help from the male partner and the economic pressure to provide a livelihood that the women are under. Together with the omnipresent, stupefying media that promotes quasi-moral models. Young people are weak and lost as never before ... The best example would be my unemployed, 30 year old son, who still runs away from life and responsibilities.

Divorce isn't easy for anyone. But it's not so much the separation itself that affects young people's perceptions of trust as it is how the parents handle the situation. Many children lose faith in relationships because they watch their parents become emotionally unstable and react irrationally, sometimes violently. Before the battles become overt, children often witness bickering, humiliation and other negative social confrontations between their once loving parents.

This is the pattern many kids observe right now: man and woman meet, fall in love, get married and make babies. Enter stress. Babies take over lives. Distance grows between man and woman; communication was never great to begin with but is now much worse. Enter stress-relieving but relationship-destroying behaviours, such as physical abuse, drug and alcohol use, and emotional and physical infidelities. Everyone is unhappy. Divorce follows. One or both parents now are struggling and are emotionally, mentally and/or financially broken. Is that not a sad scenario for any child to observe and become a part of?

Many stay-at-home mums today express resentment and, while happy they had kids, wished they had maintained a career so that when they got divorced they weren't in such a tough position, having being out of the workforce for too many years to readily catch up. Only 10 per cent of mothers surveyed in a 1962 Gallup poll hoped their daughters would follow the pattern of their – often traditional – lives.[25] Fifty years later, not a whole lot has changed. Those daughters of 1962 now have daughters of their own, and the messages that those young women are getting from their own mothers is terribly inconsistent; on the one hand they say they wouldn't trade their kids for anything, but on the other hand they send the message that a career is more sustainable than having a family. Certainly there are few real-life examples of women who are able to do both well – by their own standard.

Daughters also pick up on the higher levels of unhappiness and stress that accompany divorce and single motherhood, and sometimes resent the position it puts them in growing up. As one young woman from our survey commented: 'my mother was not empowered by the separation [from my father]... This happened when I was 15, and I felt like instead of becoming a young woman, I took over as man of the house, but my opinion of women suffered.' A Pew Research survey conducted in 2012 revealed that even after taking into account ethnicity, income and education, just 23 per cent of unmarried mothers and 31 per cent of working mothers say they 'are very happy with their life these days', versus 43 per cent of married mothers and 45 per cent of non-working mothers who felt that way.[26]

The other, deeper message, that is passed on is guilt; when mothers talk about how their lives would have been different (better) had they stayed in the workforce or communicate to their daughters that they do not want them to repeat 'their mistakes', they are indirectly telling their children that their existence is part of the mistakes, and has impeded the success they could have had in their prime years. Thus the children must live according to her wishes as a form of payback for Mum's mistake in having given birth to them.

Those messages from Mum, one of our most important mentors, along with the slew of celebrity mothers, such as Sofía Vergara, Gwyneth Paltrow and Heidi Klum, being toted as 'superwomen' who do it all and have it all, and still look hot at 40 and 50 years old, leaves ordinary young women feeling anxious and confused, and eventually leaves them feeling disappointed when they realize they won't have it all – and not even much of what they had imagined and hoped their lives would be. The problem with these messages given to young children is that they erode the underlying beliefs necessary for a trusting and caring relationship to be built around. In short, it's divorce training. Daughters who do not take on a full-time career can feel like they are betraying their mother's wishes. Sons observe their mothers and wonder if they'll ever be able to make a woman happy; how could they when Dad failed miserably in doing so? After all, nearly seven out of ten divorces are initiated by women.[27]

On the other side of this sad ledger are all the dads who have watched their marriages disintegrate into a series of alimony and child-support payments. Only 10 to 15 per cent of men win in custody battles,[28] and many men end up feeling like they are spending their lives working for people who have been turned against them. When a man works long hours to try to keep up with payments and is then called callous, he feels misunderstood. If he has any blemish on his personal record he could be deemed unfit to parent; if he takes up a new hobby he's called selfish; and if he shies away from new intimate relationships out of fear that the cycle would repeat itself, he is told he has a fear of commitment. It's not a stretch to say these men have a deep sense of despair, their suicide rates after divorce being ten times higher than the suicide rates of women.[29] While this might initially suggest that marriage must be more rewarding for men than for women, and many women undoubtedly feel they have to take on the bulk of the child care and household chores, it's clear from the health benefits alone that both men and women benefit from being married. However, because men are conditioned not to ask for help or reach out to others, they have more pent-up emotions and are likely to take more drastic action in times of crisis.

Since most children today are still brought up on a diet of Disney movies and fairy tales to think that conventional marriage is for everyone and that marriages are supposed to last for ever, the break-up is devastating to the entire family. As a kid you think, Is this what I have to look forward to? Then as an adult you think, Why bother? What's the point? The entire burden will fall on me in the end anyway.

It doesn't have to be that way if the divorce is amicable and both parties communicate to their children their love for them and respect for the other parent, but that's usually not what happens. Young people are not growing up seeing great role models for trust and reliability, especially in intimate relationships. Long-term monogamous relationships are now thought of in terms of what you lose rather than what you gain; they're seen as a restriction on independence and freedom, and commitment is seen as sacrificing your own goals and passions for something that will most likely fail in ten or twenty years, if not sooner. Some kids also feel that they are one of the reasons why their parents' marriage ended, and avoid having children of their own in an effort to spare any potential future children the pain they witnessed and experienced.

Young people are still expected to want these things even though they say they are never taught properly how to talk about or handle the challenges that come with these commitments. Ultimately they wonder who they can trust. They wonder, 'If I can't trust those closest to me, whom can I trust? If Mum and Dad can't even keep it together, who can?' Learning how to trust others starts with our primary relationships, so when our primary role models are unreliable and don't deliver on their promises or aren't there for one another, we will find it harder to rely on others or allow ourselves to be depended upon by others.

No doubt a precursor to a thriving marriage is trust. But another thing to consider is just how much else in society is built on top of that foundation. George Vaillant, professor of psychiatry at Harvard Medical School, ran the longitudinal Harvard Study of Adult Development, informally known as the Grant Study, for over forty years (since 1966). It was started in 1938 as a way to measure not just pathology, as was trendy at the time, but how nature and nurture influenced mental and physical health outcomes in men. The original researchers wanted not just to observe health over time, but 'optimum' health.[30] All the participants were sophomores from the all-male Harvard College. In his latest analysis, marking the seventy-fifth year of the study (many of the remaining participants now in their nineties), Vaillant mentions on multiple occasions the importance of a warm childhood – one that had a stable home environment where the child was close to his parents, parents were supportive and encouraging of initiative and autonomy, and the child was close to at least one sibling – and its role in the development of trust as well as future happiness and success. He noted that 'children who fail to learn basic love and trust at home are handicapped later in mastering the assertiveness, initiative, and autonomy that are the foundation of successful adulthood.'[31] Men with the warmest childhoods also made 50 per cent more money than the men who had bleak childhoods.[32] He noted that the most independent men were those who came from the most loving homes: 'they had learned that they could put their trust in life, which gave them courage to go out and face it,' and that a 'lack of hope and trust in other people made [a man] extremely vulnerable to loneliness'.[33] A young man in his mid-20s who replied to our survey, and who largely grew up without a father, echoed this sentiment, telling us that he had been unable to leave home or finish his education until this past year: 'It has only been since I started really taking a look at the underlying network of issues I had [growing up] that I recognized my false beliefs, which has really been a major step in my personal growth.'

In a 2008 survey by the National Fatherhood Initiative, 56 per cent of mothers who were married or lived with the father of their children said the father had a 'very close and warm' relationship with the children versus 15 per cent of mothers who did not live with the father, and just 3 per cent of mothers who were married or lived with the father of their children said the father had a 'distant and unemotional' relationship with the children versus 47 per cent of mothers who did not live with the father.[34]

Although it seems like the warmth of a lone individual's childhood or their ability to trust and their choice to marry or not is not such a big deal, on a mass scale there are significant ramifications. More than mere social implications stem from this lack of trust; countries in which citizens don't trust each other don't do as well economically. As Paul Zak, professor of economics at Claremont Graduate University said: 'countries with a higher proportion of trustworthy people are more prosperous . . . In these countries, more economic transactions occur and more wealth is created, alleviating poverty. So poor countries are, by and large, low-trust countries.'[35] It is primarily the Nordic nations that have seen an increase in trust since the 1980s, with Danes being the most trusting of their fellow citizens (76 per cent). Several nations with rates of trust below 20 per cent include Mexico, France, South Africa and Argentina.[36]

In his book *Trust: The Social Virtues and the Creation of Prosperity*, Francis Fukuyama wrote: 'Liberal political and economic institutions depend on a healthy and dynamic civil society for their vitality,' which all builds on a strong and stable family structure.[37] Charles Murray shared a similar view in *Coming Apart: The State of White America, 1960–2010*, arguing marriage is one of the foundations of a nation's strength and financial resilience. He wrote that families with children are the core of communities, which are the core of society. It is around these families that communities must be organized, he says, because families with children have always been 'the engine' that makes society work.[38]

There is a strong correlation between partner status and employment status. Married men spend 17 per cent more time than single men and 9 per cent more time than cohabiting men in the labour force. For women, there were no significant differences found in the number of weeks worked and partner status, though women with no children spent 17 per cent more time in the labour force than women whose children have left home. By 27 years old, eight times the number of single women have a child living in their household than single men. These trends are more pronounced for those of minority backgrounds, the less educated and the unwed (see endnotes for specific statistics).[39] Overall, the US unmarried population grew 41 per cent between 2000 and 2010. The main alternative for unmarried couples, cohabitation, has grown 1400 per cent in the US since 1970.

In the UK, 68 per cent of women between the ages of 16 and 64 have jobs while 78 per cent of men in the same age range have jobs, as of 2014.[40] The proportion of never married women aged 18 to 49 went from 18 per cent in 1979 to 43 per cent in 2011. The number of women cohabiting with a partner also increased, from 11 per cent to 34 per cent. The number of people living alone nearly doubled from 9 per cent in 1973 to 16 per cent in 2011 – for the 25- to 44-year-old age range the rate had increased five-fold from 2 per cent to 10 per cent.[41] The number of opposite sex cohabiting couples increased from 2.2 million in 2003 to 2.9 million in 2013 – 41 per cent of which had dependent children living with them. Women accounted for 91 per cent of single-parent households with dependent children.[42]

Though it can be a convenient set-up for adults, it is well established that cohabiting and single parents do not provide as stable a foundation for children, who often end up living in two different worlds. Compared with children in intact, married families, children in cohabiting families are about twice as likely to drop out of high school, use drugs or become depressed. Compared with marriage, cohabitation also provides less commitment and safety to children (who are three times more likely to suffer physical, sexual or emotional abuse) and romantic partners. Consequently, cohabiting couples are more than twice as likely to break up and four times more likely to be unfaithful to each other.[43] Thus, whatever benefits may accrue to cohabitation, there are clear negative costs and consequences.

There may also be a strong correlation between family trauma – like divorce – and being overweight. In a survey of almost 300 morbidly obese patients, researchers found a very high occurrence of severe family dysfunction, particularly sexual abuse. About half of the men and women reported they were sexually assaulted or abused as children. That rate is 300 per cent higher than the general male population. Pretty much all those surveyed reported experiencing some lasting form of childhood trauma. Weight gain often immediately follows a distressing life event. Examples of this on a large scale include divorce, and divorce rates increased considerably just before obesity began to soar.[44] Young boys often have more difficulty adapting to a parent's divorce than young girls

– especially if the father leaves the home, putting them at higher risk. For example, a recent Norwegian study revealed that children that had frequent and positive interactions with their father, such as the father paying attention to the child's interests, offering encouragement and smiling, during the first year of their life were calmer and better behaved than other children at age two. This was especially true for boys. Both mothers and fathers were equally positively engaged with their daughters, but fathers were more often positively engaged with their sons than mothers were.[45]

Interestingly, Vaillant found that, although recovery may take decades, with the passage of time the good things that happened in childhood outshine the childhood traumas, which become less important: 'A warm childhood environment appeared to be a far better predictor of future social class and of adult employment (or unemployment) than was either childhood intelligence, parental dependence on welfare, or the presence of multiple problems within the family.'[46] Even as the Grant Study men aged into their seventies, their level of contentment 'was not even suggestively associated with parental social class or even the man's own income. What it was significantly associated with was warmth of childhood environment, and it was very significantly associated with a man's closeness to his father.'[47] This relationship is now what is missing in all too many homes these days.

Where's Dad?

A woman simply is, but a man must become. Masculinity is risky and elusive. It is achieved by a revolt from woman, and it is confirmed only by other men.

– Camille Paglia, professor of humanities and media studies at the University of the Arts in Philadelphia and author of *Sexual Personae: Art and Decadence from Nefertiti to Emily Dickinson*

If we do not initiate the boys, they will burn the village down.

– African proverb

As mentioned earlier, many children are now born and raised by single mothers. Forty-four per cent of millennials and 43 per cent of Gen Xers think that marriage is archaic,[48] which begs the question: what will commitment look like in the twenty-first century? And how will those attitudes affect future generations and how those children are raised?

America leads the industrialized world in fatherlessness[49] – not something to put on a banner and salute. In the UK, a young person is more likely to have a television in their bedroom than a father in the house by the end of their childhood.[50] Among those who have fathers, the average school-age boy spends just half an hour per week in one-to-one conversation with his father, according to David Walsh, founder of Mind Positive Parenting. 'That compares with forty-four hours a week in front of a television, video game screen, [and] Internet screen,' he says. 'I think that we are neglecting our boys tremendously. The result of that is our boys aren't spending time with mentors, with elders, who can really show them the path, show them the way of how it is that we're supposed to behave as healthy men.'[51]

Jeff Perera, who does community engagement for the White Ribbon movement in Canada and founded the blog Higher Unlearning, both of which involve discussions on men, masculinity, fatherhood, healthy relationships and working to end violence against women and girls, spent a morning in Toronto talking to 8- and 9-year-old boys from around the city about what they liked and didn't like about being a boy. One group came up with this list for what they didn't like about being boys:

- Not being able to be a mother.
- Not supposed to cry.
- Not allowed to be a cheerleader.
- Supposed to do all the work.
- Supposed to like violence.
- Supposed to play football.

- Boys smell bad.
- Having an automatic bad reputation.
- Grow hair everywhere.

Perera said many of the boys 'usually share thoughts such as how they don't like that boys get very competitive, leading to aggressive behaviour or cheating to be labelled a "winner"'. In all respects, it is all about being a winner for boys, sometimes at all costs. Some will talk about how boys always are in trouble, as one boy indicated here with '[having] an automatic bad reputation'. Perera asked the boys if they could explain what they meant by not being able to be a mother. Most of the boys agree that they like that they don't have to give birth, but felt they would be missing out as parents. One boy stood up and said in commercials it's always girls playing with the dolls and boys don't get to be mothers. When Perera mentioned to the boys that they could be fathers, the boys looked confused. Perera writes:

> My mind raced as I wondered just how many of these fifty boys had physically-present but not emotionally-present fathers or role-models, or had fathers who were present at all. If they did hang out, they did little more than throw the ball around. We need more Maps to Manhood. When we reinforce outdated codes and ideas of manhood, these young boys will strive to achieve a standard of being a man that ensures they will fail as a human being.[52]

The effect of fatherlessness and the lack of modern rites of passage are both underestimated as having negative casual influences on the social-emotional development of boys. Boys suffer when there's no father in the home or no positive male role models in their lives; they start to look for a male identity somewhere else. Some young men find it in a gang, other young men find it in drugs, alcohol, playing video games or objectifying women. For example, it could hardly be a coincidence that all three of the gamers featured in the

2014 documentary *Free to Play* are young men who grew up without their fathers around. One of the gamers, 'Dendi', whose father passed away when he was young, poured himself into video games after his father's death – he said it was the 'push to play more'. Another gamer, 'Fear', whose father walked out on his family when he was very young, started spending large amounts of time gaming after he wasn't picked for a basketball team, saying that his father's absence in many ways made him what he is today. The third young man, 'Hyhy', said his father worked 15–16 hours a day when he was growing up and had 'pretty much given up on everything else in his life'. The documentary follows their individual journeys as some of the world's best Defense of the Ancients (DotA) players competing to win a one million dollar tournament prize.[53]

Another side effect of fatherlessness is increased incidence of attention and mood disturbances. A 2010 study of more than a million Swedish children aged 6 to 19 found that children raised by single parents were 54 per cent more likely to be on ADHD medication.[54] The National Center for Health Statistics reports that children of unwed or divorced parents who live with only their mother are 375 per cent more likely to need professional treatment for emotional or behavioural problems.[55]

Craig McClain, co-founder of the Boys to Men Mentoring Network, offers an unfortunate view of why men do not often engage teenage boys:

> Men are afraid of teenage boys, deathly afraid, and they don't want anything to do with them. I saw it in a lot of my talks to men's groups, saying, 'Hey, how many of you guys want to go up on a weekend with 30 teenage boys with me? Raise your hand.' And one of them will raise their hand, and I'll say, 'That's the problem.' Men are afraid of teenage boys because all they remember about their [own] teenage years is pain and sorrow and sadness and being alone, and when they see teenage boys in that place, that's where they go, so they back off.[56]

What are young guys to do? The 2007 documentary film *Journeyman* followed two Minnesota teenagers – Mike and Joe – as they went through the Boys to Men mentoring and rites of passage programme. Initially both young men were very distrusting of the world. Neither one had a father figure in his life. Mike and Joe were both individually matched with a male mentor. Both of the male mentors also had absent fathers and struggled with feelings of shame and guilt about who they were in their youth. Dennis Gilbert, one of the mentors, was unsure of his abilities as a mentor:

> At first I was like, 'I don't know if I want to be a mentor.' I had some issues then that I didn't know I had with adolescent boys, particularly in groups. I had this fear thing. A lot of times, we'd just sit in the car and we'd stare, and [I'd get] almost no response back from [him]. After about six months I thought, Am I doing this right? I'm not noticing anything. We're not feeling like good friends, I'm just somebody who picks him up because he's bored sometimes. So I called Charlie. I said, 'I think I'm failing at this mentor thing. He doesn't like me, we don't talk about anything…Maybe there's somebody out there better to be a mentor here.' And Charlie said, 'Dennis, you're doing…exactly what you need to be doing.' He was right. It passed…In another three months he started opening up.[57]

One of the most crucial things for these young men transitioning into manhood was simply having an adult male around who enjoyed their presence and could guide them so that they could be loved for who they were but also held accountable for what they did. Being loved simply for who they are is the unconditional love that mums usually give, and love based on performance and effectively trying to achieve something is typically dad's domain. In this case, the mentors gave both.

After two years, Mike went from failing in every class to getting top marks across the board, and he did his first staffing on a Boys to

Men weekend. He said the experience was transformational; he said he could see himself having a future now, whereas he couldn't before. Joe now had a child of his own and was looking forward to raising his family. The boys' mentors also found that they went on an emotional journey of their own to face unresolved issues from their youth that came to light through their interactions with the boys.

With involved dads or positive male role models, kids are more open, receptive and trusting of new people. Compared to kids not living with Dad, one group of elementary school children surveyed who were living with their fathers scored better on 21 of 27 social competence measures.[58] And perhaps as a result, they also have more playmates.[59] They're also more likely to do better and go further in school. Elementary school children raised with their fathers also do better on eight out of nine academic measures, and a father's impact remains significant through high school.[60]

There's no question boys need men in their lives. A mother's role is extremely important, too, but 'there's not one thing a single mother can do to help her...sons in adolescence to calm down and to be moral,' says Michael Gurian, author of *The Minds of Boys*. 'Boys need a father. And why? Because that's how nature's set up. Because it's human nature. There's maternal nurturance and there's paternal nurturance, and they're wired differently. Males nurture in a somewhat different way than females do, and children – girls and boys – need both maternal and paternal nurturance.'[61]

Guys also need to learn that it's OK to want to be in their son's life. Gender issues researcher and activist Warren Farrell suggests that a more balanced perspective about what is possible for young men will benefit everyone, not just young men:

> Prior to the women's movement, girls learned to row the family boat only from the right side (raise children); boys, only from the left (raise money). The women's movement helped girls become women who could row from both sides; but without a

parallel force for boys, boys became men who had still learned to row only from the left – to only raise money. The problem? If our daughters try to exercise their newfound ability to row from the left, and our sons also row only from the left, the boat goes in circles. A family boat that goes only in circles is more likely to be sunk by the rocks of recessions. In the past, a man was a family's breadwinner and he might be with one company for life. In the future, advanced technologies make economic change the only constant, increasing the need for a family boat with flexibility – with our sons eventually able to raise children as comfortably as our daughters now raise money.[62]

Only a few decades ago, boys had not only dads but also uncles, grandfathers, older cousins, male family friends and next-door neighbours who provided an extended, tribal family system that was often an informal source of social support. Facebook, Twitter, gaming forums and a host of other Internet social media sites now try to replace those functions – but they cannot do so. Young men need more than 'contacts'. They need confidants. They need people who will be there when they are down in the dumps, who can sense their need because they interact with males enough to recognize changes in their moods without them having to ask for help. It is hard and awkward for anyone to ask for help. Given that this is true for most people, most of the time, we should all be alert to ask if we can help others when we perceive that help is needed. This is another reason why young men need compassionate friends and family who are likely to notice they need help and who come to their aid. It is also important to have others recognizing when young men positively contribute to a situation, or achieve goals – to offer warranted praise and build up their sense of pride and honour.

Media influence

What does it mean to be a man? And where do young men get their information about what it means to be manly? Many males who we have surveyed said they felt most like a man when they were honest about who they were, confidently made decisions and actively pursued their dreams. Men are naturally risk-takers and explorers, they like to master things. Knowing that they're needed motivates them, and they want respect from their peers, specifically from other men. Again that respect is based both on who they are and what they do.

But that meaningful respect needs to come from doing pro-social things that make life better in some way for others. It should not derive from out-drinking their buddies or doing some stupid shit better than them. Popular films and television shows, unfortunately, present few alternatives to this latter asshole image of males.

We strongly believe that television programmes could use more men with triple-digit IQs. Why the overwhelming majority of male characters are testosterone-driven meatheads, douchebag detectives, obsessed chefs, vampires, womanizers or overweight men with really hot wives is perhaps not such a mystery. A recent University of Maryland study concluded that unhappy people watch significantly more television.[63] That makes sense – television is passive, provides an escape and is an easy way to tune out of one's life. Drama is an amazing distraction. When you can watch tanned guidos duke it out like two betta fish in a small aquarium, you feel less inadequate about your own life. Disharmony seems to be appealing, too. As Leo Tolstoy wrote in *Anna Karenina*: 'Happy families are all alike; every unhappy family is unhappy in its own way.'[64] Watch one show about happy people and you've seen them all.

The problem is, without better role models in real life, young men become confused about what is and is not acceptable male behaviour. Violence and sex, two over-represented topics in media and under-represented topics in conversation, become especially unclear. 'It's very confusing to little boys . . . all around them they see violence on the news, on television, on video games – and at the same time, they're getting the message that the fantasies that boys seem to have always had are bad . . . I think the danger is giving the boys who are having those thoughts the idea that it says something bad about them as people,' says Jane Katch, kindergarten teacher and author of *Far Away from the Tigers*.[65]

Warren Farrell elaborated on this point by saying many young boys unconsciously learn that sex is dirtier and worse than killing, because parents will allow their kids to watch a Western in which people kill each other but will turn off the television or change the channel when there's nudity or sex. No doubt the graphic pornographic images that many young boys have access to today online do little to counter the sense of sex being dirty and void of love or emotional connection.

By 13 or 14 years old, the message comes across to boys that they want sex more than girls do – or that the girls who initiate sex are untrustworthy – so they feel they must take on the role of initiator. Naturally, there is a huge fear of rejection, which is a potent motivation inhibitor. Sex on television and porn reduce that fear of rejection. If a young man doesn't perceive himself among the best performers, he believes the girl he is most attracted to will reject him. Watching television and porn requires no commitment and has a zero rate of rejection; it provides instant gratification that can alleviate the fear to some degree. As a side effect, however, it also reduces the motivation to get the skills needed to attract the girl, creating further distance between a man and his ultimate goal.[66]

The flawed welfare system

In 2013 an average of 4.1 million people in the US received welfare, known as Temporary Assistance for Needy Families (TANF), or State Supplemental Program (SSP) benefits each month during the fiscal year; most were children.[67] A recent report from Pew Research indicated 18 per cent of American adults have received assistance from the Supplemental Nutrition Assistance Program (SNAP), or 'food stamps', at some point in their lives, and Democrats were twice as likely as Republicans to have used food stamps. Women were about twice as likely as men (23 per cent vs 12 per cent), and minorities were twice as likely as whites to have received food stamps. People over 65 years old were the least likely age group to say they had received food stamps (8 per cent), while people with less education – a high school diploma or lower – were three times more likely than college graduates to have received those benefits.[68]

Over the last twenty years, the amount of cash assistance provided for the poorest families has grown weaker, not stronger.[69] The lifetime limit of receiving benefits is five years, and many people have reached the imposed TANF limit in the most recent financial crisis. Whether or not you believe that welfare promotes out-of-wedlock childbearing, destroys the motivation to seek and attain an income, or does not offer adequate support to those most in need, most people can agree that the current system is flawed in many ways. Particularly in the way that it is not balanced by adequate federal investments in public education, job training and support, and job creation. Many nations are in desperate need of these programmes, not just the US.

The current system also discourages single mothers from establishing a stable two-parent household, despite a portion of welfare funds allocated to promote this kind of family structure. Surveys from the Office of the Assistant Secretary for Planning and Evaluation (ASPE), part of the US Department of Health and Human Services (HHS), show:

> that the incentives of TANF-eligible women with children to cohabit or marry are affected by TANF program rules. The way in which incentives are affected depends on the financial resources of the male with whom the woman might cohabit or marry and on the male's relationship to the children. The relevant TANF rules that affect these incentives are those governing eligibility, how the basic grant is structured, how blended families are treated, how unrelated cohabitors are treated, and work rules.[70]

Women who marry or maintain a home with the biological father of their children can face the reduction or loss of their benefits:

> Our main finding is that if a male has financial resources, TANF provides the greatest disincentive to form and/or maintain a biological family, and the least disincentive, if not an incentive, to form an unrelated cohabitor family. In a biological family, where the male is the father of all the children, he must be included in the unit and his resources counted. In an unrelated cohabitor family, where he is father of none of the children, he is not included and his resources are not counted. In addition, most states disregard unrelated cohabitor vendor and cash payments to the TANF recipient and her children.[71]

Although the previous Aid to Families with Dependent Children (AFCD) system allowed states to base the receipt of welfare on the perceived sexual morality of the mother, using phrases such as 'suitable home' and 'man in the house' to disqualify many single black mothers,[72] the current structure of TANF actually promotes having nearly any man *but* the biological father heading the house, regardless of ethnicity.

In the UK, close to 11 per cent of the population between the ages of 16 and 64 claimed out-of-work benefits in 2014.[73] Associated with this high number is the large number of single parents. Britain has more single-parent households than the majority of European countries (only surpassed by Estonia, Ireland and Latvia). Of the 1.8 million single-parent households in Britain, over a third of them are not employed or searching for work. On average, single-parent households in the UK claim more than double the amount of government benefit support as two-parent households,[74] and are 2.5 times more likely to be in poverty.[75] The Centre for Social Justice (CSJ) estimates that the cost of 'family breakdown' is at least £46 billion a year, more than the entire

Defence budget, though there is only £30 million a year invested by Parliament into preventing family breakdown.[76] The CSJ also notes the penalties married couples currently face in the welfare system:

> public services may inadvertently inhibit family formation and even encourage family breakdown. Fathers frequently feel excluded from services that are largely geared towards mothers and children and which – in some cases – automatically suspect men of domestic or child abuse. There is often a perception that a man's role is one of providing but not nurturing and caring, or that positive father involvement can be an added bonus rather than something obligatory. This is also further reinforced by law, which does not require unmarried fathers to be named on the child's birth certificate . . . Any saving couples receiving welfare make by living together, in terms of rent and bills, are more than swallowed up and the tax and benefit system does not even encourage parents to live together . . . Where two people both living in social housing want to move in together, they are faced with the prospect of losing one of their houses – moving in together constitutes a significant risk. Finally, the UK tax system provides no recognition of the social, economic and health benefits of marriage – the most stable family form – as such is an outlier across Europe and the wider group of OECD countries.[77]

Essentially, the current systems are not helping people get out of poverty, and often the cycle continues from generation to generation. Children who experience family breakdown growing up are less likely to stay in school or get secondary education. A person with a poor education is more likely to rely on benefits and less likely to enter or stay in the workforce, and as a result is more likely to have debt and live in poverty eternally.

Helicopter parents

On the flip side of absent parents are 'helicopter parents' – often of a higher socioeconomic status – who are reluctant to relinquish control over their children's environment, to allow them to grow up, develop resilience, and find solutions to their own problems. Lori Gottlieb, a clinical psychologist in New York, wrote in *Atlantic* magazine about the role parents play in shaping their child's sense of happiness. She wondered whether protecting children from unhappiness while they were growing up actually robbed them of happiness as adults. The rise of so-called helicopter parents, who hover over and around their children in school settings to be sure they are doing the right thing, supports this idea. The University of Vermont has even hired 'parent bouncers' to help keep these parents at a healthy distance.[78]

Although their intentions may start out as good, helicopter parents' surveillance tactics not only undercut their kids' independence, they prevent them from soaring on their own. This problem is seen in the extreme in modern China in the form of 'sitting mothers'. Mums accompany their prized only child to college, especially the male, who must become the pride of the family and its legacy. They take apartments near the school and keep a keen eye on all the comings and goings of Junior. In some cases, when mums cannot live close by and dads have business to attend to, a 'sitting grandmother' will do the job instead.

Failing is an inevitable and much underrated part of life, but many parents aren't letting their sons learn that it's OK to fail at most things some of the time. A life without failure is a life without risk-taking; it is settling for the sure thing and not the best thing. This costs them later in life. One male college student from our survey offered this suggestion:

> Let men fail when they are young. That way it doesn't seem like the end of the world if they do when they are older. I think a mistake my parents made when I was young is they always rescued me from the brink of failure. My biggest

problem moving on to college is I never learned to learn from
my failures. I see men around me fail over and over because
they seem incapable of deriving any lessons from it.

Another perception that has come from helicopter parenting is the
belief that neighbourhoods aren't safe places any more, deterring
their kids from playing pick-up sports games outside their parentally
managed and supervised teams, and indirectly robbing them of the
opportunity to practise social organization skills as well as learning
to resolve conflicts on their own. People generally spend time in
nature to improve their physical, psychological and spiritual sense
of well-being, but kids aren't learning that. The fear-based mentality
being passed down from their parents has effectively made kids
neutral or apathetic towards the outdoors. From 2008 to 2012, 16- to
19-year-olds were the least likely age group to go to a National
Forest or Wilderness – they accounted for just 3 per cent of the total
visits.[79] Again, we believe strongly that everyone's human nature is
enhanced by regular connections with physical nature, with feeling
part of the external environment. Being in a forest, or desert, or in
the mountains or ocean often generates a sense of awe that
contributes to a feeling of aliveness.

Gay parents

While co-parents are not as effective as parents with intact
marriages, the effectiveness of gay parents is a question that remains
not fully studied. Do children need to have a married mother and
father to have the brightest future, or will two same-sex parents
who are in a marriage-like relationship and have been with the
children since birth produce similar results? Gay marriage is legal
in several US states and countries around the world, but many other
gay couples who wish to marry are not allowed to do so. This
means that some children with gay parents grow up with married
parents while others grow up with parents who are technically
cohabiting but perhaps model an analogous family dynamic.

The slim amount of research on the parental efficacy of gay couples who have children has not been sufficiently studied, and the current data is conflicted. One highly criticized study found that children with gay parents who began a same-sex romantic relationship later in the child's life were more likely to smoke marijuana and cigarettes, were more likely to have been arrested, were more likely to be in therapy or counselling for anxiety or depression, and watched more television than the children in intact biological families.[80] In contrast, other studies with their own limitations suggest that the children of gay parents are just as happy[81] and healthy,[82] and develop normally sexually and socially (although they are more likely to experience bullying[83]), when compared to children with biological parents in intact marriages. The American Psychological Association says there's no scientific basis for believing that gays and lesbians are unfit to be parents based on sexual orientation alone.[84]

We expect that as the number of desirable men of marriageable age becomes a scarcer commodity, there will be an increase of women living in unconventional or bisexual cohabiting arrangements, as witnessed in the rise of the non-monogamy movement.[85] Throughout history, when there has been an oversupply of women, a lower value is placed on marriage and family, and sexual relationships outside marriage increase and become more openly talked about and accepted as the norm.[86]

Family dynamics are changing at a rapid pace, and the ripple effects from this evolution have yet to be fully felt. Education, on the other hand, is one institution that is lumbering along at a painfully slow speed, as we will discuss next.

9

Failing Schools

Young men are not failing at school; the school system is failing them. The US spends more money per pupil than the majority of other developed countries,[1] but it achieves less gain per buck. And now that many schools receive federal and state funding based on test results, teachers teach for those outcomes, but not for stimulating student curiosity or critical thinking, nor for learning non-specific principles or values. Over time such training to focus on fact memorization may come to lower the intellectual level of the teachers themselves, not just their bored students.

'The quality of teachers has been declining for decades, and no one wants to talk about it...We need to find a more powerful means to attract the most promising candidates to the teaching profession,' said Harold O. Levy, chancellor of the New York City Public Schools, back in 2000.[2] There are a lot of amazing teachers out there, but in general, the current batch of teachers are less intelligent than earlier peers, buried in the bottom third of the SAT class.[3]

IQ is definitely not the sole predictor of good teaching, but the difference between having a strong or weak teacher lasts a lifetime. Kids who have a good teacher at nine years old are less likely to become teenage parents, are more likely to go to college and will, on average, earn $50,000 more over a lifetime.[4] This research most likely could have used any other grade and got similar positive correlations.

But because there are few tangible incentives to being a dedicated teacher (poor wages, less status), over time many educators get discouraged and don't invest the effort to make their classes engaging or relevant to current events. Thus many kids end up just dumbed down by rote memorization to achieve teacher approval and school-targeted results. Much education is not problem-focused or solution-oriented, or relevant to real-world challenges, as many people believe it should be.

What else is wrong with school dynamics? Too much boring homework, and too many overworked or absent parents who are not interested in their kids' progress or academic problems, only the results on the report card. Too many schools have eliminated gym class and structured playtime, which means there is no longer a time or place to release pent-up energy, socialize at recess or develop imagination. Financial constraints have led to science courses without labs, dropping courses with any kind of creativity altogether, and limiting nearly all field trips to places like natural history museums. And as kids are less challenged in their classroom, there arises the ever tempting option to text and surf the Internet in class, which swamps directed attention away from the lesson.

Thirty years ago elementary schools offered recess twice a day. Many US schools now have recess only once a day, and some schools are eliminating play or free time completely. In the UK, Chief Inspector of Schools Sir Michael Wilshaw is concerned that there is not enough strenuous physical activity in physical education lessons. Many of the teachers, he notes, have low expectations of their students, who are not being engaged or challenged. And some students were even being prevented from exercising because their teacher interrupted them or took too much time to explain new tasks.[5] So all that restless energy that young boys have now has nowhere to be released – except in the classroom. Older school administrators have told us that playtime at recess was critical in the development of social bonding for many kids, as that was the place where friends were made and social groups had the chance to interact.

Kindergarten now resembles what used to be a first-grade class. Since boys' brains develop differently from girls', they aren't receptive to the intense reading exercises now given to kindergarteners. If a boy is forced to learn before his brain is ready, he is unintentionally conditioned to dislike the task, and early negative experiences create resistance and resentment for learning in particular and school in general. Since 1980, there has been a 71 per cent increase in the number of boys who say they don't like school, according to a University of Michigan study.[6] That dislike is both the cause and effect of poor academic performance. This means schools must take into account variation in children's learning styles, and differential rates of knowledge acquisition, as well as gender variations by age and subject matter. One size education does not fit all and may end up 'mis-fitting' boys more than girls.

One female teacher from our survey commented:

> I taught in private schools in the USA for eighteen years. Overwhelmingly, teachers were women and I found the learning environment much more suited to girls than to boys encouraged by the requirement to sit still for long periods of time to 'color inside the lines,' etc. Boys also tended to be placed on Ritalin and other drugs at a far higher rate than girls, probably to make them conform to a gynocentric environment. The notion that gender is socially constructed – while true to a large extent – only complicated the attempt to tease apart the complexity of being a boy in America.

We see this in the evidence that the US ranked 36th on maths and 24th in reading, while Britain ranked 25th on maths and 23rd in reading on international comparative tests in 2012. Commonwealth nations such as Canada ranked 13th and 8th, Australia ranked 19th and 13th, and New Zealand ranked 22nd and 14th, respectively.[7] In Finland, which is one of the highest ranked countries in Europe, children don't start formal schooling until they are 7 years old,[8] but they are learning much at home from their families. Earlier education has many advantages when it recognizes individual differences by age and gender and type of material being taught. Children as young as 2 and 3 have been shown to learn a great deal of maths and even basic science principles in Montessori-based schooling, which highlights tactile skills (hands-on manipulation of objects representing various things, like numbers or events) as an effective way into a child's mind, for boys as well as girls.

Since Bs have become the new Cs – it is now unacceptable to be 'average' – has the pressure from having to perform turned boys off from trying in the first place? Many young men from our survey said 'yes'. In particular, 64 per cent of boys aged 12 and younger agreed that 'pressure to perform combined with fear of failing causes young men to not bother trying in the first place.'

One middle-aged mother with both a son and daughter commented in our survey:

One of the most difficult things for small children to accomplish is to focus. Once a child's ability to focus has reached its coping limit, they start to fidget, wiggle, roll around. Anything but sit still. They literally move away from the activity that requires focus. They move away mentally, physically, and their heart is no longer in it. The more mature their brains are, then the longer they can sit still and focus. When I am with a child that starts to wiggle uncontrollably, I instinctively know that it's useless to continue trying to teach them anything. If pushed beyond that point, then that is when the child starts to get turned off of learning. If they are pushed past the good-focus-point too often, then they will reach for any distraction to avoid learning. Video games are a convenient and tantalizing distraction. Unfortunately, they are also 'numbing' and socially isolating.

In the US, SAT scores are often seen as a valid predictor of college success.[9] But guys' SAT scores are the worst they've been in forty years! In the UK, nearly three-quarters of girls got A*–C grades on their GCSEs, while fewer than two-thirds of boys did that well.[10] With more and more diverse test-takers than ever before, a decline in scores is somewhat expected. But these scores affected boys of all races and SES (socioeconomic status) levels. So why this regression?

We will paraphrase the Public Broadcasting Service (PBS) article, 'What's the Problem with School?', which sums up the situation well:

- In general, boys will be more physically active, but less socially and verbally mature, than girls when they begin school. Since boys are more active than girls, they have more difficulty sitting still for long periods of time. (As a side note, much of the active time kids used to have during school has all but vanished. Children spend about half as much time outdoors today as they did in the 1980s. In recent years, 40,000 American schools have eliminated recess, with only 12 per cent of states requiring elementary schools to offer any free time and only 13.7 per cent of elementary school students having gym classes at least three times a week.[11])

- Children are now being taught to read in kindergarten, and boys, being less verbally skilled than girls at that age, are not developmentally ready to be receptive to reading exercises as girls are.

- Girls are, on average, initially stronger than boys in language, and elementary classroom lessons are four-fifths language based. Thus, boys feel like they are not good at literacy, and that perceived deficit becomes a part of their new negative self-identity.

- Boys tend to learn best with hands-on learning activities, and schools don't offer enough opportunities to manipulate actual things. Furthermore, diaries and first-person narratives, writing styles preferred by girls, are often favoured over comic books and science-fiction, themes favoured by boys.

- Fewer than one in nine schoolteachers is a man[12] (in the UK it's fewer than one in five[13]). Most teachers in elementary schools are women, which leaves fewer positive male role models for learning as a masculine pursuit. We would add that this is even truer in high school classes.[14]

Once students are in college, they face other kinds of challenges. The late Clifford Nass, distinguished communications professor at Stanford University, saw consequences of the ubiquitous digital life:

> You walk around the world and you see people multitasking. They're playing games and they're reading email and they're on Facebook, etc...On a college campus, most kids are doing two things at once, maybe three things at once...Virtually all multitaskers think they are brilliant at multitasking. And one of the big discoveries is, You know what? You're really lousy at it! It turns out multitaskers are terrible at every aspect of multitasking. They get distracted constantly. Their memory is very disorganized. Recent work we've done suggests they're worse at analytical reasoning. We worry that it may be creating people who are unable to think well and clearly.[15]

And that is true of some of the brightest college students in the world – the 1,500 select few who are accepted to Stanford from among the 30,000 applicants annually. If they can't multitask, but believe they can, what chance is there that less talented students can do so effectively? The short answer is – they can't.

All of us are forcing our minds to do a juggling act. The ability to have multiple monitors and Internet browsers open at the same time combined with the belief that we can multitask means we have rejected the intellectual tradition of solitary, single-minded concentration, which actually reduces the amount of content we remember. And with libraries reducing operating hours,[16] the traditional location to concentrate and study without distractions is slowly becoming defunct.

Focused effort makes success possible

Another factor that may underlie the pressures that turn young men off could be a lack of a good work ethic, which many parents in Western countries no longer make a priority to teach to their children. Students in Shanghai were number one in both maths and reading on the international PISA tests. Other places in East Asia such as Hong Kong, Singapore, Japan, Taiwan and South Korea directly followed.[17] Students in China take academics very seriously, and both parents and schools are determined to prepare children for success. Sometimes it's to an extreme, such as with the 'sitting mothers'. In Vietnam, which ranked eighth place in maths, half of all parents keep in touch with their child's teacher throughout the year to monitor their progress.[18]

The 'all work and no play' philosophy has its trade-offs, such as the Japanese statistics on sexless marriages that we noted previously. In China, suicide is the leading cause of death in young people aged 15 to 34,[19] mostly due to the stress young people feel in school, rising social inequality, as well as the difficulty in finding jobs after school is done.[20] Excessive Internet use and excessive gaming are also well documented in South Korea and China, which have hundreds of treatment programmes and boot-camp-style inpatient facilities to regulate sleep, diet and exercise and rid the patients (mostly young men) of their compulsions.[21] It is obvious that parents and societies must develop a balanced approach of promoting a solid work ethic in schools and in careers, but within the context of developing a more rounded child. Excessive stress on children to perform up to parents' overly high expectations can be devastating. In contrast, the laissez-faire approach, as in the US and UK, of many parents can lead to chronic underachievement and failure to make the grade, not only in school, but with life's endless demands.

School's out – now what?

Today, all fingers are pointing towards STEM (science, technology, engineering and mathematics) careers as guaranteed jobs. Nearly twice as many students from China and the European Union are getting engineering and science degrees than students from the US. The National Science Foundation (NSF) actually puts the US 20th out of 24 industrialized nations in terms of 24-year-olds who got their first degree in the 'hard sciences'.[22]

The same idea was emphasized in a recent Casey Daily Research report: 'intellectual capital' will be the most important factor not only for the job market but also for growing national economies. To remain competitive, nations must make STEM studies a priority, such as investing in computers, electronics, biosciences, engineering and other growing high-tech fields, because more jobs require advanced technical skills. In essence, there are too many liberal arts majors![23]

A study from Georgetown University lists the five college majors with the highest unemployment rates (crossed against popularity), with clinical psychology, miscellaneous fine arts, US history, library science, military technologies and educational psychology topping the list – all were above 10 per cent. Unemployment rates for STEM subjects hovered around 0 to 3 per cent: astrophysics/astronomy, around 0 per cent; geological and geophysics engineering, 0 per cent; physical science, 2.5 per cent; geosciences, 3.2 per cent; and maths/computer science, 3.5 per cent. Parenthetically as psychologists, these are personally worrying statistics.

STEM jobs also pay more. The list of the twenty highest mid-career median salaries, by college degree, features no careers from the liberal arts. Liberal arts degrees provide few prospects for graduates. Yet the bubble continues to inflate. In the 2009–10 school year, around 690,000 non-US citizens were enrolled at US colleges, the highest level in the world and up 26 per cent from a decade ago. Non-US students constitute 2.5 per cent of bachelor's degree students, 10 per cent of graduate students, and 33 per cent of doctoral candidates, with 18 per cent of non-US students enrolled in engineering programmes – nearly triple the level of US students.[24]

Anyone from our survey who selected 'Young men in America will not be as innovative or capable as their peers in other First World countries' may have rightly noticed these trends that are a neon sign of the times not to be ignored except at one's future peril. We believe this conclusion may also be applied to young men in the UK.

Women climb, men decline in college landscapes

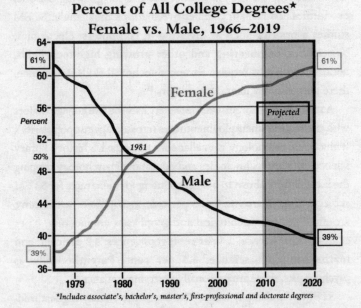

Percent of All College Degrees*
Female vs. Male, 1966–2019

*Includes associate's, bachelor's, master's, first-professional and doctorate degrees

(Source: US Department of Education (Institute of Education Sciences), 2009)

This graph is one of the most powerful visual representations of our message throughout this book – that guys are declining in academic proficiency as girls are rising, even soaring above previous generations of women.

Sex education versus porn 'education'

> The high availability of Internet porn combined with a lack of sex education means many young guys don't know what they're getting into. They're going to have challenges later with women because they don't realize how it's impacting or shaping their sexuality. For them, sex becomes an objectified experience. I have talked with guys that have to fantasize about being with their partner when they're actually with their partner because they're disconnected from the sensation of their own body connecting with another body.
>
> – Celeste Hirschman, sex and relationship therapist, co-creator of the
> Somatica Method[25]

Sex education is to porn as reality is to fantasy. There's a lot of fantasy material freely available, but very few informative resources out there for young people regarding real-life sex. We cannot label porn as all bad, but when young men are on a regular diet of it – watching it *before* they've actually started having sex or even kissed a girl – one has to wonder how it affects their views on normal – or reality-based – sexual behaviour. Almost all people can recall the first erotic image they saw; like a flashbulb memory it is forever emblazoned in our minds. Ogi Ogas and Sai Gaddam explain the kind of lasting impact that erotic cues can have:

> Many male sexual obsessions appear to form after a single sexual exposure... almost all life-long sexual interests in men first form during adolescence. Clinicians report that it is very rare for an adult man to form a new sexual obsession with a visual object. If the male desire software was operating solely

according to the principles of conditioning, then age should not be a significant factor. Instead, there appears to be a special window of time when visual sexual interests can form – what neuroscientists call a critical period.[26]

When this critical period gets hijacked, it seems men can suffer from what one Italian study called 'sexual anorexia', which occurs after watching copious amounts of online porn. Many of the young men in this large-scale 28,000-person survey started 'excessive consumption' of porn sites as early as 14 years old and later on, in their mid-20s, became inured to 'even the most violent images'.[27] The problem worsens when young men's sexuality develops independently from real-life sexual relationships. As they develop reduced responses to habitually watched porn sites, their libido drops, and then it becomes nearly impossible to get an erection. A lot of young men in our own 20,000-person survey said that porn distorted their idea of a healthy sexual relationship and that 'the script' of porn was always playing in the back of their mind when they were with a real female. Many women however, reject the scripts, especially when men try to enact certain scenes without any prior communication.

Surely those views would be tempered by better sex education and conversations about what to expect from real-life sexual relationships. Here's how one male high school student from our survey responded: 'I think that our society, one which allows the display of blood and gore and viscera on a network television but gawks at the slightest implication of a nipple, likely due to lingering protestant ideals, should become better acquainted [with] and less ashamed of its sexuality, especially considering how much more common and useful it is than a desensitization to death and disembowelment.'

The average age at which children first view porn is 11 years old.[28] Sexual education in non-religious public schools tends to begin around the same time, and in the US it is taught mainly in two forms: abstinence-only and comprehensive. The abstinence-only approach promotes the abstinence from sex before marriage. Comprehensive sex education promotes abstinence but also informs students of the benefits of contraception and how to avoid sexually transmitted infections (STIs). Neither the comprehensive nor the abstinence-only approach discusses porn. According to a 2010 report from the Centers for Disease Control and Prevention (CDC), almost all teens in America have received a formal sex education by age 18, but only about two-thirds have been taught about birth control methods.[29] Amazingly, only 13 states require that instruction be medically accurate and 19 require information on condoms or contraception, while 37 require that information on abstinence be provided.[30]

The UK government currently requires that primary schools cover anatomy, puberty and the biological aspects of sexual reproduction and use of hormones to control and promote fertility, and later, secondary schools are required – at minimum – to provide students with information about STIs and HIV/AIDS.[31] Many students describe their sex education as 'poor' or 'very poor', and many feel ill-equipped to navigate the physical and emotional landscape of sex. In a 2013 study, more than half of those polled said the sex education they received at school didn't cover what they really needed to know. More distressing is the fact that a quarter of British school children hadn't received sex education of any kind.[32]

Not surprisingly, neither the comprehensive nor the abstinence-only approach is very effective in its stated objectives. People are marrying later than they ever have; the average age in the US is 28 for men and 26 for women.[33] In the UK the mean age at first marriage is 32.4 for men and 30.3 for women.[34] At the same time, 30 per cent of 16- to 24-year-olds in the UK say they first started having sex when they were 15 years old or younger[35] and 88 per cent of teens who pledge abstinence and 90 per cent of Americans overall will have sex before marriage.[36]

Obviously, nations with a strong religious orientation within their political realm, like the US, have pressures to downplay sex altogether, as something reserved only for marriage, and the topic is not discussed openly in civilized conversation.

Making contraception less available to teens tends to backfire, says Marty Klein, author of *America's War on Sex: The Attack on Law, Lust, and Liberty*. Teens that receive an abstinence-only sex education have the same amount of sex that other teens are having, except they don't use protection as often. Where abstinence-only sex education fails to impact sexual behaviour, it still shapes how teens perceive their actions. Young people that get less sex education understand less about sex and their bodies, have lower self-worth and are less open to talking about their sexual feelings and experiences with an adult.[37] It has been shown that when young people are given a comprehensive education about sex they don't have more sexual partners than those who didn't receive sex education, rather sex education programmes help delay the onset of sexual behaviour, and when they do begin having sex they use condoms more often, have fewer unplanned pregnancies and contract fewer STIs.[38]

In the US 15- to 24-year-olds made up about 25 per cent of the sexually active population, yet they acquired nearly half of all new STIs.[39] In 2012 there were 29.4 births per 1,000 women aged 15 to 19 – a higher teen birth rate than in almost every other developed country.[40] An estimated 84 per cent of women who had abortions in 2008 were unmarried. Abortion rates have been decreasing every year since 1990.[41] The United Kingdom has a slightly lower 44.2 conceptions per 1,000 women aged 15 to 19, nearly half of which (49 per cent) resulted in abortion, bringing the UK teen birth rate to 27.9 per 1,000 women.[42] It is the highest rate in Western Europe.[43] Despite the overall trend of declining teen births, approximately five out of six teen mothers in the US are unmarried, whereas approximately one out of six teen mothers in 1960 were unmarried.[44] In the UK, 57 per cent of all conceptions occurred outside a marriage or civil partnership.[45]

Teen childbearing cost the US about $3 billion in public expenditures and $6 billion in lost tax revenue each year, says the CDC.[46] The direct medical costs of STIs among 15- to 24-year-olds are estimated to cost another $6.5 billion annually.[47] Yet the grand total for funding all abstinence education, pregnancy/STI/ HIV prevention and education programmes, and family planning services annually is only $874 million.[48] The UK spends roughly £125 million annually in income support alone for teen mums (excluding other costs such as assistance with rent and council tax).[49] If it's not already obvious, these numbers on their own clearly indicate that it is worth it to make these programmes more effective.

Students want better programmes, too, but unfortunately they have little influence on what information schools give them. With few public resources and no help from parents, the Internet has become the main go-to resource for unanswered questions and curiosities. Porn, being as accessible as it is, is now serving as both sexual educator and safe haven for emerging sexual needs.

One complicating factor in all this is the insidious intrusion of time-perspective personalities in sexual decision-making, in particular the present-hedonistic orientation that typifies many teenagers. Many teens act on impulse without concern for future consequences – they leap before looking. And they are curious, which is only natural.

Young people are going to learn about sex one way or another, and technology is here to stay, which begs the question to parents: would you like to educate your children about sex – or would you rather let the industries, like porn and other popular media, which exploit your failure to do so, be their primary source of education? 'Don't do it,' or 'be safe,' isn't an education. Although condoms tend to break less than vows of abstinence, kids need more grown-ups they can talk with and readily accessible resources they can go to for issues and questions. Parents must begin sensitive conversations about sex with their children not later than 10 or 11 years old.

10

Environmental Changes

Are young men less fertile than their fathers and grand-fathers were? New research is suggesting that this is the case. Richard Sharpe, a male reproductive health specialist at the University of Edinburgh, found from a series of synchronized studies that one in five young men in northern Europe has a sperm count low enough to negatively affect his fertility. Why such a dramatic change in a short time frame? Sharpe's observations, highlighted by the *Wall Street Journal*, were discussed along with other research from Australia that found low sperm count to be correlated with the men's own marijuana use, maternal smoking during pregnancy, having a low birth weight and being overweight or underweight in childhood.[1] Certain lifestyle choices such as alcohol and tobacco use, illegal drug use (including anabolic steroids and cocaine), stress, obesity and prolonged use of computers or video display monitors, can also contribute to these newly discovered lower sperm counts.[2]

These factors are all-important, but are only a piece of the puzzle we are trying to solve. There are other elements at play that are beyond individual control. In recent years much attention has been given to pervasive and damaging hormone-altering chemicals in our living environments, such as endocrine disruptors.

The endocrine system, also known as the hormone system, regulates all biological processes in the body from conception to death, including the development of the brain and nervous system, growth and functioning of the reproductive system, and regulation of the metabolism and blood sugar levels. It is made up of glands (mainly the female ovaries, male testes, and pituitary, thyroid and adrenal glands), hormones that are produced and released by the glands into the bloodstream, and receptors on organs and tissues around the body that recognize and react to the hormones. The hormones act as chemical messengers that bind to compatible receptors, and once attached those receptors carry out the hormone's instructions. Some endocrine disruptors mimic natural hormones, which fools the body into over- or under-producing certain hormones (such as growth hormones, oestrogen, androgens, insulin or thyroid), and in doing so throws off the body's natural balance.[3]

According to the National Institute of Environmental Health Sciences (NIEHS), endocrine disruptors are chemicals found in a variety of natural and man-made products such as pharmaceuticals, food, metal food cans, plastic beverage bottles, detergents, cosmetics, toys, pesticides and flame retardants – in the form of polybrominated diphenyl ethers (PBDEs) – that are often found in older furniture, carpets, car seats and mattresses. These products may contain dioxin and dioxin-like compounds, polychlorinated biphenyls, DDT and other pesticides, or plasticizers like phthalates and bisphenol A (BPA), which, at levels yet to be determined, interfere with the body's endocrine system and have detrimental immune, reproductive, developmental and neurological effects in all animals, including humans.[4]

As far back as 1950, researchers noted that the pesticide DDT could hinder the sexual development of roosters, leading to 'chemical castration', and other reproductive peculiarities, say Theo Colborn, Dianne Dumanoski and John Myers, authors of *Our Stolen Future: Are We Threatening Our Fertility, Intelligence, and Survival? A Scientific Detective Story*. Since then, more and more incidences popped up around North America and Europe; birds, otters, alligators and fish had undergone noticeable hormonal and reproductive abnormalities because of exposure to PCBs – chemicals that are used to insulate electrical equipment, and other synthetic compounds.[5]

In a 2002 article for *New Scientist*, Julie Wakefield described how in the 1980s Mike Howell, a fish biologist at Samford University in Alabama, observed female mosquitofish in Florida rivers developing the same kind of enlarged anal fins that their male counterparts used in mating. Investigating further, he found the fish were downstream from a paper mill. A year before Wakefield's article, Howell and his team analysed samples taken downstream in the polluted water of another paper mill. They found traces of androgens, particularly androstenedione, which is a precursor to testosterone and an anabolic steroid popular with body-builders. In this particular instance, sterols in the wood pulp that were churned out by the mill had reacted with bacteria in the water, causing the presence of androstenedione, making Howell's team wonder if similar biological processes were releasing more androgens into the environment. Wakefield went further, saying that we shouldn't just be concerned about androgens, but anti-androgens too, which are chemicals that prevent the usual activity of male hormones in the body. Anti-androgens are capable of halting the testosterone production, blocking its ability to communicate with cells that turn on key genes, or even tampering with the activity of genes testosterone usually turns on. 'This is worrying,' says Wakefield, 'because testosterone is vital for the normal development of the male sex organs'.[6]

The biggest unknown is the cumulative effect of endocrine disruptors. Michael Skinner, who runs a research laboratory at Washington State University, shed some light on how biological instructions are transferred to subsequent generations when he conducted an experiment with pregnant rats in 2005. The experiment was supposed to test whether exposing them to a fungicide would affect the sex of the unborn foetus, and although he and his colleagues found lower sperm counts and decreased fertility in the male offspring, there was no effect on sexual differentiation. Afterwards, one of the research fellows mistakenly bred the grandchildren of those exposed rats, creating a fourth generation from the original rats. Skinner told her she might as well analyse them, too. The results were astonishing. The third generation of males born after the pregnant female had been exposed to the fungicide had low sperm counts like their grandfathers, but the researchers also discovered something new.

Jeneen Interlandi explained in *Smithsonian Magazine* that the initial exposure of the pregnant rat – the great-grandmother – to the toxins would change the pattern of molecules known as methyl groups that fasten onto the DNA in the foetus's germ-line cells, which would eventually become that rat's sperm or eggs. Like 'burrs stuck to a knit sweater,' she says, these methyl molecules disrupted the functioning of the DNA and were carried down to future generations, opening them up to disease. Skinner hypothesized that in the future, medical diagnostics could involve having methylation patterns screened, as that might indicate prior generations' exposure to chemicals that are impacting the well-being of the current patient. The Environmental Protection Agency (EPA) criticized his study as having no relevancy for the risk assessment on a certain chemical because of the exaggerated doses of the chemicals, but it is provocative work nonetheless. No doubt further research will help unravel the mysteries of such genetic inheritance.[7]

To sum up, the potential short- and long-term effects of these persistent, possibly bio-accumulative and toxic chemicals being put out into our environments need further study by independent research groups. Understandably, the inconclusive results of many studies combined with the rising rates of chronic and fatal illnesses have made people uneasy. Around the world, for example, testicular cancer rates are twice what they were in the 1960s,[8] and cases of hypospadias, a birth defect where the penis doesn't develop normally and the urethral opening appears in an irregular position on the shaft, have also increased.

In Denmark, testicular cancer rates tripled between the 1940s and 1980s.[9] Danish researcher Niels Skakkebaek has found multiple reproductive problems such as testicular cancer, abnormally formed genitals and low sperm counts all rising simultaneously. He and his team believed unusual development of the testes was the cause, referring to the condition as testicular dysgenesis syndrome (TDS); a process that Skakkebaek believes can be affected in the womb. If hormone disruptors inhibited the natural process of the cells that developed into sperm, he said, it could predispose a person to infertility and cancer later in life.[10] Research has shown pregnant women and their newborn babies are most sensitive to the effects of these chemicals, because that is when a child's organ and neural systems are initially forming.[11]

According to Mehran Alaee, a research scientist at Environment Canada, North American PBDE levels double every two to five years; the level of PBDEs present in the breast milk of American and Canadian women is forty times higher than in the breast milk of Swedish women, where there is greater governmental concern over endocrine disruptors.[12] In the UK, PBDE concentrations in indoor dusts and air has grown in recent years, but the resulting burden on the body has not been well-studied.[13] Bruce Lanphear and researchers from Simon Fraser University found that infants of women exposed to high levels of PBDEs in early pregnancy suffered drops in IQ comparable to the detrimental effects of lead exposure in the environment.[14]

The current obesity pandemic contributes to these problems, as the more body fat a person has, the greater the potential is for toxins to be stored. Wakefield said the majority of these compounds aren't excreted by the body, but instead build up inside body fat tissues. The real problems, however, arise when body fat breaks down, because the accumulated toxins are then released into the bloodstream. 'No one understands how the chemicals in this cocktail might interact with one another to increase or reduce the overall effect on our health,' says Wakefield.[15] This should be a huge wake-up call to both consumers, who have the purchasing power, and the health authorities, whose duty it is to protect their citizens.

11

Technology Enchantment and Arousal Addiction

Technology challenges us to assert our human values, which means that, first of all, we have to figure out what they are. That's not so easy. Technology isn't good or bad, it's powerful and it's complicated. Take advantage of what it can do. Learn what it can do. But also ask, 'What is it doing to us?' We're going to slowly, slowly find our balance, but I think it's going to take time.

– Sherry Turkle[1]

'Enchantment', was the word *The Lord of Rings* author J.R.R. Tolkien used to define human beings' total immersion in a secondary world. He said that the more 'you think that you are, bodily inside [a] Secondary World [the more] the experience may be very similar to Dreaming…but…you are in a dream that some other mind is weaving, and the knowledge of that alarming fact may slip from your grasp.'[2] Tolkien was recognizing the ability to get lost in tales and stories. When you consider how much easier it is to get caught up in a virtual world where the story is told through visual stimuli than a story that was previously only written in text or spoken in words, Tolkien's revelation is alarming indeed.

The structure of language and slowness of reading text makes it more difficult to get wrapped up in the same way one can in the implicit and visceral virtual world of online games. There is no reward system in books, for example, except for the ultimate satisfaction of having solved a puzzle presented, or having understood the meaning of a message in a parable. Unlike video games there is no exclusivity, status or reward associated with page progression, and unlike porn there is no orgasm at the end – with the exception of erotic novels and books such as *Fifty Shades of Grey*, where perhaps there is some convergence.

When we immerse ourselves in a stimulating visual environment where a lot of information is demanding our immediate attention, the cognitive load overburdens our working memory, and not a whole lot is going into our long-term memory. Having a high cognitive load amplifies distractedness, and makes it more difficult for the mind to distinguish between relevant and irrelevant data. The mind gets bogged down by constant pop-ups, ads and hyperlinks, devoting more brain power to evaluating whether to click on them or not, and less attention is given to understanding whether the content is relevant or not. Watching porn can also interfere with men's working memory – especially the greater their level of arousal (and need to masturbate) is[3] – which could explain why so many of them miss class or forget to go to appointments after extended porn immersion.

Books and movies may be able to transport the reader's mind to another world but they don't offer the same satisfaction or feeling of achievement that a person can experience in the roles they play in gamified* virtual worlds. In porn, young men get to have a taste of what it's like to be a sheikh with their own virtual harem, and in video games they get to experience being the hero and the antihero without the conditions or permanence of real life, and without risking life or limb. Therefore, it's no wonder

---

* *Gamification* is a term that describes a system that is designed to motivate people and evoke their competitive drives by using rewards, feedback loops and publicized status indicators (i.e. leader boards, progress graphs, ability to 'level up', friend counts).

that many young men consider the thrill-packed worlds of online porn and video games far more exciting than anything they encounter on a daily basis in their real lives.

Video games offer virtual rewards at regular intervals, often after a certain level has been reached or a specific skill has been mastered. This schedule of reinforcement fits in perfectly with the kind of operant conditioning used by psychologist B.F. Skinner in the 1940s to motivate pigeons to press a lever endlessly for extra food in his specially designed 'Skinner Box'. Behaviour that is positively reinforced tends to be repeated, especially if it comes at variable ratios, and in video games, after the required amount of effort and skill has been made, the reward is guaranteed.

Some games are designed to give rewards sporadically along the way to the goal. Similar to the bait-and-switch technique, these games reward behaviour only some of the time in order to keep a person engaged. Throwing in the occasional punishment – like taking away hard-to-come-by weapons – is another way to effectively control a player's behaviour as well as motivate them to improve their skills so they don't make the same mistakes again.

Maressa Orzack, who was a clinical psychologist and assistant clinical professor of psychology at Harvard Medical School, determined that the process of character development and reward systems within video games are a facet of operant conditioning, and are deliberately being incorporated into the games by their sophisticated designers.[4] The problem, say Neils Clark and P. Shavaun Scott, authors of Game Addiction: The Experience and the Effects, is that a 'person who is initially motivated by their own intrinsic reasons for achieving may become dependent on these outside rewards and actually lose their innate internal motivation to achieve things in life'.[5]

Exacerbating this problem is the fact that these sources of stimulation and thus, this type of conditioning, are now totally pervasive. The Internet, television, video games and porn are available twenty-four hours a day on a variety of devices (computers, laptops, phones, TVs, iPads and so on). One of the reasons why boys default to these seductive worlds more easily than girls is that we are telling boys their inner mental worlds – filled with sex and aggression – are unacceptable and scary, therefore they have no other outlets for their natural impulses. This is all contributing to an overall decrease in motivation to contribute or partake in real-world events and in complex, social relationships that contain multiple layers of verbal and non-verbal code.

One young man we interviewed told us:

> With porn and video games' instant gratification, other pursuits such as women, physical activity and school become far less enticing. Young men now yield to the power of pressing play, and subsequently need to go no further than their television or computer screens for endless enjoyment. The variety of stimulation that those two activities provide has the potential to leave little desire to take part in the aforementioned pursuits (I should note that this desire is further diminished by marijuana and other drug usage greatly).

Gabe Deem, a recovering porn addict turned public speaker and counsellor for youth in Texas, echoed a similar sentiment:

> I always thought video games and porn were amazing. Besides the pleasure they gave me, video games also fulfilled my competitive nature and intrinsic drive to cultivate and produce things as a man. Instead of desiring to get a good job, lead a family, and participate in a community, I wanted to improve my rank online, lead my team of gamers, and spend all my time chatting with guys I have never met.
>
> Besides the pleasure porn provided...well...I only watched porn because of the pleasure it provided. I never used porn or video games because of issues in my life, I used them because I had access, and enjoyed them. I had no clue they

could potentially have a negative physiological impact on me. Growing up I almost constantly had a girlfriend and I did not have a traumatic experience as a kid, never was abused, and had no history of addiction in my family.

I was what some call a 'contemporary addict' who just had unlimited access to supernormal stimulation and over years of chronic over-consumption became hooked and numbed. I was not your 'classic addict' who turned to a behaviour or substance to 'ease the pain of life', I turned to the behaviour and substance to 'experience the pleasure of life'.

I often hear this myth thrown around, that only guys who get hooked on porn have other issues in their life that they are running from or trying to medicate. This was not the case for me and many other guys I know who watched a lot of porn and played countless hours of video games; in my case the 'issues' came after the consumption.[6]

Our regularly engaged-in habits cycle back to our brains, creating not only behavioural patterns, but also physiological changes in neural circuitry. Nicholas Carr discusses just how malleable our brains are, and how well they adapt to new stimuli in *The Shallows*. He tells us that: 'Virtually all of our neural circuits ... are subject to change ... The plasticity diminishes as we get older – brains do get stuck in their ways – but it never goes away. Our neurons are always breaking old connections and forming new ones, and brand-new nerve cells are always being created.'[7]

Essentially the brain is capable of re-programming itself from moment to moment, modifying the way it functions. This is what neural plasticity means. Despite its massive plasticity, over time the deeper any brain groove is the more ingrained behaviours become and the harder they are to modify via retraining. Carr references a couple of fascinating examples. In the 1970s biologist Eric Kandel used a large species of sea slug called Aplysia to demonstrate that synaptic connections can change. He found that even if it is lightly touched the sea slug will reflexively recoil, yet, provided it is not being harmed, when exposed to repeated touch it will quickly habituate and its recoiling instinct will disappear. Kandel observed the slug's nervous systems and found that this learned behaviour (or lack of it) was mirrored by a gradual weakening of the synaptic connections between the sensory neurons that 'felt' the touch and the motor neurons that signal the gill to withdraw. In the beginning of the experiment, about 90 per cent of the sensory neurons in a slug's gill had connections to motor neurons, but after the gill was touched forty times, only 10 per cent still had links. Kandel won the Nobel Prize for this series of experiments and its theoretical implications.

Alvaro Pascual-Leone, a neurology researcher at Harvard Medical School, offered additional clues as to how the way in which we perceive something affects the connections in our brains. He recruited a group of people who had no experience playing a piano, and taught them a basic verse, then he divided the group in two. One group was instructed to practise the music on a keyboard for a couple of hours every day for the following five days. The other group was told to sit in front of a keyboard and just imagine playing the music – and not touch the keys – for an equal amount of time. Pascual-Leone used transcranial magnetic stimulation (TMS) to map the participants' brain activity over the duration of the experiment and found that both groups exhibited identical changes in their brains; in other words the brains of the group that just imagined playing the verse had been altered solely because of their thoughts – without taking any overt action. In this case, thinking or imagining made it so. Both Kandel's and Pascual-Leone's research show the remarkable ways in which the brain habituates to repeated familiar experiences after just a short period of conditioning.[8]

The implications of this kind of conditioning with regard to porn are shocking when you think about the ease of habituating a person to respond to sex that is only a collection of pixels, but it could also provide a silver lining to those wishing to retrain their brain to become more responsive to their real-life sexual partners. The good news appears to be the same as the bad news. Just as synaptic links between neurons become stronger and more abundant due to specific and repeated experiences, releasing higher concentrations of neurotransmitters for example, the brain also becomes less responsive to less familiar experiences.

Many people who watched Phil's TED Talk commented that porn and video games should not be lumped together. Gamers are not necessarily porn users, and vice versa. In many obvious ways, porn and video games are very different entities, but they share many non-obvious characteristics. Both video games and porn are entertaining and have interesting and useful applications, but they can also be a huge waste of time and potentially psychologically and socially damaging to some males. We are concerned about young men who are excessively using porn and/or video games in social isolation. There has been no established guideline about what constitutes an excessive amount of video games or porn;[9] ultimately, if the user is unable to control their gaming or porn habit despite negative social, emotional, interpersonal, academic or professional consequences, there's a problem.[10] The determination of the severity should revolve around the individual's response.

Both video and online porn are relatively recent forms of digital entertainment that have been added to the social environment. The industries are increasingly merging and becoming particularly seductive to gamers, as Andrew Doan, author of *Hooked on Games*, points out:

> The combination of sex and pornography in a video game has the potential for explosive growth and has already proven to become so. In Second Life, it's reported that there are over 20 million accounts with more than half of those being active gamers …There are people making significant amounts of real money by providing a virtual escort service, some are making six-figure incomes. By day, a woman could become a

mom, lawyer, or other professional. But by night, she is the
voice behind an avatar that charges twenty dollars an hour for
a man to have a virtual companion and virtual sex.[11]

The California-based start-up Sinful Robot was also in the process
of designing virtual reality sex games for the Oculus Rift, a 3D
technology that completely covers a user's field of vision like a ski
mask.[12] The company disintegrated some time in 2013,[13] but it's
only a matter of time before someone else creates immersive 3D
games that incorporate virtual sex.

Eroticism and motivation are both fuelled by arousal. If there is
lust, arousal veers in a sexual direction, and if there is a need to
triumph, arousal sends one down the path of goal setting and
long-term success. Real life is competing with digital alternatives
for nearly every aspect of existence, since porn and video games
are readily accessible, burden-free, pleasurable and entertaining.
The choice for lots of young men is often the digital alternative to
the physical, existential-reality version.

Futurama's 'I Dated A Robot' episode comes to mind, where
Fry, a young man who accidentally ends up in the year 3000,
creates a Lucy Liu robot who is programmed to love everything
about him. After a short time he becomes disinterested in doing
anything other than spend time with her, at which point his friends
intervene and show him a propaganda video warning against
human–robot romance. In the video, a young man, Billy, becomes
infatuated with a Marilyn Monrobot. All Billy wants is to make
out with her. Even when his neighbour Mavis, an attractive young
woman, asks him if he'd like to come over later and make out
with her, he tells her that walking across the street is too far to go
for making out. The narrator of the propaganda video sombrely
asks, 'Did you notice what went wrong in that scene?' Before the
robots, says the narrator, Billy probably would have worked hard
to make money with his paper round, which he'd then use to take
Mavis out on a date, thereby earning him the chance to have sex

and reproduce. 'But in a world where teens can date robots, why should he bother?' Naturally, aliens destroy the planet shortly afterwards.[14]

Though nearly every social need in reality now has a complement in the digital world, it is unclear whether the digital alternatives satisfy those needs in the same way. In Abraham Maslow's 'hierarchy of needs' – which depicts the stages of human development often as a pyramid, with the most basic needs at the bottom – the primary two levels of physiological and safety needs must be met in physical reality. Is it possible, however, for the top three needs in Maslow's hierarchy – belongingness, love and esteem, and self-actualization – to be met in digital reality? Could a person be just as, if not more, fulfilled in digital reality? The answer is yes and no. Surely, some needs can be achieved in the digital world, but because these needs are met without risk of consequence, and frequently in social isolation – as if in a dress rehearsal – a person who is, for example, gaming alone may well be able to achieve their esteem needs yet completely bypass a sense of belongingness and fail to address their love needs.

Gamers may think they have 'hacked Maslow', but it does not come without a major side effect: entitlement without the ability to relate to others. As one person from our survey commented, games put 'you in fictional MATURE situations, but without any of the consequences. You can feel powerful and "experienced" without all the failure leading up to real-life success in those areas.' So a gamer could be 'hot shit' in one world, and develop a sense of superiority, but most people will have no idea who they are or what they have 'accomplished'. Furthermore, self-actualization could not be reached without the fulfilment of the other needs, so a lack of intimacy and appreciation for others creates a distorted sense of potential and actualization that is not based in any shared social reality.

Maslow's hierarchy

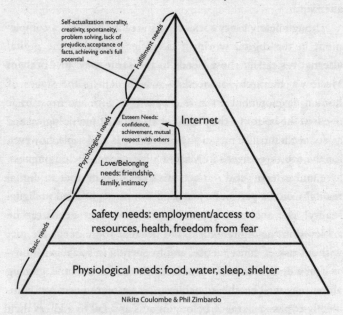

Hacked Maslow: An Unstable Pyramid

Self-actualization morality, creativity, spontaneity, problem solving, lack of prejudice, acceptance of facts, achieving one's full potential

Fulfillment needs

Esteem Needs: confidence, achievement, mutual respect with others

Internet

Psychological needs

Love/Belonging needs: friendship, family, intimacy

Safety needs: employment/access to resources, health, freedom from fear

Basic needs

Physiological needs: food, water, sleep, shelter

Nikita Coulombe & Phil Zimbardo

A 25-year-old male gamer we spoke with reflected this idea:

> The PC gamer mentality is very elitist, though really it's a combination of a superiority and an inferiority complex. Many of them feel inferior to people on the 'outside', so they have to compensate. They have a need to portray a badass online, so they can feel superior to others. A lot of them will berate you if you mess up in a game. People used to say GGWP – good game, well played – now that hardly ever happens. People love to mock others when they fail and call them out on it. Even if it was a close match, your opponent might tell you to uninstall the game or say 'easy game, easy win,' just to try and piss you off and get a reaction out of you. They also might gang up on you and put you in a low priority queue, which stalls your game play, not because you are a 'troll' but because they blame

you for the team's loss, or the other players decide they don't like you. This attitude is common in DotA [*Defense of the Ancients*] and in other games I've played, and not just in MMOs [massive multiplayer online games].

When we asked him how feeling superior in games translated into the real world, he said that many gamers had below average social skills to begin with, yet felt they were 'the LeBron James of their respective game'. (LeBron James is an NBA basketball superstar.) He said they still hit a wall, socially, in the real world, and the growing divergence between their online persona and their real-life reputation drove them to play even more to excel in their gaming world since it was easier to achieve their desired status there than in daily life.

Jeremy Bailenson, director of the Virtual Human Interaction Lab at Stanford University, and fellow researcher Nick Yee, call the phenomenon of adapting one's real-life behaviour to that of their digital persona the 'Proteus Effect'.[15] On the positive side, the Proteus Effect has been shown to help people change drug and alcohol problems, and meeting up in a virtual space for support in conquering real-life addictions shows promise, especially for those who might have difficulty getting to a physical treatment centre.[16] On the negative side, it could create or reinforce an inflated ego that clashes with the demands of reality, promote de-individuation or manipulate the way a person thinks.

In real life, when people interact with each other they automatically mimic the other person's speech and posture patterns. In one study, Bailenson, Yee and Ducheneaut showed that if an avatar in a virtual setting was able to mimic the head movements of the participant during a conversation, the participant was more likely to agree with the avatar's point of view than the real-life participants who were in the playback condition. In another study, in which the avatar was trying to persuade a participant, and the avatar's face was morphed to contain 20 to 40 per cent of the participant's features, the facial similarity was such a power-ful cue that it could sway the participant's choice of political candidate, even in high-profile elections. The attractiveness and even the colour or style of the clothing worn by people's charac-ters in a game can alter how they perceive themselves and affect how they interact with others, both inside and outside the game.[17]

Beyond the clash of virtual egos meeting real-world standards, it's unclear how well children can move between reality and digital worlds. Katie Salen, director of design at the Quest to Learn school in New York, says:

> People talk about this distinction between the virtual world
> and the real world, and there's concern that there is an inability
> on the part of young people to separate the two. I actually
> think that that distinction is a very adult idea, an idea that has
> come from a generation of people [for whom] virtual didn't
> exist and it was something new that was then added to the real
> world. But kids have that ability to move kind of seamlessly
> between the digital and the real.[18]

Bailenson says that the distinctions between virtual worlds and reality are becoming blurred to the point where they can even be interchangeable. In the documentary *Digital Nation*, Bailenson makes a realistic-looking avatar of host Douglas Rushkoff:

> In one study, we made you 10 centimetres taller than you actu-
> ally were and had you conduct a negotiation with someone.
> Having 10 centimetres difference in height from your normal
> self causes you to be three times more likely to beat someone
> in a negotiation in virtual reality...Regardless of our actual
> heights, you'll then beat me face to face when we have a nego-
> tiation...A small exposure inside the virtual reality carried
> over to their behaviour face to face...We've done studies with
> children [in which] they see themselves swimming around

with whales in a virtual reality; a week later, half of them will believe that they swam with whales.[19]

It brings to mind the phrase 'fish out of water' – the fish are not aware of the water being swum in, and growing up in the digital age, the virtual 'water' looks and feels like the real 'water'. The youthful eye that has become immersed in an artificial visual world may not readily distinguish elements existing in real life from those in visual media.

Dynamics of porn

In his 1975 film *Love and Death*, Woody Allen said, 'Sex without love is an empty experience, but as empty experiences go, it's one of the best.' Or is it? In the moment, porn can be very gratifying, but the potential negative after-effects must be considered too.

A male high-schooler from our survey shared his thoughts: 'I think the on-demand pleasure, gratification, control and stress release of pornography and video games reduces our patience, makes us hold ourselves to unrealistic expectations and cripples us socially.'

Pornography is the explicit portrayal of sexual subject matter meant to stimulate sexual arousal and satisfaction. Unlike art or erotica, modern porn videos have little artistic merit and are focused solely on the graphic, physical aspects of sex rather than on the beauty, feelings and emotions that accompany intimacy. Depictions of sex have been around since prehistoric times, but the concept of pornography was not widely understood until the latter half of the nineteenth century. The large-scale excavations of Pompeii in the 1860s kicked off discussions on what exactly qualified as obscene, resulting in many of the erotic objects discovered being carted away to private museums – for the eyes of more privileged members.

The production of pornographic films quickly followed the invention of the motion picture in 1895. Soon after that, sexually explicit materials were deemed obscene and made illegal to show publicly, which continued through the 1960s. David Sipress, a long-time cartoonist for the *New Yorker*, summed up the situation well in a drawing that depicted an older man talking to his son and grandson, who were both using laptops, telling them that when he was their age, he 'had to hike 10 miles through the ice and snow to a store when he wanted to look at dirty pictures'.[20] It was a different time.

Today, the anonymity of the Internet means anyone anywhere can watch porn and they don't have to interact with anyone to get access to it. Technically access to pornographic material is limited to people over 18 years old, though enforcing 'community standards' is tricky, especially online. Most people would agree that hard-core pornography should not be available to children, but access to it – voluntary and involuntary – is difficult to regulate, and less likely to be enforced.

Despite what appear to be billions of dollars in profits, industry executives say the business of porn is suffering these days due to the weak economy, piracy and free or inexpensive porn available online.[21]

While huge profits used to be made from hotel room adult entertainment and DVD sales, the market has shifted in favour of the affordability and anonymity that the Internet provides; porn is now only a click away. Technology has also made it easier to enter the industry; anyone who wants to have sex on camera can be a porn player – and if they're any good at enticing viewers, a woman or teen girl can become a well-paid porn star.

Can young men learn about sex from watching porn videos? Sure, somewhat. They can learn that sexual acts can be quite varied and, thereby, a continual source of pleasure over one's lifetime by consensual experimentation with one's partner. Beyond that, the take-away message from porn viewing is likely to be ego-deflating because of the assumption that what you see is what is the norm, the only acceptable way to perform, the appropriate way to relate to a sexual partner; worst of all, you see that size not only matters but it dominates everything.

Several young men from our UK student survey weighed in:

> I believe without a doubt this creates paranoia and unrealistic expectations for boys as it is not addressed at all within sex education (at least in the sessions that I have had). Therefore it means that boys explore it [for] themselves and will then feel demasculated if they don't look the same …

> [Male friends] were disappointed when the girl was quieter than they have seen, and when they didn't reach a single orgasm, when they have seen girls orgasm numerous times before the guy [in porn] … Girls … were disappointed at the guys' stamina lasting only a few minutes, instead of the half-hours they were [used] to seeing in porn.

> I currently do not receive sex education. I do, however, believe that online porn creates an unrealistic expectation of sex as it encourages certain 'porn-star' images that are not in the slightest way representative of the average person. Not only does this damage young people's self-esteem, as they may become depressed with their image, but it damages the way sex is perceived, as there is a huge emphasis on selfish pleasure and physical attraction, disregarding emotional attachment to the partner.

Several young women shared their observations, too:

> I took a feminist studies class that emphasized the impact media has on a woman's reflection of her body. This is true, although it angered me that this professor believed it had no impact on men as well. When my boyfriend and I first started dating, sex was a really difficult aspect of our relationship for him. It resulted in him deciding to go to therapy to work out issues he had about his body and his ability to satisfy me sexually. I believe that this has a lot to do with what media such as video games and porn portrays as masculinity and

what is needed to be a sexually appealing man. It saddens me to think that these outlets have painted a picture that caused a man, who I love and am very attracted to, to think so lowly of himself. Cognitive-behavioural therapy did wonders for his performance anxiety and we're doing great now.

Because the older generations never had to deal with this, they don't understand that young men need to be educated about sex as an act that is enjoyable to both parties. There are a lot of men who have no idea that women need to be engaged in sex as partners and not as porn stars. Young men are GENUINELY confused about this distinction and don't understand why we won't do 'that thing' they saw in a porno.

Porn does create unrealistic expectations about sex for young people (mainly males) as it promotes an artificial image of 'perfection' which does not necessarily exist and therefore leads to disappointment. Similarly, it portrays sex as an emotionless, meaningless act which may create problems in future sexual relationships.

Porn cheapens sex and discourages men from romance and real intimacy. It teaches them to ignore a woman's emotional needs and view sex in a selfish way.

In my opinion, the roles of men and women seem to be changing rapidly. For example when out at a club you can easily observe how the need for men to chase after women is rapidly decreasing as women seem to be becoming far more desperate and therefore are the ones acting out and throwing themselves at the men who mainly use them and then move on; as highlighted in the porn industry. However despite the fact that I strongly disagree with porn and everything associated with it, one can't blame men for this as it is the women who are becoming easier and aren't helping themselves when wanting to be respected by men.

Most Internet porn has no storyline and no build-up to the sexual performance. There are no words, just actions. There is no suggestion that in real life there are romantic precursors, negotiations, discussions, tender moments, kissing, touching, complimenting and even just talking. Then there is the implicit understanding that the female wants sex as much or more than the male in the video, and she might even initiate unzipping him, take his pants off and start oral sex. That is not going to happen often in the real world.

Imagine learning to play football by watching the best players in the English Premier League destroy their adversaries, or baseball by watching all-star baseball hitter Albert Pujols smack three mammoth home runs in the World Series. They are exceptional athletes with dominant bodies trained for years to be among the best in their profession. So they might inspire, but you learn the game by diligent practice on Little League fields or on playground courts with coaches and peers whose ability level, age and size are comparable to yours.

In porn, nearly all the male actors have enormous penises. They are selected for their size and stamina, and then likely take medications to enhance their arousal. What you don't see are breaks in the action to change camera angles during which they may get 'fluffed' by an assistant, take meds, or get secondary assistance from vacuum pumps or penile injections. So, too, their seeming ability to perform non-stop for twenty minutes may also include off-screen timeouts.

Through watching porn men also feel pressured to fulfil what they believe are female fantasies, mainly having a giant hard cock that lasts for hours. A lot of young men think there is something wrong with them if they have a normal-sized penis or think they have premature ejaculation if they orgasm after ten minutes. It's like putting a treadmill on the highest speed on the highest incline – pretty much no one is going to be able to do that for any extended period of time. Nevertheless, a lot of young men develop sexual performance anxiety when preparing to have sex with a real in-the-flesh woman because of this set of false expectations that are built up as normative over successive viewing of similar scenarios.

Another certain negative effect of boys watching lots of porn is a growing feeling of penis envy, of not measuring up, so to speak. That self-consciousness in a realm so important for male identity is surely a source of disguised discontent. This can be seen in public locker rooms, where many young men refuse to disrobe, undressing in the showers and covering themselves when they come out. When the male sexual enhancement drug Viagra was first promoted, its advertisements featured white-haired older men. Now consider that more men under 30 years old are being prescribed Viagra than ever before to ensure adequate sexual performance.[22] Once such drugs are perceived as necessary to sexual success, it becomes meds over matter in that realm. So those former ad campaigns that started with old-timers years ago have shifted to ever younger looking – even physically active – men who want to be ready for action at the hint of sex.

Chronic stimulation, chronic dissatisfaction

Sex is an undercurrent of Western society, as it is in most religiously oriented nations, but it is not looked at holistically. Love is promoted but lust is denied, even ignored by mainstream media. Lust, however, is hardly out of sight; rather, it's in plain sight, on thousands of online sites. The Internet is the great collective unconscious that provides insight into our needs, desires and fantasies. And while porn may initially help people become more excited about sex, over time it appears to have the opposite effect. A recent study from the Centers for Disease Control and Prevention (CDC) found that 'frequent porn users are more likely to report depression and poor physical health than nonusers, suggesting that by substituting for healthy in-person interactions, porn may start a cycle of social and sexual isolation.'[23]

Porn is an attempt to make up for the under-representation of lust in most domains in our culture; however, it's represented very, very well online. According to the web traffic-reporting site Alexa, 24 out of the top 500 most-viewed general websites world-wide are dedicated to porn – that's nearly 5 per cent. In the UK, 22 out of the top 500 most visited websites are porn sites. To put this in context, nearly 47 of the top 500 sites are different countries' Google homepages. Now consider that the most popular porn sites, LiveJasmin and XVideos, had more traffic than 36 of them, including Google Canada, Mexico, Australia and Germany.[24] LiveJasmin and XVideos are also visited more often than CNN, AOL, Myspace and even Netflix.[25] However, unlike many of the other popular sites, which have a general audience, the porn websites' audience is primarily males under 24 years old, most of whom are viewing in isolation from home or secretly at school.

All of the 24 most popular porn sites offer free content and also offer more exclusive features, such as higher quality high-definition (HD) videos or live webcam viewing for a small fee. You can pretty much find anything you want free of charge, and you can access these videos nearly any time, anywhere in the world that Internet exists.

A buffet of arousal awaits – PornHub has 56 categories listed conveniently in alphabetical order; the average category hosts 5,832 separate videos. The most viewed videos among these categories average 22.3 million views and are about twenty minutes long. On average, it took 33 per cent of the way through the video before there is vaginal or anal penetration. In only a quarter of the videos is there a discernible female orgasm, whereas in 81 per cent of the videos there is a discernible male orgasm – the male orgasm typically is the highlight of the final scene.

Not once in any of the most viewed videos is there a discussion of safer sex practices, or of physical or emotional expectations or boundaries. Condoms are used in only one of the most viewed videos – one in which lesbians are using strap-ons. And many times a man will receive oral sex from a woman and then penetrate her vagina – and then her anus and then move back to her mouth or vagina (known as ATM, for ass-to-mouth), a practice that puts the woman at much higher risk for sexually transmitted infections (STIs) and bacterial infections such as urinary tract infections (UTIs). Very seldom is there a close-up on the man's face, yet there are many close-ups on the woman's.

A commonly used camera angle focuses the lens directly on the genitals while the woman's breasts and/or face are visible in the background. Often the woman is positioned so her facial expressions can be filmed. The man often ejaculates on the woman's breasts or face, or in her mouth, rather than inside her (with the exception of 'creampie' videos). Porn videos usually end shortly after the man has ejaculated, suggesting male ejaculation is the pinnacle of sex, and everything else is secondary. The old 'fade to black' that ended movies has become 'face to black,' as porn ends with the woman's face covered with cum.

These videos insinuate that sexual fantasies never involve conversation. There is very little emotional intimacy portrayed in any fashion, and the few verbal exchanges, if present, are awkwardly scripted. Surprisingly, for all the bad rap porn gets, there are very few instances in which derogatory language about women (such as 'slut', 'cunt' or 'bitch') is directed at the woman – at least that is the case in the most viewed videos. Such language occurs more in gang-bang, rough-sex and interracial multiple penetration scenes. There is also very little physical intimacy, because if partners were actually close to each other, the camera would not be able to capture such graphic close-ups. Another hugely popular category is teen sex with a sub-category of 'college girls being exploited', where the filmmaker asks the ages of the girls, and they say on camera that they are over 18 years old, though they look much younger.

The overall message is that porn is not about sex or making love, it's about 'fucking' in a visually appealing way primarily for the male viewer. That's not to say that women don't enjoy watching people have sex; many do, and there are a good number who watch porn. Simply put, most women just don't enjoy shot after shot of graphic close-ups of body parts bashing together without any context. Porn is not about romance, sexual foreplay or gradual building up to ever greater intimacy. It is about on-demand performance of oral sex initially, then vaginal or anal sex, then variations in positions or partner arrangements. That is not as appealing to most female audiences as it is to most male viewers.

On a positive level, porn can be an outlet for exploring fantasy or for realizing the possibilities during sexual play. Or, porn can serve as a substitute for a lack of sexual partners in real life, for shy men, and for men who cannot afford erotic massages or escorts, or who do not want to deal with the emotional repercussions of a sexual encounter with a woman who expects something more than a one-night stand (or ten-minute body friction exchange). The problem is that isolated porn viewing could set off a progression into further seclusion or emotional distance in romantic relationships. In a recent poll in the UK, a third of light porn users (one hour or less a week) and seven out of ten heavy porn users (more than ten hours a week) said that their porn use caused relationships problems.[26] Overuse of porn could also cause other, unwanted, undesirable changes, which young men are typically unaware of until it is too late.

Dude, where's my erection?

The most powerful sex organ is the brain, and for men, that's where an erection starts. So what happens to your brain when you watch too much porn? Gary Wilson, of YourBrainOnPorn, compares chronic overconsumption of Internet porn to other behavioural addictions such as excessive gambling, video game addiction and food addiction. He points out that there are already more than ninety *brain* studies on Internet addiction, gaming addiction and online porn addiction – all of which reveal the kinds of brain changes seen in drug addiction.[27]

This makes sense because the part of your brain where arousal happens is the same place where addiction occurs: the reward circuitry. Most of this circuit lies behind your nose in evolutionarily ancient structures. It's where you experience the motivation to achieve your desires, to eat, to have sex, to take risks and to fall in love. It's also where you get turned on – or off – or addicted to something, because cravings also arise here.

On his site, Wilson explains that because dopamine is the primary neurotransmitter that turns on the reward circuit, the more aroused you are sexually, the higher your dopamine surges. For example, an erection won't happen if there is not enough dopamine to signal the reward circuitry, but porn-related sexual problems related to dopamine dysregulation can show up in a variety of ways:

- Lack of spontaneous erections.

- Lack of arousal by static porn or previously viewed porn. Often guys need to escalate to more extreme material just to get aroused – a sign of addiction.

- Decreased penile sensitivity – indicating the brain has become numbed to pleasure.

- Delayed ejaculation or the inability to orgasm during sex with a real partner.

- Copulatory impotence – the inability to maintain an erection with a real partner.

- Eventual inability to get any erection, even viewing extreme porn.

- Erectile dysfunction drugs lose their effect. Viagra and Cialis only dilate the blood vessels to sustain an erection; they don't create arousal in the brain. Without arousal, nothing can happen.

Dopamine skyrockets with novelty, so Internet porn can veil creeping sexual performance problems for years before young men realize they have an underlying problem. With every new sexual scene or 'partner', there is another surge of dopamine. If your dopamine starts to decline – that is, your erection starts to dwindle – you just click on something else to boost it back up. And with Internet porn, there is always something new, exciting or shocking.

In the first-ever brain study on Internet porn users, which was conducted at the Max Planck Institute for Human Development in Berlin, researchers found that hours and years of porn use correlated with decreased grey matter in regions of the brain associated with reward sensitivity, as well as reduced responsiveness to erotic still photos.[28] Less grey matter means less dopamine and fewer dopamine receptors. The lead researcher, Simone Kühn, hypothesized that 'regular consumption of pornography more or less wears out your reward system'.[29] This helps explain why some users become dependent on new, or more extreme, porn. They need more and more stimulation to become aroused and get an erection.

Bombarding the reward circuit is the cue to 'fertilize' all those two-dimensional cyber mates. So, the brain creates special pathways that activate the reward circuit without relying on dopamine – but only respond to this specific 'valuable' activity, such as watching Internet porn or playing video games.

The sorry result is that daily life, and often sex with a familiar partner, grows duller and less rewarding. At the same time, stimulation from online porn becomes the only thing the brain registers as worth engaging in. As mentioned earlier, some users have trouble climaxing during real sex, or even getting or maintaining an erection (i.e. erectile dysfunction). Or, even if they are aroused at first (because of the partner's newness), they might soon find their partner no longer turns them on. Their brains now require constant screen-based novelty. Until they retrain their brains, they're stuck.

Wilson says:

> Internet porn is now a powerful memory that calls to you at a subconscious level – because it's the most reliable source of dopamine, erections and relief from your cravings...This is what happens with all addictions. The more you overstimulate the reward circuitry by jacking up your dopamine...the less it responds. Think of a flashlight with fading batteries. In simple terms, your reward circuitry isn't providing enough electricity to power your erections.[30]

An easy way to think about what's happening is that porn is numbing the very thing it intensifies. Or, as Nicholas Carr said, 'when we extend some part of ourselves artificially, we also distance ourselves from the amplified part and its natural functions'.[31]

Arousal addiction: give me the same but different

The addictiveness of video games and porn is a real concern for many reasons. As with all addictions, the activity becomes all-consuming and preferable to anything else in life – as every compulsive gambler, alcoholic or druggie will tell you. Video games and porn, however, are different from drinking and drugs. We can think of them as 'arousal addictions' – seeking out novelty in order to achieve or maintain a high level of arousal.

Before high-speed Internet people consumed porn much differently. Arousal addiction wouldn't have been as possible as it is today. Sixty years ago, it was small photos of native women's breasts revealed in *National Geographic* magazine. Thirty years ago, it was flipping through spreads in a *Playboy* or *Penthouse* magazine, to see full naked bodies of beautiful women. *Hustler* magazine introduced 'pink' views into the vaginal area. Men could also be found secretly paying a premium at a theatre specifically for full-length adult films, like *Deep Throat* or *Behind the Green Door*. Twenty years ago, it was a pile of VHS tapes, and ten years ago it was a burned DVD mix of selected clips. But today, you can have as many windows open as you want on your computer screen with a dozen high-definition videos streaming, and all you have to do is click back and forth between them.

Everyone can remember the first sexual image or movie they saw, it leaves an everlasting impression. So if you're a young sexually inexperienced man growing up watching hard-core porn (really, any person watching a lot of hard-core porn), and you masturbate exclusively to it – often with a 'death grip' – imagine how that will affect your future sexual experiences. If you've trained your brain and body to become aroused by multiple hard-core porn scenes, most likely real-life sex partners will not turn you on nearly as much as they would if you hadn't watched porn. You might objectively find the other person attractive, but they won't physically or mentally arouse you.

Many young men run into problems when they come to rely on porn to become aroused because the things that turned them on when they first started watching porn will no longer turn them on the same way. This happens when the old image or scene isn't doing it for them and they look for newness, variety, the surprise factor in the content, more hard-core and stranger material, anything they haven't seen in order to attain a sexual climax.

Sameness is soon habituated; differentness is attention-sustaining, even if it means morphing porn tastes that don't line up with a person's sexual orientation, such as gay or 'shemale' porn. Unfortunately the potential downside for what is best for an individual's long-term needs conflicts with what's good for business. The video game and porn industries are supplying an endless variety of new material via online instant streaming; so porn addicts can always get their 'fix'. Neutral stimuli and events that are associated with the addictive substance or its process, such as gambling casinos or drug-taking sequences, can become conditioned to generate further arousal and add to the body's chemical reaction.

Arousal addiction traps users into an expanded present-hedonistic time zone during this quest for the fix. Past and future are distant and remote as the present moment expands to dominate everything. And that present is totally dynamic, with images changing constantly. Brains on porn are being digitally rewired in a totally new way to demand change, novelty, excitement and constant stimulation. And those brains are being catered to by porn on demand and by video games at a flick of the switch or a click of the mouse. When excessive porn viewing becomes addictive, the brain lights up as if it were on heroin. The more aroused you are, the higher your dopamine level. The higher your dopamine, the more you crave something.

Though the impact of arousal addiction on behaviour and physiological responses is going to vary from individual to individual, it is worth examining the potential physiological, mental and emotional effects of watching too much porn because few people consider how it is affecting their brains and their ability to become aroused during porn-watching sessions and in real-life sexual encounters.

The subtle and not so subtle effects of arousal addiction can negatively impact any part of a person's life that are static, repetitious, involve planning, delaying gratification and long-term goal setting. The young men we've spoken with who demonstrated signs of arousal addiction feel very anxious in social situations in general, have less motivation to set and complete goals, feel out of control, and even discussed suicide. They are becoming totally out of sync in traditional school classes, which are analogue, static and interactively passive. Academics are based on applying past lessons to future problems, on planning, on delaying gratifications, on work coming before play and on long-term goal setting.

Do you sense misfits in a mismatch here? They're also totally out of sync in romantic relationships, which tend to build gradually and subtly and which require interaction, sharing, developing trust and suppression of lust at least until 'the time is right'.

The Coolidge Effect

Normally, every male experiences what is called a post-ejaculatory refractory period after an orgasm. Translation: he needs a break, a time out, after sex before getting it on again. But that period of time gets massively reduced with a novel sexual opportunity. As far as your brain is concerned, porn is like having your own harem. Although the experience only exists in fantasy, each new clip is like having a new sexual opportunity.

The Coolidge Effect is the phenomenon where this idea is observed. It all goes back to an unverified story about former US President Calvin Coolidge and his wife, Grace Coolidge, being shown separately around a government farm. When Mrs Coolidge came across a rooster having sex with the hens, she asked the attendant how often he did that. The attendant replied, 'Dozens of times each day.' Mrs Coolidge then said, 'Tell that to the President when he comes by.' Upon being told, the President asked whether it was the same hen every time. The reply was, 'Oh, no, Mr President, a different hen every time.' The President then said, 'Tell that to Mrs Coolidge!'

So you get the idea. The Coolidge Effect is a peculiarity seen in mammals where males (and apparently females to a lesser extent) show renewed sexual interest if they are introduced to new sexual partners. In a study of habituation in sexual arousal conducted at State University of New York in Stony Brook in 1985, forty male volunteers were divided into two groups; one group was shown images of five different heterosexual couples in sexual situations while the other group was shown the same image five times. The arousal in the first group increased while the arousal of the second group gradually diminished.[32]

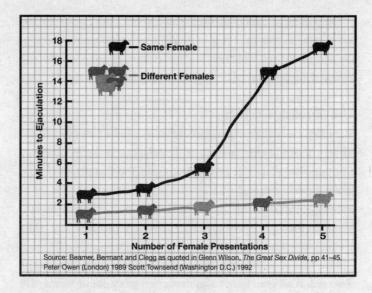

Source: Beamer, Bermant and Clegg as quoted in Glenn Wilson, *The Great Sex Divide*, pp 41–45.
Peter Owen (London) 1989 Scott Townsend (Washington D.C.) 1992

Pornography is a dopamine-producing machine. Dopamine's presence helps initiate feelings of enjoyment and pleasure. Rewarding experiences such as eating, taking drugs and having sex release dopamine into two main brain regions, the nucleus accumbens and the frontal cortex. However, once a person develops an addiction, the dopamine pathways become pathological.

Due to their abundance, once desirable female porn stars can lose their novelty and commercial value quickly. In what is known as the 'New Girl Effect', many webcam performers, much to their chagrin, make the most money they'll ever make in their very first week.[33] But how does the preference for novelty and interchangeable parts affect real-life intimate encounters?

Dating and the objectification of women

'Your nails are pretty,' he said as he examined her hands. 'Are they fake?' In the world of pick-up artists, back-handed compliments like this are known as 'negs'. Pick-up artists purposefully use psychological tactics such as negs to entice a girl into being attracted to them.

The young woman we spoke with didn't know about this strategy when he asked her the question. 'Of course not!' She was flustered and caught off-guard. This guy has no tact, she thought to herself. But he had a formula. And the formula worked, sort of. They ended up making out at the end of the night, but the chemistry was fleeting. Perhaps she just had buyer's remorse and his game needed work, but her attraction to him quickly waned when they moved beyond the script into the world of genuine human connection.

Many books like *The Mystery Method* and *The Game* have emerged lately, offering some very effective, sometimes offensive, and generally entertaining advice on how to pick up women. It is admirable that males would go to such elaborate lengths just to get their foot in the door, but unfortunately their solutions don't address other key aspects of a relationship, such as finding areas of mutual interest, transitioning from stranger to interested date or becoming a long-term partner. Maybe tackling these other areas is not the purpose, but at some point, when a male does want a real relationship, it can be difficult to transition out of the 'game' into creating the relationship. Their whole mindset has to change from approaching the girl or woman as a 'target' of possible conquest to being with a 'person' of potential value and enduring interest. And in the old-fashioned ending, to actually fall in love with someone other than oneself.

The key is staying mindful of ways in which to balance immediate desires with long-term goals, and monitoring the effects one's approach has on oneself and others. When the spontaneity of connecting with someone from the opposite sex is snuffed out, the motivation transforms from meeting an interesting girl to bedding 'tens'. It goes from building self-confidence to 'peacocking'. It's not even about connecting any more; it's about escalating the game in order to score. Other people involved become interchangeable objects for one's pleasure as the game takes on a new identity more like fantasy football than fantasies about making love with a real-life, flesh-and-blood woman.

In our survey, both sexes weighed in on the effects of these negative attitudes:

[Male]   I believe these behaviours may 'raise the bar' for pursu-
           ing relationships – instead of being 'just what you do' as
           a young man, there begins to exist a cost/benefit sort
           of analysis. If you can get your entertainment and
           sexual needs met via video games and porn, without
           the 'baggage' and 'drama' that often accompanies inti-
           mate relationships, young men may not be as motivated
           to seek those relationships out.

[Male]   Some sexism in society plays a role. Boys are taught to
           NOT respect women, because that is what they see in
           media . . . the interactions of their role models. If a man
           does not respect a woman, why should he go out of his
           comfort zone to talk to her or get involved in a roman-
           tic relationship?

[Female]   Hands down, not one man I know who uses porn has a
           healthy, respectful relationship with women. They
           may be able to 'behave' appropriately for a limited
           amount of time in social situations, but it ALWAYS
           affects their attitudes and underlying values. There are
           ALWAYS diffident attitudes and remarks that are
           evident to the women who live and work with men
           who use porn. There is an old phrase, 'sys in, sys out'
           [in this context, similar to 'garbage in, garbage out'].
           No human brain can feed on the self-gratifying con-
           sumer habits of pornography and also pursue a
           mature, complex, comprehensive, enduring relation-
           ship with another human.

Since the joy of romantic connection doesn't lie in prefabricated interaction, what do males who use these methods really want? In the world of young men, the desire for happiness and fulfilment has somehow morphed into the need for stimulation, amusement and control.

Tucker Max, bestselling author of *I Hope They Serve Beer in Hell* and *Assholes Finish First*, posted a dating application online that received many responses. His multiple-choice form asked potential dates questions such as, 'What will my friends say when they see you?' Below are some of the options responders could choose for that question:

> 'Another tall, hot blonde with no self-esteem – he's getting laid tonight.'

> 'Tonight's forecast calls for scattered clothes, with a significant chance of intense, passionate humping.'

> 'My Lord – she smells like the fish market.'

> 'Well, she's too ugly for him to date…$10 says he sleeps with her anyway.'

> 'I wouldn't call her fat, but he's gonna need the Jaws of Life to get out of this.'

> 'She's just a cheap hooker. I wonder how much smack she cost him.'

> 'Should have been a blow job.'[34]

On one level, it's a joke. But it makes you wonder why Max's writing turned into a No. 1 *New York Times* bestselling book in a time when many people are embarrassed to buy condoms or don't know how to have an honest conversation about sex – with anyone.

We see sex everywhere, so why is it so hard to talk about? Is being crude – thus lowbrow and easily dismissible – the only way to make it acceptable? A lot of young men in the Westernized world have developed a Madonna–Whore Complex in part because of this strange divergence. Described as love without sex and sex without love, these men want a wholesome woman as their mate and a whorish woman as their lover. When they come across a woman in the real world who is nice *and* sexual, they become anxious and often push her away – for them, sex must be impersonal. This creates hugely challenging intimacy problems for everyone involved.

We spoke with one woman in her early 20s who described a recent three-year relationship with a young man that embodied this internal struggle:

After about seven months of dating we moved in together. Our sex life was never good. He had problems maintaining an erection throughout the relationship. Sometimes he would get an erection, but when it was obvious we were about to have intercourse his erection would go away. He said he had these problems with every girl he had been with. In the morning he had 'morning wood' and he was able to successfully masturbate – clearly the problem was in his mind. He enjoyed cuddling and holding me, and we got along great otherwise. We talked pretty candidly about everything. He had a massive porn collection on his computer. The collection itself didn't really bother me except there is no doubt in my mind that all the pornography influenced his perceptions on sex in a really negative way – he had major performance anxiety and could never get into the moment. In middle and high school he went to a boarding school and stayed in a dorm with all boys; he said they watched A LOT of porn there. And this is before any of them actually had any real-life sexual experiences. I think that is the key in why he has had erection problems (and performance anxiety) his whole life – the fact that he was exposed to hard-core porn before he experienced what sex was like in reality totally confused him. He said it was difficult for him to perceive me sexually (that is he couldn't reconcile the idea of someone he loved being his sexual partner too); he saw sex as something that happened with someone he didn't care about, a sexual object rather than a real person. By the end of the relationship we were living like roommates.

Relationships used to be viewed as a precursor to setting up a family together, and people treated their potential partners as such. But today, with fewer reasons to become romantically committed, young men are no longer looking beyond women as temporary, interchangeable sex objects.

Dynamics of video games

Several decades ago, if you had glasses you were called 'four-eyes' and kids with too many books were hurled other vintage insults. For baby boomers, the smart kids were only cool just before exams, and showing an interest in good grades or electronics meant you were a nerd, and nerds were in a league of their own – at the bottom of the social hierarchy.

In the old days, prior to pinball machines and arcades, *Donkey Kong* and *Doom*, and long before *Call of Duty*, when teenage guys got together they would play sports, ride their bicycles, drive around aimlessly, and play cards. They drank and smoked and nearly died running around with BB guns and building rafts to float down rivers that would fill up after heavy rains. This was an era when neighbours knew each other's names, families ate dinner together, you couldn't live too far beyond your means and people had to entertain themselves.

Everything changed in the 1970s and 1980s. The nerds were busy doing what nerds do best: designing innovative technologies and pioneering new ways to control and explore the known universe. The first arcade games, gaming consoles and general-purpose computers were created by nerdy guys for nerdy guys. Most of them knew more about technology than social graces, and not much attention was paid to style. Some nerds were just passionate about building things, others were socially awkward and needed something to do. They were not designed by the men who could get women, because those men were out chasing them. But when gaming companies became legitimate businesses with stronger capabilities, better graphics and improved usability, nerds suddenly had the opportunity to become geeks, and geeks were cool. Go to the launch party of any game or electronic device nowadays and you'll see beautiful models and sexy go-go dancers as the sideshow attraction.

It could be said that this dramatic transition happened in 1977, when the first *Star Wars* movie came out. That same year, the Apple II was debuted at the first West Coast Computer Faire held in San Francisco, an event some refer to as the birth of the personal computer industry. A year later, Midway released *Space Invaders*, in 1979 Atari released *Asteroids*, then in 1980 Namco released *Pac-Man*, the most popular arcade game of all time. In 1981 the first magazine about video games, *Electronic Games*, was published. There was a brief hiccup experienced by the video game industry in the early 1980s, but Nintendo overcame it several years later. All the while Jack Tramiel, founder of Commodore International, was producing simple but economical computers for the 'masses, not the classes'.[35] The availability of computers, the Internet, touch screens and motion control revolutionized the way people were able to interact with each other and play video games.

After the prices became more affordable, the power of technology was realized in mainstream society, there was rapid innovation, and the world ate it up. Electronic consumerism stimulated tech growth, and as Intel's 'Sponsors of Tomorrow' ad demonstrated, a new form of rock stars emerged. No doubt that pocket-protector-wearing nerd the baby boomers made fun of has many people answering to them today. Hence the scene from the new *21 Jump Street* movie, where the undercover cops (played by Jonah Hill and Channing Tatum) are met with scorn when they try to get in with the popular crowd by parking in the handicapped spot, projecting a blasé attitude, and punching a gay student. They were playing by the old rules; little did they know the bad boy attitude no longer sent quite the same message. When we stop and reflect on the exponential growth in the last few decades, we can appreciate 'the crazy ones, the misfits, the rebels, the trouble-makers, the round pegs in the square holes...the ones who see things differently', as Apple visionary Steve Jobs so eloquently put it.[36] The underdog has been our mascot since.

There are a lot of benefits to playing video games – mainly, they are a lot of fun, and there can be a fair amount of social bonding, problem solving, strategy and even exercise involved. Online games provide the opportunity to become more computer literate too, a skill that should not be underestimated in the future job market. Many online games also allow people to interact with other people around the world, providing an opportunity to learn about many other cultures. But these benefits extend only up to a point, and a large portion of people don't take advantage of these positive features.

As mentioned earlier, we're mostly concerned about people who play video games excessively and in isolation. In a recent *AskMen* survey, when asked, 'Who do you play video games with most often?' only 24 per cent of respondents said they play with their friends in person, while 37 per cent said they play either completely alone or with strangers online.[37]

The disadvantage of playing video games, especially a lot of exciting video games, is that it can make other people and real life seem boring and not worthwhile in comparison. Not surprisingly, compared with teenagers who don't play video games, adolescent gamers spend about 30 per cent less time reading and 34 per cent less time doing homework.[38] One 2010 study published in

Psychological Science found that when 6- to 9-year-old boys received a gaming system, their reading and writing scores decreased while teacher-reported learning problems went up.[39] Essentially, too much gaming is associated with decreased school performance, desensitization to violence, and potentially influencing how a person learns and socializes due to a lack of balance between time spent playing and engaging in other activities.[40]

Recall Gabe from earlier in this chapter, who told us that at 23 years old he estimated that if he were to average it out, he played four hours of video games a day since the day he was born. If that estimate is correct, that's over 33,000 hours of gaming (almost seven bachelor's degrees)!

> Looking back on my childhood, I can see now that video games and porn not only desensitized me to normal pleasures of life, but also won me over due to the supernormal stimulation they provide and ended up replacing my real world desires and passions for virtual ones. The levels of excitement and stimulation I could achieve in a video game eventually made real-life sports seem boring.
>
> In my opinion, the way games today are made are a recipe for addiction. With leader-boards that take countless hours and skill to be at the top, and constant releases of 'bonus packs' to add on to the game (novelty), they keep a guy hooked and once you feel as if you might be getting bored with the game they add more levels or an ability to improve your rank even more. Over time the real world around me just could not keep my attention because all I could think about was when I was going to be able to get back home and game.[41]

Neils Clark and P. Shavaun Scott suggest reasons why games have the ability to draw players in, unlike slower and more introspective forms of entertainment:

Games aren't as passive as other media...they connect us to other living people...this word 'game' no longer really does justice to what's happening in today's digital living room. Whether you want to call it interactivity, agency, autonomy, or anything else, the most painfully obvious advancement is that games have taken us past passively watching television and reading books. You can watch a car chase on television, but it's kind of different when you're the one going 150 MPH and outrunning the cops in your red Ferrari. With games we're in the driver's seat. That level of control changes things, making them look and feel different to the brain...Stories on a television screen can inform us, but short of reality, a game is what teaches. Being able to see what happens when we make those dangerous choices, being able to then make our own spontaneous choices has made history's games inviting, exciting, and lasting.[42]

The question is, How do these imaginative fantasy adventures *feel* different to the brain? In *Boys Adrift*, Leonard Sax points out that video games actually can affect the brain in ways that compromise motivation. The nucleus accumbens operates in conjunction with another area of the brain called the dorsolateral prefrontal cortex (DLPFC); the nucleus accumbens is responsible for directing drive and motivation, and the DLPFC provides context for that drive:

A recent brain imaging study of boys between the ages of seven and fourteen years found that playing video games puts this system seriously out of kilter. It seems to shut off blood flow to the DLPFC...Playing these games engorges the nucleus accumbens with blood, while diverting blood away from the balancing area of the brain. The net result is that playing video games gives boys the reward associated with achieving a great objective, but without any connection to the real world, without any sense of a need to contextualize the story.[43]

It's not just the brain that is suffering either. Members of the Association of Teachers and Lecturers in the UK said that some older children have had difficulty finishing traditional pen and paper tests because their memories had deteriorated from overexposure to screen-based technology. Some young children had lost dexterity in their fingers because of how much time they spent using a touch-screen tablet. A 4-year-old who had been exposed to digital devices since birth even required therapy for compulsive behaviour.[44]

There is increasing evidence of bidirectional causality between gaming, attention problems and impulsiveness. Child psychologists Douglas Gentile, Edward Swing, Choon Guan Lim and Angeline Khoo recently examined the effects these variables have on each other in more than 3,000 youths in Singapore over a three-year period. They found that even when sex, ethnicity, age, socioeconomic status and earlier attention problems were statistically controlled, the kids who spent more time gaming later had more attention problems. They also noted that even when the initial time spent gaming was statistically controlled, the kids who were more impulsive or had some level of attention problems to begin with would spend more time playing video games, exacerbating the problems.[45] This data could help explain why boys are more likely than girls to be diagnosed with ADHD and spend more time playing video games; it also suggests attention problems could be altered by environmental factors and might be reduced by less game time, or by playing different kinds of games.

Several years ago, Allan Reiss and his colleagues at Stanford used fMRI imaging to look at what happens inside people's brains during a gaming session. They discovered that males get greater feelings of reward during video game play than females, and are two to three times more likely to feel addicted to video games. The game Reiss tested involved gaining territory eliminating balls from the screen before they approached a vertical line called the 'wall'. Although the female participants understood the game and appeared motivated to do well, 'the males were just a lot more motivated to succeed,' said Reiss.

Their research revealed that the male participants had far more activation in the brain's mesocorticolimbic centre, a region that includes the nucleus accumbens, amygdala and orbitofrontal cortex, and that the activation was correlated with how much territory was gained. Those parts of the brain were also shown to influence each other during the gaming session much more in the men's brains than in the women's brains, and the better connected that circuit was, the more the men excelled in the game.[46] The findings could explain why games that involve conquering or acquiring territory are more popular with males, and why they are motivated to play more hours than women; perhaps the mesocorticolimbic centre would be more activated in women's brains in a game that had a different objective. As one young woman in our UK student survey commented, 'If there were more female-targeted games, we might purchase them and play them more than males.'

We would like to see more brain imaging studies done that measure the internal rewards for more neutral or female-oriented video games. We also think it would be interesting to measure the possible effect puberty has on competitiveness in various themed games, as we have casually observed that girls tend to play more video games prior to maturation.

When video games go right

> Play is the answer to how anything new comes about.
>
> – Jean Piaget, Swiss developmental psychologist

There's a reason why video games are so popular – they make challenges fun and interesting. When video games go right, they provide a stimulating environment for learning, triumph, offer some social bonding, and rewards are derived in the process of playing. Players in MMORPG (massive multiplayer online role-playing games) also develop reputations, allowing them to build trust with other players, something that may not be as easy for them to find or build with people in the real world. Games like *World of Warcraft* and *Second Life* are very social, even if players are in the guise of an avatar. Positive gaming may also take the form of a learning or training programme and make real-world impacts.

Dance Dance Revolution initially started out in arcades in the late 1990s and was later released for video game consoles. Players get up onto a small dance platform and tap on coloured arrows that are coordinated with musical and visual cues in the game and light up under their feet. A player's score is based on how well they time their movements to the musical and visual cues, and they are allowed to select more music to dance to if they receive a high enough score.

Jane McGonigal's *World Without Oil* is another step in the right direction. With the mantra 'Play it – before you live it', more than 1,500 players started visualizing and living their lives as if there were a true oil crisis. The result, as described on the website, was an 'eerily plausible collective imagining of such an event, complete with practical courses of action to help prevent such an event from actually happening... More than mere "raising awareness", *World Without Oil* made the issues *real*, and this in turn led to real engagement and real change in people's lives.' Visit worldwithoutoil.org to learn more.[47]

Foldit is another game that has intrigued many users. The game requires users to solve puzzles for science by designing proteins. It turns out that humans' pattern-recognition and puzzle-solving abilities are more efficient than existing computer programs at pattern-folding tasks, so the scientists behind *Foldit* are using players' answers to teach computers to fold proteins faster and predict protein structures. The combined effort of players actually helped solve a problem related to HIV that had puzzled scientists for more than ten years. Check out http://fold.it for more information.

The Xbox Kinect and Nintendo Wii gaming systems are other great examples of positive gaming. Wii has a broader demographic than other gaming consoles and typically involves more exercise and socializing, too. The whole family can play together, but the games are fun enough that teenage guys play by themselves or with each other. I (Nikita) have even seen 90-year-old grandmas playing Wii Bowling in a nursing home. It's one of those 'kid-tested, parent-approved' kind of things that creates a win-win scenario. One-fifth of 16- to 24-year-olds surveyed said they'd give up their gym membership if they played Wii regularly, and parents believe that social gaming platforms like the Wii are having a positive influence in their home in addition to encouraging kids to do more exercise, reported a recent TNS Technology study.[48] In one study where overweight and obese children followed a weight management programme, but some of the children were also assigned to play active games on an Xbox Kinect, those who played the video games lost more weight than the children who just followed the weight management programme alone.[49]

For some people, directing attention towards a virtual world may be a very good thing – even therapeutic, which researchers at the University of Washington and Loyola University have found to be the case with burn victims. Patients who played video games were distracted from their pain and reported feeling far less pain than when they were not distracted. This was confirmed by analysis of their MRIs; being in a virtual world actually decreased the amount of pain-related activity in the brain.[50] In paediatric dentistry, children are encouraged to watch a favourite television show or game on an imaginary screen while their teeth are being drilled. This kind of hyno-therapeutic treatment has been shown to be very effective, especially with patients who could not receive anaesthesia.

When gaming goes wrong

> [The current state of the gaming industry is] too dark and derivative
> for my taste. The console and computer gaming business is too
> narrowly-defined by the 14 year old male mentality and all his not-
> so-honourable fantasies. It's being driven by what has worked and
> afraid of what a 10 million dollar development bust will entail. It has
> lost its moral compass.
>
> – Bob Whitehead, game designer and programmer[51]

Few things unite people like a common enemy. In the past, a common enemy might have been a neighbouring tribe or country, but a gamer's enemy today is social obligation: responsibilities, time management, dealing with real people and taking real risks.

Like the *Futurama* episode, 'Billy is in his room' is a common scene. Visiting relatives are welcomed by their aunts and uncles and cousins, whom they have not seen for some time. After the hugs and kisses and gift giving, the teenage son of the host family disappears – and never returns, even to say goodbye. The relatives ask, 'Where's Billy?' His mum answers with what has become a familiar family refrain: 'Billy is in his room.' That is the explanation for the failure to respect minimal social graces, or what used to be accepted as minimal family obligations to come out from seclusion even to say, 'See ya, Cuz,' and buzz back to his gaming dungeon. For anyone who values family and its rituals, this is unacceptable behaviour not only from Billy but even more so from Mum and Dad, who should know better and not be covering up for their son's lack of civility. In one sense, as such scenes get replicated widely, such behaviour becomes part of the negative fallout from excessive, isolated gaming and porn absorption, effectively creating the new 'cavemen'.

Video games go wrong when people play alone for long periods of time on a regular basis. With gaming experiences that can satisfy so many physical and mental needs, the gaming–life balance can spiral out of control. A couple of grown men loaned their perspectives in our survey – they were prepared to risk burn out, and sacrifice sleep and other commitments in order to get their daily gaming fix:

I believe myself to be a member of the first generation of Internet gamers, and I used to be a hard-core MMOG (massively multiplayer online game) addict spending 12 to 16 hours a day playing games. So I will share some personal thoughts. It started with bulletin board systems online, where you could play simple games and leave messages to other people, and gradually progressed into online chat rooms and then interactive games with chat rooms and now into online societies where you can literally spend all of your daylight hours inside and there will be people there wanting to play and chat with you. This alternative to spending time with people in the physical world around them offers easier access to gratification of social needs. The direct consequence of this is a degeneration of one's ability to socialize in person. Especially when it comes to new people and women. We have nothing of interest to talk about. No one wants to hear about our characters or things that happened during an online battle, or how we have designed our online house. And so we are left behind others who are not as interested in online gaming. Another horrible side effect is poor physical health. Many gamers (when I say gamers, I am referring to ones I know and have met) have underdeveloped upper-body muscles and poor eating habits and health as a direct consequence of the time spent behind a computer. Once you find yourself addicted to the Internet, it feels pointless to change your habits, because you get no gratification for doing so. If you manage to break away from the computer screen, you will not know what to do with the time you normally spend playing. There are no tools available online that I have found to offer a path to freedom from this kind of addiction. I believe the best solution is prevention, and the only way to do that is to inspire children.

I am a physician with a research background in neuroscience, who battled his own addictions with video games. I was an addicted gamer who, at my peak, invested over 20,000 hours of playing games over a period of nine years. My reckless compulsion to play games transformed me into a monster that almost destroyed my family, marriage and career. Without attention to this quickest-growing addiction, our society will suffer from the creation of Generation Vidiot, millions of people devoid of innovation and skills to live in the physical world.

Video games also go wrong when the person playing them is desensitized to reality and real-life interactions with others. After several tragic school shootings in the late 1990s, a videotape of the two Columbine High School shooters surfaced showing them talking about how their acts would be like the popular computer game, *Doom*. Two weeks later a Senate hearing examined the marketing of violence to children. Lieutenant Colonel (ret.) Dave Grossman, a former Army Ranger who taught psychology at West Point and author of *On Killing: The Psychological Cost of Learning to Kill in War and Society*, spoke on one of the panels, saying there had to be a bridge between being a healthy citizen and having the ability to 'snuff' out someone else's life:

In World War II, we taught our soldiers to fire at bull's eye targets. They fought bravely. But we realized there was a flaw in our training when they came on the battlefield and they saw no bull's eyes. And they were not able to transition from training to reality.

Since World War II, we have introduced a wide variety of simulators. The first of those simulators were pop-up human targets. When those targets appeared in front of soldiers, they learned to fire, and fire instinctively. When real human beings popped up in front of them, they could transfer the data from that simulator.

Today we use more advanced simulators. The law enforcement community uses a simulator that is a large-screen television with human beings on it, firing a gun that is identical to what you will see in any video arcade, except in the arcade the safety catch is turned off ... The industry has to ask how it can market one device to the military, whoever is marketing it, and then turn around and give the same device to your children, and claim that it is harmless.[52]

Some violent video games that are licensed to the military can be superior devices for teaching soldiers battle tactics. *Call of Duty: Modern Warfare 2* proved to be excellent 'training-simulation' for the Norwegian mass-murderer Anders Breivik, who bombed government buildings in Oslo and went on to murder sixty-nine more people, mostly youths, at a summer camp on the island of Utøya in 2011. The killer admitted that he played *World of Warcraft* to relax. Simon Parkin, a video games journalist for the *Guardian*, argued *Call of Duty* was a medium for his psychopathy, not the cause: 'broken humans will no doubt draw whatever inspiration they are seeking from it to feed their own madness,' and that no creator can ensure that their creation is not misused.[53] Others see it as adding gasoline to the fire.

One study that measured social rejection's impact on narcissism and any resulting aggression found that when people who were narcissistic were rejected by their peers (or perceived that they were rejected) they were highly aggressive towards others after the rejection – not unlike patterns found in mass shootings.[54] After the Virginia Tech shooting, journalist David Von Drehle aptly pointed out that the extreme self-centredness of these kinds of killers is the 'forest in these stories', and that all the other elements – guns, games, lyrics, pornography – 'are just the trees'.

'Only a narcissist', said Von Drehle, 'could decide that his alienation should be underlined in the blood of strangers.'[55] The more time a narcissist spends alone in those 'trees', however, the more carried away in his self-absorbed thoughts he will get, and the more justified he will think his acts are.

Speaking at the University of Pittsburgh's Western Psychiatric Institute in 1982, Surgeon General C. Everett Koop warned that video games might be detrimental to the health of young people: 'More and more people are beginning to understand [the games'] adverse mental and physical effects ... There's nothing constructive in the games ... Everything is eliminate, kill, destroy.'[56] That was thirty years ago, when *Dig Dug* and *Ms. Pac-Man* – a 2D game in which a player would earn points by eating pellets and avoiding ghosts within a maze – were a couple of the top arcade games.

Today, many would agree that violent video games are synonymous with successful video games.[57] Children with more propensities to be aggressive are more attracted to violent video media, but violent media, in turn, can also make them more aggressive. This could be related to the fact that most video games reward players for violent acts, often permitting them to move to the next level in a game. Yet recent research suggests a link between violent video games and real-life aggression; given the opportunity, both adults and children were more aggressive after playing violent games. And people who identify themselves with violent perpetrators in video games are able to take aggressive action while playing that role, reinforcing aggressive behaviour.[58] Like the Proteus Effect, there is an increasing amount of data that suggests our brains instinctively mimic the states of the other minds we interface with, even if those other minds are imagined.[59]

The desensitization and mirroring effects combined with the addictive qualities of games can be a recipe for disaster for some players.

Steven L. Kent, author of *The Ultimate History of Video Games: The Story behind the Craze that Touched our Lives and Changed the*

World, says pinball machines, the precursor to video games, began to incorporate the idea of 'pay-outs' – combining games with gambling – in the 1930s. Politicians were quick to prohibit all forms of pinball; the ban was upheld for decades until pinball enthusiasts were able to demonstrate that the game involved more skill than luck, bringing more legitimacy to the industry. Much like the joystick and buttons on a controller, the flipper – the spring-powered levers invented by engineer Harry Mabs in 1947 – allowed greater user interaction with the game as well as the opportunity to develop skill.

Three decades later video arcade games were the new trend, and in order to make money locations depended on a player lasting less than two minutes per game. Therefore it was necessary for companies to create games with interesting graphics, original plots and simple objectives. Something that was easy to learn but difficult to master* that people would want to play over and over again once they got started. The formula was effective. In the late 1970s so many people were playing *Space Invaders* in Japan that there was a national coin shortage, and people would huddle around players who could succeed further along in whatever game was most popular.[60] There was also a level of public prestige and personal satisfaction that went along with attaining a high score.

Flash-forward another thirty years to today's video games for which top talent is recruited – from the designers to Grammy-winning composers – and they look just as good, if not better, than big-budget Hollywood films. The most popular themes in movies and games that appeal to young men revolve around driving, sports and war, except in the video game the user gets to control everything. Even if they don't like the rules of the game

---

* *Bushnell's Theorem* or *Nolan's Law* is an aphorism by game designer and Atari founder Nolan Bushnell about video game design: 'All the best games are easy to learn and difficult to master. They should reward the first quarter and the hundredth.'

they can use cheats (such as secret codes and hacks that give players an unfair advantage) to operate the game beyond their skill level and exert even greater control over the game. Social games like *World of Warcraft* are designed to be on-going by rewarding character progression, and as players acquire more weapons and skill levels, they have greater social status and the game becomes more gratifying. There is a certain comfort knowing these infinite worlds exist where accomplishments can be revisited and picked up where they were left off at any time. When these illusive worlds replace reality, however, comfort can turn into dependence.

Uncle Sam goes 2.0

As mentioned by Lieutenant Colonel (ret.) Grossman at the 1999 Senate hearings, violent video games are having more and more practical applications. For example, realistic violent video games set in a warlike environment are being used to treat veterans who have post-traumatic stress disorder. Video game-like applications of digital technology are also an integral part of military operation. P.W. Singer, author of *Wired for War*, raises some considerations:

> Technology is wrapped up in the story of war. You look at all the things that surround us, everything from the Internet to jet engines; these are all things where the military has been a driver for technology. And technology opens new frontiers, new directions we can go in, but it also creates new dilemmas, new questions you need to answer... Going to war meant that you were going to a place where there was such a danger that you might never come home again, you might never see your family again. Now compare that experience to that of a Predator drone pilot. You're sitting behind a computer screen, you're shooting missiles at enemy targets, you're killing enemy combatants. And then at the end of the day, you get back in your car, and 20 minutes later, you're at the dinner table talking to your kids about their homework.[61]

Singer alludes to important questions. How will identifying with a violent avatar, or removing oneself from direct violent action that's actually happening in the real world, affect the way we view each other and affect our real-life behaviour? Could video games desensitize players not only to others' feelings but also to their own?

Rye Barcott, author of *It Happened on the Way to War*, told us that in the Marine battalion in Iraq in 2005, during heavy firefight periods, young Marines returning to barracks would rush to play violent video games all night, going back into battle the next day like 'exhausted zombies', and that was a common pattern among many of them.[62]

'Video games are never going to replicate the real thing,' says Lieutenant Colonel Larry F. Dillard Jr, of the US Army.[63] But you never know.

In the popular children's science-fiction novel *Ender's Game*, by Orson Scott Card, Ender gets enrolled into Battle School, eventually reaching the school's top rank through his intelligence and cunning.[64] Ender's practice sessions, in which he commands spaceships in a 3-D battle simulator with his fellow students, gradually escalate into battle after battle against an enemy alien race known as the Formics, also known as Buggers. Ender is on the brink of exhaustion and is having horrible nightmares that haunt him during his waking hours. In his 'final exam', Ender's crew is outnumbered nearly a thousand to one near a small planet. Ender decides to use a deadly weapon to destroy the planet itself, annihilating all the ships in orbit. He's hoping his ruthless actions will get him kicked out of the school. Instead, he learns that all the battles had taken place with real fleets and his actions effectively ended the war with the aliens.

The questions foremost in our minds are: could Ender have killed the Buggers if he knew that it wasn't a game? If being one step removed from action makes for more effective and less endangered soldiers, why wouldn't the military be moving in this direction?

Not to mention how obsessed young people, especially young men, are with gaming. Noah Shachtman, contributing editor of *Wired*, said that the military understands it must embrace today's digital-obsessed youth in order to recruit the kind of soldiers, airmen and Marines that will be needed in the next century.[65] But will the youth of today understand the impact of their actions as they use indirect technology to execute their orders?

Soldiers using this technology today may have actually had first-hand experience in real combat situations, and they come to work wearing their uniforms as a constant reminder that a button they press in one location could have real-life consequences at another location on the other side of the planet. Yet we should be wary of the fact that kids are growing up immersed in realistic digital entertainment depicting violent scenes, which they are physically removed from but feel they are participating in. These kids, who have spent too much time in the 'trees', likely will not have the same capacity to empathize with other people and thus may make less humane decisions; especially as drone technology presents itself as a deadly real-world extension of gaming technology.

12

Sour Grapes:
Entitlement vs Reality

A hungry fox saw some fine bunches of grapes hanging from a vine
that was trained along a high trellis and did his best to reach them
by jumping as high as he could into the air. But it was all in vain, for
they were just out of reach. So he gave up trying and walked away
with an air of dignity and unconcern, remarking, 'I thought those
grapes were ripe, but I see now they are quite sour.'

– Aesop, 'The Fox and the Grapes'

I n stressful situations, many of us adjust our understanding of
what's going on to preserve our sense of self. The core message
of 'The Fox and the Grapes' tale is not in the fox's failure to get
the grapes but in his reaction to that failure. He maintains his pride
with a wee bit of self-deception. 'And therein lies the appeal,' says
D.L. Ashliman, professor emeritus of the University of Pittsburgh.
'Each individual reader can respond to the fox's self-deception
according to his or her own expectations and needs. We can criticize
the fox for his dishonesty and inconsistency, or we can congratulate
him for his pragmatism and positive self-image.'[1]

The fox's response preserved the integrity of his self-image to
himself. Stanford University social psychologist Claude Steele was
the first to describe the theory of self-affirmation, in 1988. His
students, psychologists David Sherman and Geoffrey Cohen,

described its powerful role in their own research, nearly two decades later:

> [The theory] asserts that the overall goal of the self-system is to protect an image of its self-integrity, of its moral and adaptive adequacy. When this image of self-integrity is threatened, people respond in such a way as to restore self-worth... One way that this is accomplished is through defensive responses that directly reduce the threat. But another way is through the affirmation of alternative sources of self-integrity. Such 'self affirmations,' by fulfilling the need to protect self-integrity in the face of threat, can enable people to deal with threatening events and information without resorting to defensive biases.[2]

In a sense they are saying that people can respond negatively to such threats by going on the defensive, or that a better way is to go on the offensive to bolster one's self-integrity.

Young men's attitudes are similar to the fox's. The ego reigns king in Western society today, and our delusional self-perceptions have dissociated us from mundane reality. Most people confuse comfort with happiness, preferring familiarity to truth. Our politically correct culture has become stifling for any form of critical analysis. Although stigmatizing people with labels can be damaging, such labels also allow people to externalize their problems and avoid taking personal responsibility to improve themselves. The avoidance of reality has pervaded our language and even the way we understand what's happening around us, as the late comedian George Carlin pointed out. People have invented a 'soft language' to insulate themselves from the truth, he said, 'toilet paper became bathroom tissue... The [garbage] dump became a landfill... Partly cloudy became partly sunny.'[3]

Western culture is presenting a confusing and unfulfilling reality full of distorted ideals. In the US, for example, over the last thirty years the average high school student's performance has not improved yet their grades have undergone excessive inflation. In 1976 only 18 per cent of students had an A- average or better, but in 2006 33 per cent said they did – that is an 83 per cent increase! At the same time, 20 per cent fewer students did fifteen or more hours of homework per week than in 1976.[4] In other words, the illusion of success is supported. They got rewarded for doing less.

In the UK, too, many suspect grade inflation. From 2012 to 2014 the number of university students who were awarded higher than a 2:2 went from 25 per cent to 70 per cent.[5] Is it just because students are better prepared? Or are universities facing pressure not to lose fees from full-paying students, not to fall behind in the league tables, and to produce enough students who can meet the 2:1 minimum standard that is required by three-quarters of the top 100 UK recruitment firms?

Young men are told they can be anything they want to be, but it doesn't feel that way. With modern pressures to constantly perform flawlessly in all areas of life – school, career, socially, sexually – we can't blame them for seeking validation and approval in other environments like porn and video games or even gangs, or for being relieved when their anxiety or depression is diagnosed and given a label that other young men also share, such as ADHD.

This estrangement creates a different set of rules and perception of self for young men that does not translate into the real world, however. Developmental psychologist Erik Erikson saw identity as a combination of the ego's dealing with the outside world and the unconscious mind. He believed a stable sense of self could be achieved when there was a successful balance between the two. Adolescence, Erikson said, was the most important time for this development,[6] which makes us wonder how stable adolescents' identities are when they are searching for them though imitations of life rather than in the real world's daily trials and tribulations. The assumption that high self-esteem automatically translates into real-world success is deeply untrue, and as much as a young man can seek refuge in his parallel world and spend the majority of his time behind a screen/gang/label – which can essentially act as a buffer or mask separating him from the social majority – he will eventually come up against an unavoidable reality, which could very well trigger a severe identity crisis.

Poet and philosopher Robert Bly and psychoanalyst Marion Woodman call this confrontation 'The Great Disappointment'. Leonard Sax says our culture does a terrible job of preparing kids for the moment when they realize they're not going to be the next big thing:

> The spiritual condition of the child before the onset of puberty [is] characterized by the feeling that 'something marvelous is going to happen.' Then sometime after the onset of puberty, navigating through adolescence, the teenager is hit with the awareness that something marvelous is not going to happen. That's the moment of The Great Disappointment. In our culture, that moment is often postponed until young adulthood, when the 20-something finally realizes that she isn't ever going to compete in the Olympics or be the next American Idol or a movie star.[7]

Adolescence, Sax says, is the period when children should be learning about their own abilities and limits. In a world with such a massive population as ours, the vast majority of us are going to have to come to terms with the fact that we are no more special than anyone else. Being a mature adult means recognizing that you're not going to be famous or on the cover of popular magazines. This subpar job of preparing young people for this realization leads to a rocky transition into full adulthood. Playing video games regularly can make the gamer the master of that universe, and for many young men that is all the satisfaction they need.

The young men who game to excess often avoid anything that undercuts that means of achieving validation because it is so woven into their identities. Therefore it is doubly threatening when their activities are being questioned because they themselves are being critiqued at the same time. Virtual actions and ego become interchangeable. Distraction and immersion into their preferred virtual space serves as a shield around them, pushing any ego-puncturing inconsistencies out of sight.

Truthfully, most of us have started doing this to some degree – pretty much all of us have some kind of online persona. As the pace of life picks up, the new instantly becomes the familiar, and soon it is old and then obsolete. More and more, Western culture takes technology for granted and we feel entitled to distraction. As the comedian Louis C.K. lamented on *Late Night With Conan O'Brien*, 'Everything is amazing right now, and nobody's happy.'[8]

These days, it literally is all about 'me'. In an analysis of over 750,000 books published between 1960 and 2008, Jean Twenge and her colleagues found that the use of first person plural pronouns (i.e. We, Us) decreased 10 per cent, while during this same timeframe, the use of first person singular pronouns (i.e. I, Me) increased 42 per cent, and second person pronouns (i.e. You, Your) quadrupled.[9] It is easy to get turned off and become dismissive of anything that isn't serving our individual needs, or serving them fast enough. But there's something else, an uncomfortable gnawing feeling that accompanies any moment where we don't have our face buried in some external device. It's not exactly loneliness. It's more like an itch we can't scratch. We know we could just stop and sit with ourselves if we really wanted to, or fix whatever problem has come up, but we couldn't be bothered to figure it out or put the effort in to apply the solution. So we complain or dismiss whatever is causing the gnawing feeling. This is what is commonly referred to as 'first world problems'.

One reason why young men may feel entitled to things these days is because very few of them actually participate in the process of building or maintaining the things they take for granted. It used to be only wealthy gentlemen who didn't know what was under the hood of their cars, now hardly any young men do. They just take their vehicle to an auto mechanic where it can be diagnosed electronically and fixed with specialized tools. The process of creation and upkeep is out of sight. Most young men who have cars never even look at the engine under the hood, not even to know where the battery is until their car stalls and they realize they are missing the cables to jump-start it.

Just as it is necessary to humanize a person to have empathy for them, in order to fully appreciate any given 'thing' there needs to be a sense of the efforts and resources that went in to making it. When a young man gets handed things constantly during his early years or bailed out of trouble during his adolescence, he doesn't learn to appreciate things or take pride in cultivating stuff, only in owning stuff. What he learns is to expect everything and to manipulate others to get stuff he believes he needs. Nowadays, many young men have no sense of awe. They have become disconnected from the physical reality around them. At the same time, they develop a belief that any sort of blue-collar jobs are beneath them, whether it is skilled or unskilled, or even pays more than many of the jobs in white-collar industries, as in plumbing or being an electrician.

In 1969, the Rolling Stones sang the song, 'You Can't Always Get What You Want', but, they assured listeners, if enough effort was put in, a person could get what they needed. The song was a hit. Today a song like that would never get made. Hard work appears to be for someone who doesn't know how to work the system – a sucker – and young men no longer have the patience or desire to learn how to build the foundations for success, nor are they inclined to expose themselves to ridicule if they were to fail along the way.

In the 2013 CIRP Freshman Survey, a survey of incoming college freshmen from around the US that is conducted annually by the University of California in Los Angeles (UCLA), the researchers noted that while freshmen perceive themselves as cooperative and tolerant of those with different beliefs, they rated themselves poorly when it came to being open to having their own beliefs challenged.[10] Similarly, in a Josephson Institute of Ethics survey on the moral attitudes of young people, 45 per cent of boys (versus 28 per cent of girls) 'agreed' or 'strongly agreed' with the statement. 'a person has to lie or cheat sometimes in order to succeed', and twice as many boys as girls agreed or strongly agreed that 'it's not cheating if everyone is doing it'.[11] Stop for a moment and repeat that phrase to yourself. If there is some consensual activity it becomes acceptable even if it is immoral or unethical. That attitude becomes a stepping stone for good people to justify doing worse things, if others are doing so.

Why buy the cow when you can have the milk free?

Mara Hvinstendahl, author of *Unnatural Selection Choosing Boys Over Girls, and the Consequences of a World Full of Men*, says that it is a myth that there are fewer men than women in the world. Women tend to outlive men, but at birth, the natural sex ratio is 105 males being born for every 100 females.[12] Why does the world start off with more men but end up with more women?

Roy Baumeister, social psychologist and author of *Is There Anything Good About Men?: How Cultures Flourish by Exploiting Men*, offers a provocative explanation. Throughout history, he says, the probability that an individual woman will reproduce has been reasonably high. This has been because there was always a good chance, provided a woman played it safe and went along with the crowd (which most women did), that a man would enter the scene at some point and offer sex. Women didn't need to sail into uncharted waters or explore new lands – where the likelihood of certain death was quite high – to find mates with whom to reproduce. Our female ancestors played it safe, in other words.

Men, however, had to take a vastly different approach in order to secure a mate. Most men who lived in the distant past do not have descendants alive today, and the chances of a man who played it safe and followed the crowd having living descendants is especially low. If men wanted to continue their lines they needed to be resourceful, creative, take risks and explore new options. Baumeister says:

> What seems to have worked best for cultures is to play off the men against each other, competing for respect and other rewards that end up distributed very unequally. Men have to prove themselves by producing things the society values. They have to prevail over rivals and enemies in cultural competitions, which is probably why they aren't as lovable as women.
>
> The essence of how culture uses men depends on a basic social insecurity. This insecurity is in fact social, existential, and biological. Built into the male role is the danger of not being good enough to be accepted and respected and even the danger of not being able to do well enough to create offspring.
>
> The basic social insecurity of manhood is stressful for the men, and it is hardly surprising that so many men crack up or do evil or heroic things or die younger than women. But that insecurity is useful and productive for the culture, the system.[13]

Baumeister highlights research from biologist Jason Wilder, who, through sampling the genetics of various populations alive today found that humanity's ancestors are roughly 67 per cent women, and 33 per cent men, indicating some men were able to have children with multiple women, but most men didn't have any children at all.[14] An example of this unequal distribution is recent genetic evidence that the descendants of the thirteenth-century Mongolian conqueror Genghis Khan, whose sons had large harems, may account for 8 per cent of the men living in the former Mongol empire today.[15]

Historically, perpetuating a man's genetic line motivated much of his risk-taking. On the flip side of that motivation is male laziness that occurs when an abundance of sexual opportunities present themselves. In general, as long as males have easy sexual access to attractive women, they feel no need to exert more energy, time or money to get female attention. This is particularly evident on college campuses where there are 1.33 females for every male. The imbalance also exists later in life in nursing homes where women vastly outnumber men, often more than two to one.[16] In Russia and Ukraine, there are 116 women per 100 men and 117 women per 100 men,[17] respectively. Although both of these countries also have much larger populations of older women than older men, they still have uneven ratios for those in their prime years (25 to 54 years old), with women outnumbering men.[18] With fewer men presenting themselves as viable partners, the sense that there is a 'man shortage' further perpetuates itself.

The Guttentag-Secord theory was first presented by Marcia Guttentag and Paul F. Secord in their 1983 book, *Too Many Women?: The Sex Ratio Question*. They suggested that members of the sex in smaller supply are less reliant on their partners because many potential relationships are available to them, thus they have more 'dyadic power' – the upper hand – over members of the surplus sex. When confronted with an abundance of women, men become promiscuous and unwilling to commit to a monogamous relationship. In societies with too many women, or too few 'marriageable' men, fewer people marry, and the ones who do will do so later in life. Since men take advantage of a variety of available partners, women's work and traditional roles are devalued, and because these women can't rely on their partners to stick around, more of them turn to furthering their education or career to support themselves.[19]

Not incidentally, in Eastern Europe some women present themselves as mail-order brides to foreigners, who may provide them with better lifestyles and opportunities, and many Eastern European countries have negative population growth rates despite many more women immigrants than men immigrants going into those countries.[20]

On college campuses, the number of romantic relationships has decreased and casual sex has increased. A couple of female college students we spoke with reflected these concerns:

Both men and women are extremely busy these days and technology has made it easy to access a large pool of people to find an arrangement that works for them. For example, a friend of mine in [New York] works for a top tier investment bank and is extremely successful. She wants company at times but is also extremely busy. So she 'hangs out' with a guy she likes on three days a week. This phenomenon is vastly prevalent amongst men and women in their 20s and 30s. Personally I think a lot of women grow out of this (probably a lot to do with eventually wanting to start a family) but a lot of men have realized it is easy to have non-committal relationships without having to explain yourself too much. We live in a world where we exchange bodily fluids before last names. You can be sleeping with someone but be seen as coming on too strong if you ask them if they are sleeping with other people. Modern cities like London, New York, San Francisco, etc. all offer men and women the option of having Peter Pan lifestyles – heterosexual men, especially, have one advantage – they can always go younger. None of this is meant to be a rant, it really is just the way it is.

I think one of the biggest challenges will be the effect this will have on family dynamics. Today's well-educated, empowered, successful women don't want lame, slacker husbands, and most men don't want to feel inferior to their wives. Will this push us into becoming more of an individual, rather than a family-based, society?

'Men are as good as their women require them to be,' said one 27-year-old man we interviewed. This statement made us wonder about how easy access to sex affects men's motivation to achieve other life goals. Could there be a spillover from easy sexual access to assuming other goals can also be achieved with only minimal effort and planning? It could be argued that our goals are fuelled by evolution and that the majority of our efforts are just part of one big elaborate mating ritual. But in the past, the prize – a sexual partner (and propagating one's genetics) – would have been the reward for hard work, or at least some wise planning. Today the reward is essentially free and available before any hard work has been done, so what's left? It's like downing dessert before dinner.

A young woman who Leonard Sax interviewed in his book, *Girls on the Edge: The Four Factors Driving the New Crisis for Girls*, said that these days all young men want is 'wham, bam, thank-you ma'am', that they don't have a clue as to how to satisfy a woman or care about establishing an emotional connection to build a relationship. Sax pointed out that because boys and girls are becoming sexually active at an earlier age than in their parents' generation, boys are more egocentric and less mature, and that there's been a cultural shift from dating towards 'hooking up', with young men feeling less of an obligation to care about the young women. The growing influence of porn was evident in the young men's comments. Many eagerly described the sites they visited, and told Sax that if they were given the choice between masturbating to online porn or going on a date with a real girl, they would choose the porn.[21] One young man from our own student survey said that many of his male friends were disappointed when they had sexual encounters with real girls because they were not as good looking as the porn stars.

Interestingly, a recent study published in the *Journal of Sex and Marital Therapy* suggested that both men and women who had watched porn scored higher on three commonly used narcissism inventories, and that even greater levels of narcissism were correlated with more hours spent watching porn.[22] Narcissism is the enemy of compassion, by not wanting to be a part of the social community around you, and by feeling no obligation to make life better for anyone other than Me.

13

The Rise of Women?

Since the 1960s women's earnings have grown by 44 per cent, compared with 6 per cent for men. A 2010 study of single, childless urban workers between the ages of 22 and 30 found that women actually earned 8 per cent more than men. The proportion of married women with children and with an income that is higher than their husband's has increased from 4 per cent in 1960 to 23 per cent in 2011. Women also now account for nearly 60 per cent of all college bachelor's degrees, and this upward trend will continue.[1] In the UK women are estimated to hold more than two-thirds of high-skilled jobs by 2020.[2]

American women benefited considerably from democratic laws that expanded their rights – such as Federal Drug Administration (FDA) legislation approving the use and distribution of birth control pills in the early 1960s. They also were beneficiaries of Title IX of the 1972 Educational Amendments to the Civil Rights Act sanctioning equality for the sexes in education, causing educational institutions to support women in sports; the 1973 Roe v Wade ruling allowing women the right to a safe and legal abortion; and the 1993 Family Medical Leave Act allowing women to take employment leave after giving birth or for other family emergencies.[3] During this same time women in the UK saw legislative changes such as the Equal Pay Act of 1970[4] and the Sex

Discrimination Act of 1975* – which made it illegal to discriminate against women having equal opportunity to acquire job training, employment or education.[5] Free contraception provided by the National Health Service no matter what a woman's age or marital status was also beginning in 1974.[6]

In addition, NASA began accepting aspiring female astronauts in 1976 with Sally Ride becoming the first American woman in space in 1983 (Valentina Tereshkova, a Russian, was the world's first woman in space, orbiting Earth in 1963[7]); the United Nations (UN) launched the End Violence Against Women campaign in 2008,[8] raising worldwide public and political awareness of violence prevention and policy; the 2012 Games in London were the first Olympics where women competed in every sport; and consciousness-raising of women's issues has been on the rise all around the globe.[9]

Your authors celebrate the rise in status, power and wide-ranging abilities of girls and women. Slowly but surely the glass ceiling is disappearing, enabling talented women to move up to top leadership positions in industry. There are virtually no professions today that are off-limits to women who are willing to work to make it in them. We also believe that the guardians of that corporate glass ceiling are older men from earlier generations who are still living in the 'old boys' club' system. When they retire, we believe more capable women will rise up to the tops of their industries.

Still, there are many areas where the situation could be improved. As of 2014 women held only 18 to 20 per cent of seats in the US Congress, the Senate and the House.[10] In the UK, just 21 per cent of board positions in FTSE 100 companies are held by women (though that is a large jump from 12.5 per cent in 2011),[11]

---

* The Equality Act later replaced these Acts in 2010, which prevented additional discrimination against religion, disability, sexual orientation, pregnant women and age. (See www.legislation.gov.uk)

and less than a quarter of Members of Parliament are female.[12] Feminist Laura Bates pointed out that this puts the UK 74th out of 186 in terms of female representatives in Parliament, ranking behind Sudan, where sharia law is in effect, and China, where the term *sheng nu* – 'leftover women' – is used to urge professional women to get married.[13]

Despite earning more than men in their twenties, women still lag in perpetual earnings. There has been a lingering statistic that claims women earn 77 cents per dollar that a man makes for the same work. This statistic – circulated as recently as 2014 by the White House[14] – is deceptive because, as pointed out by the *Economist*, if employers could really get away with having women do the same work for 77 per cent of what they would pay a man, they would do just that, and their shareholders would 'gleefully pocket the extra profits'.[15] In reality the 77 cents statistic takes the average of salaries made by full-time female and full-time male workers. Some of the reasons for this apparent difference in pay includes men working more hours per week than women (in the UK, for example, 18 per cent of employed men work very long hours, compared with 6 per cent of employed women[16]), men not taking as much time off work after the birth of a child, as well as a greater concentration of men in higher paying careers, such as engineering.

The *Economist* soundly suggested that policies that enable women to remain in the workforce (if they choose to do so) would be a huge step in the right direction. The US is an exception among Western nations in not permitting statutory paid maternity or paternity leave or offering affordable childcare.[17]

Do we need a democracy of gender?

In *The World Split Open: How the Modern Women's Movement Changed America*, University of California professor emerita Ruth Rosen wrote that women are 'both like and unlike men', and a society that doesn't honour women's ability to bear and raise children is 'clearly violating their rights to fully participate in society'. Rosen argued that a society that compels women to live as men do is not a true democracy. A true 'gender democracy', she said, must honour the life of the family as much as it honours the life of work.[18]

Honouring the commitment to family makes sense, but the philosophy should be applicable to both mothers and fathers. In a recent Pew Research Center survey, more men said working full-time was the ideal situation for them, but about the same number of men and women said they would prefer to be at home raising their children rather than working. Fifty-six per cent of mothers and 50 per cent of fathers surveyed found it difficult to balance the responsibilities of their job and their family, and while 23 per cent of mothers said they spent 'too little' time with their children, 46 per cent – or double that amount – of fathers wished they could spend more time with their children. This disparity helps explain why, overall, more women than men believe they are doing an excellent or very good job as a parent.[19]

Despite having higher confidence in their parenting abilities, women still experience internal tension with how they prioritize their career and family. In the *Atlantic*'s most read article of all time,[20] 'Why Women Still Can't Have It All', Anne-Marie Slaughter, an academic who was a former Director of Policy Planning at the State Department, agreed that the notion of work–life balance needed to change. She wrote about how she found it very difficult to perform at the level she wanted as a high government official and be the kind of parent she wanted to be, even though her husband was willing to take on the bulk of parenting responsibilities for the time she was in Washington. She said that she believed women (and men) could have it all, and have it all at the same time, but not with the way that Western society and economy are presently structured. She said it was time for women in high-powered and leadership positions to recognize that 'having it all' is hardly a function of personal ambition and discipline, and that many working women are just struggling to make ends meet or support partners who are unable to find work. Additionally, the cost of good day care can break the bank and children's school schedules and activities often conflict with work demands. She references research by economists Justin Wolfers and Betsey Stevenson, who show that women are less happy than they were forty years ago, despite the gains women have made in wages, educational opportunities and social status. To create a society that actually works for women, Slaughter suggests closing the 'leadership gap' by electing a female president and fifty female senators, so that women may exert power evenly and be equally represented in judicial and executive positions.[21]

We agree that it would be a very good thing to have a greater number of women in political and leadership positions, and companies would attain and retain more talented female employees if they adopted 'family-friendly' policies. We also surmise that the work–life balance will improve for everyone only when both mother's *and* father's rights are supported. For example, in the UK, men only get one to two weeks of paid paternity leave, while women get fifty-two weeks of maternity leave, and paid 90 per cent of their earnings for up to thirty-nine weeks plus additional support from the government if needed.[22] To create genuine fairness and partnership between the sexes we must move beyond the current female-centric conversations that so often alienate men towards more human-centric conversations that strive to include everyone. The things that women are really looking to have happen can happen if men's roles in the family are supported, as doing so will alleviate some of the work–life crunch many women feel while allowing men to be more involved in their families and communities.

More and more women are finding that, although it may not necessarily be what they want, they don't have to have a man in their life to achieve many of their personal, social and romantic goals. This is a liberating feeling for many women, as it should be. Something to be mindful of, however, is that as feminine confidence grows, it could proportionally and inversely affect the harmony between men and women; the more women separate their long-term goals from men the more the social chasm could widen between the sexes. In order to minimize that chasm it is crucial to allow men and men's issues to be welcomed and addressed in discussions on equality.

Overlapping challenges

The negative trends in male behaviour that we noted in Part I are hardly one-sided. The number of women who are overweight is also quite high – obesity rates are about the same as men's in many developed countries, and often higher in less developed nations.[23] Jean Twenge and W. Keith Campbell noted in *The Narcissism Epidemic* that narcissistic personality traits rose rapidly among college students from the 1980s to today, 'with the shift especially pronounced for women'. While young men still score higher on narcissism, young women are quickly catching up.[24] Just think about all the 'princess' propaganda pushed on girls – and strangely, embraced by parents who think it's 'cute'. They are not thinking about how movies like *Frozen* or *Cinderella* condition their daughters to feel entitled romantically and financially later in life.

When it comes to media, although young men spend more time on the Internet and playing video games than young women, women aged 18 to 49 watch roughly eleven hours more television per month than men.[25] This aligns with the research on women's overall unhappiness levels and the data that unhappy people watch more TV.

Just as the media shows few alternatives to the slovenly male, it also presents few alternatives to the boy-crazy female with nothing better to do than seduce the male protagonist. The Bechdel Test is an informal rating system that classifies films with three simple criteria: to pass the test a movie must 'have at least two [named] women in it, who talk to each other, about something besides a man'.[26] Very few video games pass all the criteria of the Bechdel Test,[27] and just over half of movies do.[28] The test is imperfect, as a film could pass the test but still include sexist content; nevertheless some cinemas and organizations – such as the Swedish Film Institute – are taking the rating seriously, and using it to highlight gender bias against women.[29]

Girls are more obsessed with social networks and their mobile phones than boys are. For example, one woman in her early 20s told us how her younger sister in high school spends hours doing her hair and make-up just to post a 'selfie' on her Facebook page so her friends would think she was going somewhere. In reality, right after taking the photo she would remove the make-up and go to sleep. The average 14- to 17-year-old girl also sends 100 or more text messages a day – more than twice the amount that boys send and receive.[30]

Despite all this 'socializing', women often have difficulty expressing their true feelings about each other and situations to one another. Whereas some men prefer socially intense situations, women prefer social pleasantries, avoiding any and all confrontation. Older generations of women, unfortunately, have passed down the habit of not saying anything – directly – when they don't have anything 'nice' to say. Recently, I (Nikita) listened to an all-too-common scene from one of my friends, who was trying to navigate a tricky text conversation with her 'bestie'. She sensed something was off between her and her friend, because her friend had planned a baby shower without her, and they hadn't been hanging out as much lately because the friend hadn't been returning all her texts. She asked her friend if she was mad at her. The friend replied, 'No, how could you think I was ever mad at you? I've just been under so much stress lately. Let's get coffee later.' My friend turned to her husband, who was sitting right next to her, and asked him how he would respond. 'I'd tell him to quit being an asshole, then we'd have a drink and move on.' Where men will tell each other exactly what's on their minds even if it's an insult, women so often say nothing and distance themselves from the other person in the hopes that the issue will resolve itself or fade to the point where it's no longer a problem.

But this attitude and aversion to confrontation carries over into adulthood. Many young women still feel uncomfortable being direct and open with each other because they have had so little practice giving and taking criticism, and have a hard time not holding a grudge against the person who gave the criticism, even when the intention behind it is good. By contrast, the way men communicate with each other lends itself to building trust because they know their male friends will be upfront with them. It also orients men towards conflict resolution and compromise, instead of trying to please everyone or 'keep the peace'. This could partly explain why, in a 2013 Gallup poll, just a quarter of women would prefer to work for a female boss while 40 per cent would prefer a male boss (a third had no preference).[31]

Why is it so hard for women just to say what's on their minds – even to their best friends? Because women's social lives, especially when they are growing up, depend so heavily on what other women think of them. Information about others is seen as power, and they fear losing not just one friend, but being alienated by other friends who are swayed by that one friend's approval. Most women also do not want to hurt each other's feelings, but in the process, what they are truly feeling doesn't get articulated, so whatever issue was really concerning them gets left unresolved for the sake of preserving the friendship and greater social cohesion of the group. So there is a feeling of social isolation that also exists among women.

Many modern women, like modern men, are also turning away from socializing, relationships and intimacy with the opposite sex. In Japan 45 per cent of women say they have no interest in sex and up to 90 per cent of young women think that staying single is better than marriage.[32] Worry over the dwindling birth rate has even prompted Japanese researchers to begin work on creating artificial wombs, in which embryos can be brought to term without a human host.[33]

In the US, the *New York Post* recently observed a trend of women in their 20s and 30s who would rather take care of a dog than get married or raise a child. Doggie-loving female readers told them that they didn't even think twice about giving up changing diapers, dealing with temper tantrums and creating college funds for the predictable affection of their four-legged 'child'. One woman said that it required less work and that she'd have more time to go out. No babysitter needed! Another said dogs were preferable, and that her little pup was 'great, except he snores a lot. He even has his own Instagram. A dog is easier to transport than a child. It's less final than having a child.' The American Pet Products Association reported the number of small dogs – under twenty-five pounds – went up 20 per cent from 2008 to 2012.[34]

For the women who would rather partner with a man, many have impractical, even otherworldly, expectations of who their suitor should be. Just like how porn gives men an unrealistic impression of sex, many women's version of porn – romantic comedies and erotic novels – gives them unrealistic expectations of what men will bring to the relationship. Though most women generally desire a man who is at least as tall, or taller than themselves, many successful young women also admitted to us that their checklist of qualities a potential partner must possess only increased as they became more educated and financially independent, further narrowing the pool of men they would give the time of day to. The reasons behind this invariably revolved around wanting to maintain a similar or better quality of life and social status once children came along in their partner-marital relationship.

Along those same lines, there are only 91 never-married men aged 25 to 34 with jobs for every 100 never-married women of the same age with jobs,[35] yet a 2014 survey of over 1,000 men and women found that 82 per cent of men and 72 per cent of women said the man should still pay the full bill on a date. Even as a relationship progresses, 36 per cent of men said they pay all the bills, versus 14 per cent of women.[36] In other words, women are becoming more educated and financially successful than men but they are less willing than men to meet their partner in the middle when it comes to sharing expenses. Perhaps this will change as men and women both become more comfortable with women leading, or with gender equality.

Landmines and eggshells: sexuality and dating

Just as most women don't want to be called sluts, most men want to avoid the label of chauvinist, particularly 'chauvinist pig'. Both names have been used unproductively for years; the difference now is men have a set of rules about what they're *not* supposed to do, but have nothing about what they should be doing, so while fewer guys are getting called chauvinists, they don't act as resolutely in the dating arena as they might have in the past. When you talk to older couples, the man will say something like, 'She was the most beautiful thing I'd ever seen,' and the woman will say, 'I thought he was the biggest jerk when I met him ... then he won me over.'

Now when a woman says 'no', men listen and back off, not knowing how to change their approach in the future, which means everyone gets fewer dates. Or they act like a jerk or resort to pick-up artist techniques because they were rejected without explanation. It is especially confusing for men when they hear women tell them they want to be with a man who is nice and respectful, yet see that the women respond more favourably to men who act more aggressively and with disregard for the woman's feelings. Some have dubbed this the 'Hero-Asshole Complex', in contrast to the Madonna-Whore Complex. It seems that desire plays by different rules that we, as a society, do not know how to discuss yet. Indeed, the majority of women want to feel overwhelmingly desired by their love interest, not logically contemplated, but this leaves a grey area for men to proceed. In a recent article on the male experience of feeling desired versus the female experience of feeling desired, Mark D. White, chair of the philosophy department at the College of Staten Island/CUNY, discussed this perplexing situation:

If I were dating and trying to achieve the appropriate balance between thoughtful consideration and spontaneous desire, I would consider the costs of failing to show sufficient respect – specifically, the risk of offending or hurting a woman – to be much higher than the costs of showing insufficient desire and passion – mainly, risking making a woman unhappy and endangering the success of the relationship. The way I think about things, I would consider the first risk much more serious than the second, and I would err on the side of respect and consideration. This may be what's behind the man Dr [Noam] Shpancer calls 'the delicate, tentative guy who politely thinks about you and asks if this is okay or that is okay,' who 'may well put you in a sexual coma – not despite these qualities, but because of them.'[37]

For a lot of guys, as much as women say 'no means no', in reality no often means maybe. Maybe as in prove or show – in a non-sexual way – why she should say yes. One Redditor commented on the article, saying:

I think men are kind of lost. The systems we've all been raised on had a very definite role for us to play. But we're told now it's dangerous. We are told to act differently, but often find that in one context or another, women want us to be cautious and respectful, and in other contexts, they want the abandon of desire. Get it wrong and you are either unaggressive (not forceful or dominant enough) and on the other end, too forceful and 'rapey'. It's difficult to know what we ought to be at any given moment. You'll see men rewarded for being respectful and egalitarian one moment, but then you'll hear a woman talk about a sexual fantasy of a man taking her without asking and just dominating her. What kind of signal do I take from these conflicting messages? Can a woman want both things? And if she does, how can she expect the man to navigate what she's wanting? Or is it that they don't really want both, they truly want one or the other, and something cultural is pressuring them to say they want the other [too]?[38]

One young man from our survey echoed a parallel view:

In a post-feminism generation, gender roles are unclear. Men in their late 20s to early 30s today were raised to be sensitive and caring, and to hide any aggressive impulses, but find this gets them nowhere. Women in their 20s to early 30s talk about feminine empowerment but are still only sexually attracted to overt displays of strength and aggression. Sensitivity, politeness and asking what a woman wants are extreme turnoffs because they are perceived as weakness. Not only is being a new kind of man a turnoff, it also keeps me from making the first move because I learned to worry about forcing myself onto the object of my desire, to not be crass or slimy, to not use pickup lines, etc. But there are no clearly defined rules for what I should be doing, just a set of things that I shouldn't do – all the things that would elicit results … I'll just go play video games, thanks.

One thing that has changed is the pressure women feel to be 'liberated'. No one can agree on what exactly that is though, and one of the reasons why feminism broke off into so many sub-groups was because there was so much disagreement about what sexual liberation was. For example, some women, such as Candida Royalle[39] and Annie Sprinkle,[40] thought porn was empowering, while others, such as Andrea Dworkin, Susan Brownmiller and Robin Morgan,[41] thought it undermined feminism's goals. Despite the efforts of religious conservatives and radical feminists to eradicate porn, societal attitudes have shifted since the 1960s from the expectation that a woman be pure and virginal until marriage to being ready, willing and able to hook up anywhere, anytime, with no strings attached. Though the current situation has debunked certain taboos, most sexual education curriculums are still stuck in the Victorian ages. 'Our bodies, our choice' sounds powerful, but what good is it when nobody understands their own body or choices?

In her book *Female Chauvinist Pigs*, Ariel Levy, a staff writer at the *New Yorker*, discussed the impact that sexual objectification and self-objectification have on the development of sexuality and identity of young women. She investigated the rise of the raunch culture and the effects of female 'empowerment' shifting from the fight for women's rights to strip dance classes. Levy writes that women of all ages are confronted with the same issues, yet: 'Whereas older women were around for the women's movement itself, or at least for the period when its lessons were still alive in the country's collective memory, teenage girls have only the here and now. They have never known a time when "ho" wasn't part of the lexicon, when 16 year olds didn't get breast implants, when porn stars weren't topping the best-seller lists, when strippers weren't mainstream …'[42]

How can society be surprised that young women act as if hotness and lust were virtues when they are barraged with images that combine sexual exhibitionism with a glamorous lifestyle? Amid the 'contradictory mishmash' of messages from parents, peers and the media, it is unrealistic to think that teenagers will pay no mind to their hormones, disregard the porn stars on television and be oblivious to all the sites dedicated to sex on the Internet. Levy says that it should be no wonder that teens are not cooperating with the traditional plan to save oneself for 'the one' or are comprehending that sex is performance given for attention, and suggests that:

> Rather than only telling teens why they shouldn't have sex, perhaps we also ought to be teaching them why they should. We are doing little to help them differentiate their sexual desires from their desire for attention...If there's a way in

> which grown women are appropriating raunch as a rebellion
> against the constraints of feminism, we can't say the same for
> teens. They never had a feminism to rebel against...Our
> national love of porn and pole dancing is not the byproduct of
> a free and easy society with an earthy acceptance of sex. It is a
> desperate stab at free-wheeling eroticism in a time and place
> characterized by intense anxiety.[43]

Levy references interviews with teen girls conducted by Deborah
Tolman, for her book *Dilemmas of Desire*. Tolman found that the girls
could not differentiate between the experiences of being wanted
versus the experience of sex. The girls also ignored or suppressed
their own arousal, in what Tolman described as 'silent bodies',
because they were terrified that really feeling 'embodied sexual
desire' would only lead to disease and unwanted pregnancy. What
the girls mostly felt was a 'great deal' of confusion and anxiety.[44]

Things have got a lot worse for women in recent decades, says
Australian feminist Germaine Greer, who wrote *The Female Eunuch*
in 1970. 'Liberation hasn't happened, even sexual liberation didn't
happen...What happened was that commercial pornography was
liberated, fantasy was liberated, but people weren't liberated.'[45]
Men and women are both looking for answers, but they can't do it
in the current political climate.

Language does not equal liberation; liberation equals liberation

We bring up these challenges and contradictions in the women's
movement as well as the distortion of statistics about sexism by
politicians because it is important for women to realize that unless
the catchy slogans actually have a basis in reality, true empowerment
for women will not exist. Despite the progress that has been made
by the women's movement, there are many real flaws that exist in
the current Western social and cultural structure for both sexes.
Furthermore, feigning concern for legitimate women's issues

through political correctness creates unfounded anger towards men and diverts attention and resources away from making long-lasting improvements or generating more effective cooperation between the sexes.

Nick Cohen, a journalist for the *Spectator*, recently discussed the detrimental effects this kind of political correctness has in a recent article:

> What distinguishes our times is the fanaticism about the power language. Starting on the post-1968 left and moving rightwards ever since, is a belief that slips in language reveal your opponent's hidden meanings and unquestioned assumptions. The wised-up need only decode, and everyone will see the oppressiveness of the elite...Indeed, your insistence that you can change the world by changing language, and deal with racism or homophobia merely by not offending the feelings of interest groups, is likely to allow real racism and homophobia to flourish unchallenged, and the sick and disadvantaged to continue to suffer from polite neglect.[46]

Instead of examining the real issues honestly, we have censored them. Which is why, in 2014, we simultaneously ended up with a Mississippi sex education class comparing women who have sex to dirty pieces of chocolate[47] and Beyoncé in a bikini on the cover of *Time* magazine's '100 Most Influential People'.[48] On one level, the bikini photos pay homage to positive body image campaigns, but on another level, it says that, as a woman, no matter what you've accomplished, what matters most is how your body looks. Women such as Malala Yousafzai and Hillary Clinton would never be asked to pose in a swimsuit – because we take them seriously. But what are young girls (and boys) who idolize celebrities supposed to think? The cover may as well have shown Miley Cyrus on a wrecking ball.

In today's world, a woman who appears in the media is expected to willingly objectify herself to stay relevant. If she is not traditionally beautiful, she can either pile on the make-up or go for a dark or edgy look – but she's still expected to try to put her sexiest foot forward. Photoshop can take care of the rest. Even actresses are sick of the status quo. Rashida Jones, one of the stars on the US version of *The Office*, wrote a piece for *Glamour* about the pornification of everything, saying that women can't possibly all be into strip dancing or showing so much skin. Owning and expressing one's sexuality has been an important step for women, she said, but most of what's out there seems so staged – '...in my opinion, we are at a point of oversaturation'. In television, this oversaturation is known as a 'tonnage issue', which TV network censors will report when there is an overuse of a certain phrase. 'When it comes to porn imagery and pop culture, we have a tonnage issue,' Jones said, but because of the ubiquity of these images and the personas that accompany them young girls who imitate celebrities may not see that personal sexual expression is related to having pride about who they are on the inside.[49]

If Beyoncé's cover on *Time* is not the tonnage tipping point, we don't know what is. Why is being a woman today so much about being 'one of the guys' with '*really* amazing hair' – as feminist Caitlin Moran puts it?[50]

Women are selling themselves short if they allow raunch culture to shape their identities and sexual expressions. We agree with Levy when she wrote:

If we really believed that we were sexy and funny and competent and smart, we would not need to be like strippers or [be] like men or [be] like anyone other than our own specific, individual selves...[to do this] would be no more difficult than the kind of contortions FCPs are constantly performing in an effort to prove themselves. More importantly, the rewards would be the very things Female Chauvinist Pigs want so desperately, the things women deserve: freedom and power.[51]

In order to do that, women must begin identifying their new ways to assert their relevance – ones that don't involve contempt for men but, rather, ways that include their own creative approaches that can benefit everyone. Men and women are different, and within both sexes there are further differences, so there is no need for each sex's definitions of success either to be the same or look the same. Echoing the words of Ruth Rosen, in a true democracy, women should not feel compelled to live as men do.

Teaching our daughters to succeed

The more women succeed monetarily, the more they will realize that men are not the sex with the power; rather they will understand that men are the sex most willing to accept the trade-offs. The truth is, no one can 'have it all'. A mistaken belief of the feminist movement was the expectation that work would equate power and self-fulfilment.

There are not many privileges that come without responsibilities and successful people learn to say 'no thank you' if a responsibility doesn't help them secure an opportunity or offer them some advantage or valuable experience. They don't accept a situation and then complain about how oppressive it feels later. Women need to be mentored for success so they don't have to rely on the law and the government to advocate for them and in some cases supplement their incomes.

In addition to creating policies that honour parenting as much as careers, the best thing society can do to allow more women to succeed in the workplace is to prepare them to overcome obstacles. The focus should be on creating safe and healthy work spaces for women (and men), instead of undermining women's strength by trying to ban the word 'bossy', as Sheryl Sandberg, COO of Facebook, has done in her otherwise positive Lean In movement.[52] We can encourage girls to lead by saying, 'You know what? Bossy people get things done. Listen to others, do your homework so you know what you're talking about, and keep voicing your opinion. The climb to the top is never easy.'

We can also take girls to watch television shows and movies that pass the Bechdel Test and get them subscriptions to magazines that advise them on how to be leaders. In 2013 *Better Homes and Gardens* was the fourth most popular magazine in the United States. Seventeen women's magazines, including *Cosmopolitan*, *Seventeen*, *Allure*, *Lucky* and *Teen Vogue* all ranked higher than *Forbes*, the *Economist* and *Working Mother* in magazine circulation. In fact, *Cosmopolitan* had more subscribers than *Forbes*, the *Economist* and *Working Mother* combined.[53] Similarly, in the UK *Glamour* had the greatest circulation of any consumer magazine – with 428,325 subscribers, followed by several other women's magazines, all of which had more subscribers than any version of the *Economist*.[54] If the number of young women who read *Cosmopolitan* or *Glamour* got a subscription to a magazine that covered finance and current events, we would no doubt see massive changes in young women's interests and a positive shift in their self-confidence.

In her book, *Committed: A Skeptic Makes Peace With Marriage*, Elizabeth Gilbert found no pattern among the hundreds of women she interviewed about how they balanced career and family. 'There was just a whole bunch of smart women trying to work things out on their own terms,' she said. In her previous book, the bestseller *Eat, Pray, Love*, Gilbert wrote about recovering from a painful divorce in which her ex-husband wanted to have children but she did not. There were other factors that contributed to her leaving the marriage, but 'the question of children was the final blow'.[55] There's no doubt a lot of heartache could be avoided if there were more honest discussions between generations of women about how different decisions affect one's life as well as who compatible partners would be for those varying paths.

If mothers and daughters read publications that covered personal finance, investing and business trends together, it would open up conversations for mums to share their first-hand experience and knowledge that will help their daughters plan a future.

Mothers can also talk to their daughters about the different challenges and trade-offs that come with having children earlier or later (or at all) in their lives, such as education loans, fertility and how parenthood affects opportunities. Daughters need these conversations. Can working mothers or overextended single mothers find the time for such conversations? We feel strongly that they must make the time for their offspring to benefit from their wisdom.

Although women outnumber men at colleges and are more likely to be involved in activities outside class, in the 2012 CIRT Freshman Survey more than twice as many incoming freshman women (41 per cent versus 18 per cent of incoming freshman men) felt constantly 'overwhelmed by all I had to do'. The overwhelmed students were also less likely than the not-at-all-overwhelmed students to believe in their abilities and have confidence in social situations.[56]

To combat this, another thing we can do is enrol more girls in team sports, which develop a unifying sense of social responsibility, and whose combination of competitiveness and teamwork creates a solid foundation for cooperating with others in business settings later on. They also help women learn that they can rely on each other, when honest and open communication is lacking in other social situations. Mothers can supplement this by having the courage to show their daughters what honest communication between women can look like – by respecting others for telling the truth, by not gossiping or displaying an entirely different attitude about someone behind that person's back, and by remaining friends with someone who offered constructive criticism. They can also model being non-judgemental of others, meaning describing others' behaviour without critical evaluations added in.

Equally important is encouraging girls to ask out the boy they are attracted to, which helps them learn how to take risks and handle rejection as well as develop character, patience and perseverance – all valuable business skills. From these experiences they also learn, indirectly, how to eventually choose a partner who appreciates a woman who takes risks. For women as well as men, we say, a life without risks is boring. A life with risks will include failures – and failures are vital learning experiences on the path to success.

14

Patriarchy Myths

Men must be needed because we can't be wanted. We believe we have to be the heroes only because we can't yet see other roles for ourselves.

– Noah Brand, editor for the Good Men Project[1]

There are numerous ways in which women experience a more acute sense of powerlessness than men. Date rape, being physically subjugated, having less socialization around negotiation and career success, physical signs of ageing and loss of the power that comes with youth and physical beauty are all examples of challenges women must navigate. But whether you are willing to admit it or not, sexism goes both ways. Boys are conditioned differently than girls, and being a man is no casual walk in the park.

Right from the beginning, when only a few days old, many baby boys undergo circumcision. It is a process some have likened to genital mutilation, and although we see the ritual of clitoral circumcision performed on baby girls in certain cultures as primitive and barbaric, the majority of boys in the US are still forced to endure it (rates in the UK are lower). As infants, baby boys take longer to be picked up after crying – giving them the implied message that complaining won't change anything. They are also sung to less, told stories less often and read to less often than girls.[2] Those *lesses* are actually negative lessons about not being worth the time and effort from parents and guardians to provide these activities.

Later, in their pre-teen and early teen years, boys learn to endure pain through rough team sports. Around the same time they become aware of what they are supposed to provide in a relationship, specifically financial expectations, so they begin taking on less enjoyable jobs because they pay more. Young men are still socialized to believe they must get a high-paying job to support a wife and kids, but young women do not get that message (hence the statistics on who should pay for a date). Boys also catch on to the stigma against stay-at-home fathers – a recent Pew Research survey revealed that 84 per cent of stay-at-home parents are women, and although 51 per cent of people say children are better off if their mother stays at home, only 8 per cent feel the same way about fathers.[3] It is clear men's roles as nurturers are overlooked, even as more men are now accepting this new role of caregiver. At some point in middle or high school when a boy starts to think about his first date he most likely starts to curb his interests in creative pursuits because he knows art and literature majors will make less money than a science, technology, engineering or maths (STEM) major. He does this based on the possibility that he might have to support a family and because he most likely cannot expect a woman – especially one he were to have a family with – to support him.

Although women now comprise the majority of college graduates, men are still the majority of STEM majors. Women, on the other hand, dominate the social sciences. In 2007, 83 per cent of engineering majors were men while more than 77 per cent of psychology majors and 79 per cent of education majors were women. For master's degrees, 77 per cent of engineering graduates were men while 77 per cent of education graduates and 80 per cent of psychology graduates were women.[4] In the UK, well over 90 per cent of students studying for a GCSE in engineering were boys while over 90 per cent of students studying health and social care were girls.[5]

Based on the proportions and differences in earnings, at first glance it could look like discrimination, yet both sexes knew beforehand that going the STEM route would most likely lead to a higher income. Women, in turn, are socialized to reinforce the gap in financial expectations by not offering to split the tab on dates; and the majority leave the workforce for at least a year after their first child is born.[6]

There are plenty of scholarships offered to people of all sexes and ethnicities, but more scholarships – both academic and athletic – are offered exclusively to women than to men. On scholarships.com – one of the most popular sites on which to find and apply for scholarships in the US – women's scholarships outnumbered men's four to one. All of the men's scholarships were restricted to a particular geographic location or university while over half of the women's scholarships accepted applicants from around the country. There were several women's scholarships just for single mothers; zero scholarships were offered exclusively to single fathers.[7] In addition, the trend of parents spending more on their sons' education in the 1970s not only equalized in the 1990s, but was reversed by the late 2000s;[8] parents now spend about 25 per cent more money on their daughter's education than their son's.[9] Why not choose the major you like if someone else is footing the bill?

Simply put, young women do not have the same reality checks young men have that the world doesn't revolve around them. It is easier to talk about equal rights than equal responsibilities; however, if we wish to see greater compassion and cooperation between the sexes that is the logical next step.

What is power?

Although the earliest stages of agriculture may have been developed by women cultivating wild grains in the ancient Middle East, as sociologist Elise Boulding suggests, many scholars, such as George Washington University research professor Heidi Hartmann, theorize men came to dominate societies after agriculture took hold, which allowed them to further constitute control over family, labour, economics, culture and religion.[10] Accordingly, power is often seen through a patriarchal lens; he who controls the purse strings controls the rest. There's no question money allows people greater freedom and control in many areas of life, but being able to exert command over a system is just one kind of power. There is another kind of power that is not as loud, but just as valid: personal power.

Real power is well-rounded. It does not just revolve around external rewards such as income, social status and material possessions. Well-rounded power includes internal rewards such as health, inner peace, spirituality, being loved and respected, emotional awareness and openness, positive concept of self, and the ability to utilize personal values to enhance the quality of everyday life, both for the person and the community.

Ultimately power comes down to having control over one's life and having access to fulfilling personal experiences. In this light, lifespan would be a reasonable gauge. The World Health Organization has listed these average life expectancies for men and women born into low- and high-income families between 1990 and 2012:

- Low-income-born male: 54.7 years.

- Low-income-born female: 57.3 years.

- High-income-born male: 73 years.

- High-income-born female: 80 years.

- Average global life expectancy at birth for males born 1990 to 2012: 64.7 years.

- Average global life expectancy at birth for females born 1990 to 2012: 69.7 years.[11]

The global average life expectancy for women is 5 years (8 per cent) longer than for men. While wealthy men will live 15.7 years (27 per cent) longer than poor women, women from wealthy backgrounds will live more than 25 years (46 per cent) longer than poor men. Women make up 81 per cent of centenarians.[12]

Slightly more men are diagnosed with prostate cancer than women are diagnosed with breast cancer, yet breast cancer research is supported by federal spending over prostate cancer at a ratio of nearly two to one.[13] The US government has also set up an online resource for women's health (womenshealth.gov) but there is no comparable menshealth.gov. Curiously, men's health is a sub-group on the women's health page (womenshealth.gov/mens-health/). On their website there is a banner announcing the National Women's Health Week where women can learn more about health concerns, but a National Men's Health Week does not exist. Some countries around the world – including Australia, Canada, the UK and the US – have begun recognizing International Men's Day (19 November) in part to raise awareness of men's and boys' health, but it has yet to be supported on the same scale as walks for breast cancer.

Men also die at higher rates from nearly all the top fifteen causes of death; the largest differences were in diseases of the heart, suicide and fatal injuries sustained from unintentional accidents.[14] Women are more likely to have suicidal thoughts than men, but suicide is four times higher among men, representing 79 per cent of all suicides in the US.[15] In the UK, men's suicide rates are 3.5 times higher than that of women, with men between 40 and 44 years old, and of low socioeconomic status, having the highest rates.[16]

Of the 4,383 people who died at work in America in 2012, only 338 were women, meaning 92 per cent of work fatalities were men. Construction accounted for the most fatalities, with the majority of accidents occurring from falls and slips.[17] In the UK, 94 out of the 99 people who died from fatal work injuries in the 2012–13 year were men.[18] Around the world men far outnumber women in dangerous jobs.

There are more women with children who are homeless than men with children who are homeless, but overall 68 per cent of the US homeless population is male, and 40 per cent of homeless men have served in the armed forces, as compared to 34 per cent of the general adult population. The National Coalition for Homeless Veterans estimates that on any given night 271,000 veterans are homeless, most of them men.[19] This national disgrace continues without any major media coverage or national dialogue about the need to pay back our brave veterans. In the UK, 86 per cent of those sleeping on the streets – the homeless – are men.[20]

From these facts we can deduce that in some ways women actually have more power than men do.

Act like a man: the heavy price of bottling emotions

For men, being physically bullied and taunted is such a huge part of the boyhood experience that it has come to be seen as normal. 'Boys will be boys,' people say. 'That's just how they are.' When young boys internalize these beliefs about themselves as being tough, that they are supposed just to take things like a man, they ultimately get cut off from the more sensitive sides of themselves that are needed later in life. As a consequence, intimacy and relationships can become a major struggle further down the road. A corollary is that they do not learn to ask for help from friends, family, teachers, coaches or others who could do so to alleviate some of the negativity they face.

When a young boy is told crying is for girls, he learns that it is not acceptable for him to express his emotions so he bottles them up. When anyone is told who they are and how they are feeling is wrong, they begin to hold back or try to change their internal experience. How this plays out in relationships is the person is never quite sure who they are or what they want. They begin to run a script that does not have any real depth or roots. Twenty years later when this young boy becomes a man who meets and falls in love with an amazing woman, he is feeling confused when she says she does not feel close to him. She wants him to open up more and he has no idea what she is talking about because he has never opened up in his life.

Other men who as boys got bullied in school can still carry anger from those experiences. When this anger goes unacknowledged it functions on a subconscious level – often as a background voice telling the person how bad, ugly or stupid they are – almost taking the place of the external bullies. This in turn damages self-confidence, and may be expressed in relationships as the man having a hard time saying no or standing up for what he wants. He might even get placed in the 'nice guy' category out of fear of ever being a bully himself. Another way this can be expressed is in keeping others at a distance due to believing other people are mean and untrustworthy, and letting them get close will inevitably hurt. On a deeper level, because they believe their peers are bad and mean, they think they are also similar, and therefore unlovable. If someone believes at their core that they are unlovable, letting love in or giving love becomes nearly impossible.

Imagine if your only experience of touch was roughhousing or someone trying to hurt you? Studies have shown that baby boys get touched less than baby girls. Many men turn to sex because it is the only place where they receive positive physical touch. Otherwise, their lives are basically void of physical contact with others. This internal personal struggle with touching and nourishment can cause sex and relationships to feel empty, lonely and pointless, effectively cutting a person off from experiencing true pleasure and connection. Again we point out that when young men turn to porn for imagined erotic experiences, they never get to see men and women touching each other in tender or caring ways.

Taboos

Belle Knox, the infamous Duke University student-turned-porn-star, recently echoed the sentiment long held by feminists that the patriarchy fears female sexuality.[21] It's an outdated message that is resonating less and less. Show us a Western man – today – who doesn't enjoy watching a woman express herself sexually, and we'll show you a gay man. As a society, we may be afraid of female sexuality ... But we are equally afraid of male sexuality and teen sexuality; we also pretend senior citizens' sexuality doesn't exist. Is the patriarchy really to blame? Or is it just that sexuality is kind of messy and nobody wants to take on the great big grey zone surrounding the traditionally socially acceptable standards?

Sexuality is like the elephant in the room that everyone is walking around: we see it but we don't talk about it. But it's getting so big that we can't ignore it any more; it is nearly impossible to avoid being bombarded by gossip magazines with an airbrushed woman in a bikini on the cover, advertisements that look like porn, or a scene from an erotic novel, and reality shows where nothing is left to the imagination. The underlying message is that we're not good enough and we're missing out. Yet all this exists because we pay attention to it, and, more importantly, we buy these things that sexually focused ads are promoting.

One major effect is that it leaves us all wanting, as if something is constantly missing, leaving us always wanting more. And for some, it creates or intensifies feelings of repression. 'Why don't I have these things? Is someone or something holding me back?' Women might say they feel objectified. Others might say it perpetuates rape culture. But a lot of this media is created by women, for women.

A French short film called *Oppressed Majority* recently reversed men's and women's roles. A lot of people were hyped about it; several feminist friends of ours shared it on social media. A man commented underneath one of the posts that he was adamantly against violence, but men and women are different and he wouldn't mind being sexually assaulted by several attractive women because he would interpret it as a desirable sexual experience. The film is trying to be funny, but all it does is show how little the director (a woman) understands men. She insinuates through the laziness and insensitivity of the women playing male characters that men don't care about sexual assault against women, which is odd considering men by and large take on the more dangerous jobs where they would be protectors of women and, indirectly, freedom. (For example, 74 per cent of the total police force in the UK is made up solely of men[22] and 90 per cent of the armed forces in the UK are also completely male[23].) We also found it interesting that the director chose to portray the women (played by men) as weak and helpless, which made us wonder what she was trying to say about women...

How come no one wants to talk about sexism against men? A blogger named Nicki Daniels wrote an open letter to bearded hipsters, deriding them for ruining her 'beard fetish'. 'Ever since I was a little girl,' she said, 'I've loved a man with a beard. To me, they meant strength, power, MANLINESS. Someone who could protect me. Unfortunately, you guys have turned it into a fashion statement. The beard has turned into the padded bra of masculinity. Sure it looks sexy, but watcha got under there? There's a whole generation running around looking like lumberjacks, and most of you can't change a...tire.'[24] It went viral, and frankly it was pretty funny unless, of course, you were a bearded hipster.

But if a man wrote a post like that ranting about women having hairy armpits or huge bushes he would be torn to pieces. Why is it that a woman can publicly discuss dumping her boyfriend for not going down on her, talk about how empowering it is to sleep with younger men, create a cab service that only employs female drivers and refuses to give men rides, or even suggest men should be taxed more, but a man doing those things is unthinkable?[25] The double standard is typically depicted as women getting the short end of the big stick, but looked at through this new lens men are getting the shaft at least as often.

If a man made a movie in the same vein as *Oppressed Majority* perhaps we'd see the flip side of gender hostility, like how men are treated as success objects (versus women as sex objects), hardly ever receive positive physical touch outside sex, and are far less likely to win in custody battles after divorce. Maybe we'd wonder why women have the right to become a soldier and the privilege to opt out if there was a draft, yet in the US every male has the responsibility to register with the Selective Service within thirty days of his 18th birthday and the responsibility to fight in the event of war[26] (which is as sexist as making all 18-year-old females register to reproduce if the country were to need more children – Nazi Germany tried something like this with the Lebensborn programme during the Second World War). In the UK mandatory conscription ended in 1960, although for several years men who were 18 to 21 years old were required to do National Service unless they were enrolled in higher education.[27] Perhaps we'd learn that a greater percentage of men are raped in prison every year than women are raped in the US.[28] When I (Nikita) mentioned this statistic to an older female neighbour of mine who is a feminist and historian, her expression was surprise, but then she firmly stated, 'Well, that's a power thing.' Is it? If rape is an extension of the so-called patriarchy and economic power why would black men get arrested for rape 6.5 times more often than whites?[29] It seems powerlessness plays a role too.

Male rape is largely ignored, downplayed or made into a joke in everyday life and in the media. The FBI does not even list any statistics about sexual assault where males are the victim; with information so hard to find, you'd think it never happens.[30] Yet it does. While far more women report experiencing rape at some time in their lives, approximately the same amount of women and men, 5.6 per cent and 5.3 per cent, respectively, report experiencing sexual violence other than rape,[31] and the ManKind Initiative in the UK reports two in five domestic abuse incidences are suffered by men.[32] Although women feel a lower sense of security than men, the Organisation for Economic Co-operation and Development (OECD) reports men are actually at a much higher risk of being victims of assaults and violent crimes.[33]

Much of the reported sexual violence against men is from unwanted advances from other males. Perhaps that number would be higher if so many adult males minded being sexually 'assaulted' by a woman or 'being made to penetrate' was included in the definition of rape. We must also consider that male victims, regardless of the sex of the perpetrator, are less likely to report the violence and seek services. The National Coalition Against Domestic Violence explained these reasons why: 'The stigma of being a male victim, the perceived failure to conform to the macho stereotype, the fear of not being believed, the denial of victim status, and the lack of support from society, family members, and friends . . . boys are less likely to report sexual abuse due to fear, anxiety associated with being perceived as gay, the desire to appear self-reliant, and the will to be independent.'[34]

We would add shame to the list. Unless it is a boy being raped by a man (as in many of the Catholic priest scandals), people seem less inclined – if at all inclined – to speak out against sexual violence against men. It could even be called taboo to do so. Even when male victims speak up, people don't really know what to do about it. There's no clear legislation around it. It also appears difficult for people to wrap their heads around a man having an erection and simultaneously being a victim. If he was aroused, he must have wanted it, right?

Wrong, said Andrew Bailey, a young male actor who posted an intense and heartbreaking account of an experience of a female teacher raping a 13-year-old boy on YouTube. At the end of the video he says he believes rape is 'hilarious' because he has to see it that way, implying there are no ways for him to process what happened to him.[35] It is supposed to be every adolescent boy's fantasy.

A female victim's orgasm during rape does not detract from her unwillingness to participate in the act, so why should a man's? If the situation Bailey described were reversed, society would be much more empathetic and capable of helping a young female student, even though the male's experience is no less serious. When you talk to men about their sexual histories, you might be surprised to learn that many of them lost their virginities in less than ideal ways. Some will admit that the first woman they had sex with forced herself on them, and they just went with it because they felt like they had to. We don't call those women rapists, but if they were men we would.

Bringing up this kind of double standard is important, because we cannot expect society to be well-equipped to handle the dark side of sexuality if we refuse to acknowledge the complex nature of sexuality or take an honest look at how, and more importantly *why* sexual assault happens. Young men especially are told that it's not OK to say no, and they are not taught how to rebuff unwanted sexual advances or instructed on what to do if they are sexually assaulted. Instead, they are socially conditioned always to be ready and willing to perform sexually with any woman who offers. So while many men might identify with the man's response to *Oppressed Majority*, many others are left without answers. In addition, denying men as victims downplays other incidences where men are expected to just handle the situation or 'take things like a man', including spousal abuse (verbal and physical), stalking and harassment.

Could the situation improve? It is helpful to have laws around consent and boundaries, but we need to teach children what real consent and boundaries look like, not just these two standard requirements: 1) Does this person want to give consent?; and 2) Is this person capable of giving consent?

Just as we are exploring and raising social awareness around areas where women are repressed, we must also allow men to examine areas where they feel silenced. Women will also need to explore and acknowledge their own biases, double standards and reverse sexism towards men. This is not a way to blame women for sexual assault against men, or undermine the significance of the sexual assault that happens to women; it is a way to let *both* sexes discover paths of communication that can unite the sexes in their commitment to end sexual assault together. Such violations of our physical boundaries are violations against human dignity.

Many men feel restrained by their gender roles, only in different ways than women, and most men aren't able to pinpoint the cause of their frustration because they are not raised to examine the roots of their challenges or insecurities. For some males, under certain conditions, this frustration turns into anger and unfortunately can get to a boiling point where they verbally, physically or sexually lash out against women. Everyone is responsible for their actions, no doubt, but at the same time we shouldn't underestimate the power of the system and situation on individual behaviour. When we only acknowledge women's vulnerabilities, telling men they are potential perpetrators and women they are potential victims, we do everyone a disservice and perpetuate imbalance.

Objectification is a prerequisite for rape. One reason why men sexually objectify women is because the majority of the time they are the ones approaching women to ask them out on dates or initiate a sexual experience. A good portion of that time they get rejected, even when they're in a relationship, and it hurts a lot less if the person they're getting rejected by can be thought of as an object. Over time this can breed contempt for whoever is not taking the initiative; it also reinforces self-doubt in the other party about what they are valued for. As more women begin to take the lead romantically and sexually, they will have a greater appreciation of the process of objectification and rejection, and men will begin to understand the flip side of objectification and rejection that has discontented women for so long. The same thing goes for other role reversals, such as more women becoming breadwinners and men spending more time with the kids. It's these kinds of trends, where men and women really get to see – not just project onto the other – what it's like for the opposite sex, that will produce the large-scale attitude and behavioural shifts we need for everyone to be truly liberated.

We were a little taken aback that Nikita's neighbour's initial reaction was dismissive. Instead of saying something like, 'Wow, that's terrible, why does that happen?' the conversation got shut down. Even asking whether rape might evolve from powerlessness, not power, makes people uncomfortable because it leads to other conversations that are not so black-and-white. But if we did start talking about it, maybe the way we think about these issues would change, and society would start addressing the causes instead of just the symptoms.

Justice for all?

In the summer of 2013 US Attorney General Eric Holder said that the current criminal justice solutions were not adequate in overcoming twenty-first-century challenges. He delivered these remarks about the US's correctional system failures at the annual meeting of the American Bar Association's House of Delegates:

> As a nation, we are coldly efficient in our incarceration efforts. While the entire US population has increased by about a third since 1980, the federal prison population has grown at an astonishing rate – by almost 800 per cent. It's still growing – despite the fact that federal prisons are operating at nearly 40 per cent above capacity. Even though this country comprises just 5 per cent of the world's population, we incarcerate almost a quarter of the world's prisoners. More than 219,000 federal inmates are currently behind bars. Almost half of them are serving time for drug-related crimes, and many have substance use disorders. Nine to 10 million more people cycle through America's local jails each year. And roughly 40 per cent of former federal prisoners – and more than 60 per cent of former state prisoners – are rearrested or have their supervision revoked within three years after their release ... and often for technical or minor violations of the terms of their release ... it's time to ask tough questions about how we can

strengthen our communities, support young people, and
address the fact that young Black and Latino men are
disproportionately likely to become involved in our criminal
justice system – as victims as well as perpetrators.[36]

In the late 1980s a sex bias was found pervading the justice system:
it seemed courts were placing women on longer probation periods
than men who were convicted of similar crimes.[37] The issue was
looked into by the judicial system. In reality, men convicted of
similar crimes were more likely to get prison sentences, not the
lighter sentence of probation, which the women got.[38] And the
women who did go to prison entered a much different environment;
Warren Farrell recalled one attorney's remarks in *The Myth of Male
Power*: 'Women felons go to a former school a few miles east of the
state capitol. The men's institutions are prisons, plain and hard.
They offer cells, guards, cell block gangs ... The women's institution
feels like the school it was built to be, and its staff encourages
reform and rehabilitation.'[39]

Today, the Female Offender Programs and Services (FOPS) of
California declared on their site that they have created a 'gender-
responsive' programme for female offenders that offers them
services, guidance and self-help treatments in order to rehabilitate
them and to make their transition back into the community more
successful when they are released. One of FOPS' goals is to treat
female offenders with dignity and respect within an ethical
institutional setting. Additionally, FOPS provides vocational and
academic programmes, career and technical education, pre-release
guidance, art classes and support groups for community
betterment projects. The philosophy behind this is to increase the
women's opportunities and to reduce the amount of incarcerated
women, while increasing public safety. There is no equivalent
'MOPS' programme for men.[40]

These issues are not exclusive to the US. In the UK women
comprise only 5 per cent of the prison population, and the

majority serve very short sentences of six months or less. Seven per cent of children will experience their father being imprisoned while they are school age, and children of prisoners are three times likelier than other children to have mental health problems or engage in antisocial behaviour. Seventy-six per cent of prisoners themselves had an absent father when they were growing up. There is a disproportion of incarcerated minorities too – 10 per cent of UK prisoners are black, though they represent less than 3 per cent of the general population.[41]

In a 2012 House of Commons debate, MP Phil Davies was quoted as saying:

> The Ministry of Justice's own figures show that women are more likely than men to get bail... It is said that 17,000 children are separated from their mothers and that 60% of women in custody have children under the age of 18. It is also suggested that about 700 of more than 4,000 women are in prisons more than 100 miles away from their children. Let us take that in stages. First, it is not the system that separates any mother from her children. It is that individual's actions in breaking the law that have led to prison and that is almost certainly 100% their fault and their responsibility alone... In addition, recently updated sentencing guidelines also incorporate consideration of the effect that custody would have on others, when the defendant is the primary carer for another. That again is likely to benefit further more women than men when they are sentenced. If we are so concerned about the children of women offenders, what about the estimated 180,000 children who are separated from their fathers who are in prison? In this age of equality, what about that much higher figure? Should we not be more, or at least equally, outraged about that?[42]

Why are there not more rehabilitation programmes for men when 47 per cent of prisoners say they have no work qualifications

– three times higher than the general, working-age population – and just 27 per cent were able to return to a job after prison? With each prisoner costing about £40,000 a year, a quarter of prisoners being held in overcrowded accommodation, and with a 47 per cent re-incarceration rate, it makes absolutely no sense that there are not more efforts made to reintegrate prisoners back into society and connect them with their families. This is especially so when 40 per cent of prisoners said that support from their family, and 36 per cent said seeing their children, would stop them from reoffending in the future (the likelihood of reoffending is 39 per cent higher for prisoners who did not receive visits). Knowing there are people outside who think you matter makes a massive difference.[43]

The sexual abuses and the consequences of those abuses that men face in prison are another story. In addition to their being raped, often gang-raped, men in prison face contracting deadly sexually transmitted infections like HIV, which is spread more easily through anal sex. HIV rates are about four times higher among prisoners than among the general population, said the authors of a 2010 article in the *American Journal of Public Health*. They were studying the handful of prisons in the US that have begun to offer condom-dispensing machines, in an effort to decrease the spread of sexually transmitted infections.[44]

If only there was more action taken to prevent rape in prison in the first place.

Why is it so hard to change the supposed 'pay gap'?

> One reason the jobs men hold pay more is because they are
> more hazardous...Just as the 'glass ceiling' describes the
> invisible barrier that keeps women out of jobs with the most
> pay, the 'glass cellar' describes the invisible barrier that keeps
> men in jobs with the most hazards.
>
> – Warren Farrell[45]

One of the reasons why the women's movement has been so successful is because it emphasized equal rights while minimizing equal responsibilities. Thus the myth fed to young women that they can 'have it all', which is misleading at best, and damaging at worst. Side-stepping equal responsibilities has resulted in women wanting the same rights top executives have but not the same responsibilities that the men doing the dangerous physical work have. Those men are invisible, which is ironic considering how much we depend on the hard work of those men every day. This book or tablet you hold in your hands, for instance, is the product of a couple of the most hazardous, and male-dominated industries: logging and mining. Even in law enforcement, a visible male-dominated profession, more police officers die each year from suicide than are killed in the line of duty.[46]

Some people make the argument that women trying for higher-level positions meet resistance from their male colleagues, blaming a sexist environment, but recent research has revealed that women are just as likely to show sexism towards other women in professional settings, including hiring practices, salaries and professional mentorship.[47]

One small Dutch study published in *Psychological Science*, for example, found both supportive and biased opinions among women's attitudes towards each other. The researchers looked at attitudes of senior policewomen and 'queen bee' behaviour. In the experiment, half of the participants wrote about a time they felt being a woman was a disadvantage at work or they experienced gender discrimination. The other participants were instructed to write about a situation where their personal abilities were valued and their gender was irrelevant. Then both groups were asked to describe their leadership style and how similar they thought they were to other women, and if they believed gender bias was a problem in the police force.

The women's answers reflected how much they focused on their gender identity at work. The women who exhibited queen bee behaviour did not identify strongly with other women at work and had been primed to think about gender bias. They leaned more towards a masculine style of leadership, seeing themselves as different from other women, and didn't see gender bias as a problem. Women who did identify strongly with other women at work and were similarly primed to believe there was a gender bias, had a greater urge to mentor other women.

The researchers suggested that organizations that want more women at the top must confront gender bias in the workplace. 'If you simply put women at higher positions without doing anything about gender bias in the organization, these women will be forced to distance themselves from the group,' researcher Belle Derks says. Otherwise, these women may discount gender bias, or refrain from helping women below them. 'If you set women up this way, so they have to choose between their opportunities and the opportunities of the group, some women will choose themselves. Why should you choose your group? Men don't have to.'[48]

The problem with suggesting that dangerous professions should adapt to women instead of women adapting to dangerous professions is that men and women who would be working together would develop two different – and incompatible – mindsets about what the job requires of them. Another way to think about the Dutch study is to consider that the perceived gender bias may actually be a generic mindset that has developed over time so that employees can meet the requirements of their profession, such as situational awareness and the willingness to respond physically to a threat. What women feel is opposition from their male peers may actually be a litmus test that everyone in the profession must endure. Their peers need to know this person – man or woman – can hack it and is tough enough to 'have their back' in the moments that count, as Warren Farrell points out:

Combat training requires the men to devalue their lives... The result? Harassment and hazing are preparation for devaluation – which is why men haze and harass one another: they are amputating each other's individuality because the war machine works best with standardized parts. Harassment and hazing are therefore a prerequisite to combat training in the 'men's army'; but in the 'women's army,' harassment and hazing can be protested – they conflict with valuing one's life. If the men's and women's armies were physically separate, these differences would be less of a problem. However, when the men are told that the women are equals but if they harass and haze the women as equals they'll have their careers ruined (and often family life destroyed), this only reinforces the men's beliefs that women want to 'have their cake and eat it, too'.[49]

Though some professions will always carry more risk than others, women don't generally go into occupations in large numbers unless it is physically safe. So the real change that needs to happen is making those industries as safe as possible, or, if men and women are going to have different standards, they need to be separated into all-male and all-female teams. The under-protection of men forces them to adopt an attitude that looks like bigotry when in fact we should be looking at what kind of climate hazardous professions create for employees. Decades of research on the power of the system and situation revealed that we cannot just look at the 'bad apples' (or individuals) in the barrel; we must look at the barrel, or situation, itself – and then move our analysis upwards to discover who are the 'barrel makers' (the systemic influencers), with deep power to create, change and terminate situations that impact the individuals operating within them.

Symmetrical relationships are not sexy

The women's movement created more well-rounded women, but put a wrench in the mechanics of relationships, because the journey was not taken together with men. Men's problems have been largely ignored or downplayed, which one could hardly say is inspiration to 'man up'. Both sexes need to be able to take an honest look at how the other experiences powerlessness and be willing to allow the other to explore all the dynamics of power.

Most top US male executives have spouses who stay at home; 88 per cent of them are married, compared with 70 per cent of top female executives, and 60 per cent of the men's spouses don't work full-time outside the home, compared with only 10 per cent of the women's spouses. The men have an average of 2.2 children; the women, 1.7.[50] Some female executives have commented that 'they need a wife', yet are not keen on the possibility of their husband taking on the role of stay-at-home parent, chef, household manager and chauffeur for the children.

In her *New York Times* article, 'Does A More Equal Marriage Mean Less Sex?', psychologist Lori Gottlieb offered an explanation as to why sharing responsibilities equally, though practical, does not currently translate into a better sex life. In one study, when men did certain 'feminine' chores around the house, such as folding laundry, cooking or vacuuming, they had less sex than when they did 'masculine' chores such as taking out the trash or working on the car. Having a more traditional division of chores also led to a higher rate of sexual satisfaction, at least for women.[51]

Gottlieb went on to say that the risk of divorce is lowest when the husband does 40 per cent of the housework and the wife earns 40 per cent of the income. Gottlieb also highlighted a survey from biological anthropologist and human behaviour researcher Helen Fisher, who told her that women's expectations for sexual fulfilment are changing so much that when Fisher conducted a survey in 2013 asking, 'Would you make a long-term commitment to someone who had everything you were looking for but to whom you did not feel sexually attracted?' the *least* likely group to say yes was women over 60 years old.

This article got quite a bit of backlash, such as Tracy Moore's response – 'What if Equality Is the Biggest Bonerkiller of All?' – but few commentators, if any, considered where we are as a society.[52] By and large women are attracted to the traditional male; they are still getting used to seeing men in other roles, and sexualizing those other roles. While men have seen women as sex objects, women have seen men as success objects, and although the paradigm is shifting, changing long-held cultural perceptions takes time. Seeing a man doing something traditionally un-masculine could be killing women's 'lady boners' just as much. No one tells girls when they are growing up that they have to earn enough money to support their husband and kids...they are told that their wage will be to support them, and maybe their children if they have them. So women still see men as success objects, and men's embracing of more traditionally feminine activities does not fit into that objectification.

In the end, maybe it's balance we seek rather than equality. What does balance look like? Most likely we need to start throwing away the ratios – the 60/40, the 50/50 – and begin to think and speak honestly about balancing individual strengths and weaknesses with responsibilities. That sense of balance will be different for everyone, so the other side of balance – what exists in the public sphere – is not feeling insecure or threatened by what works for others (i.e. turning 'Mummy Wars' into a 'War on Family Obstacles'[53]). What works best for you may not work so well for someone else and vice versa. It's not politically correct, but if it brings us closer to that elusive sense of happiness and purpose we're all after, what does it matter?

15

Economic Downturn

Students who acquire large debts putting themselves through school are unlikely to think about changing society. When you trap people in a system of debt, they can't afford the time to think.

– Noam Chomsky, linguist and social-political critic

The cost of a gallon of petrol, school tuition and a house are now way out of proportion for young people in comparison to the baby boomer generation that has parented the current generation. Perhaps not surprisingly, while the cost of education has increased at several times above the inflation rate since the 1990s, the cost of computers, televisions and toys has decreased. Regardless, it's more expensive to live in the Western world now than before the economic slump and many people are taking on large amounts of additional debt just to make ends meet.

Equity strategist Peter Bookvar says, 'The absolute cost of living is now back at a record high even though there are fewer jobs.'[1] In the US, people generally feel they have more opportunity to get ahead than their parents but are more exposed to economic risk as well.[2]

In 1970 a new house in the US cost $26,600, and the median household income was $8,730. The average yearly cost of tuition at a public four-year university was $480; private university was $1,980.[3] In 1973 the majority of the 72 per cent of Americans with a high school education or less were still able to flourish and make it into the middle classes. Having less education was not much of a hindrance if a person had a strong work ethic because manufacturing still had a very large presence.[4] Over the next several decades that path to the middle class became less attainable as companies that used to pride themselves on being self-sufficient began to focus on cost-saving measures, particularly outsourcing jobs to foreign countries with low wages, and minimal to no benefits. At the same time this restructuring of business was happening, the costs of living continued to rise and the overall median wage for men remained stagnant.

In 1971 the average salary in the UK was about £2,000, with the average house costing £5,632.[5] In 1978, 26 per cent of all jobs in the UK were in the manufacturing, mining and quarrying sectors, but today they only account for 8 per cent of all jobs. Service jobs jumped from 63 per cent of all jobs to 83 per cent of all jobs in that same time span.[6] Meanwhile, wages for the top 1 per cent of earners, who are already starting with a higher salary, increased 189 per cent since 1975 – nearly twice as much as the average full-time employee.[7]

In 1990 the average cost of a new house in the US increased to $149,800, the median household income was $29,943 and the average yearly tuition cost at a public university was $5,693 (1991–2 academic year) – three to four times more than what it was in proportion to household income twenty years earlier.[8]

Over the next decade and a half, the 'good life' drifted further out of sight. The workforce increased by almost 70 per cent while those with a high school education or less decreased to 41 per cent of workers, meaning about 2 million jobs were no longer available to those with no post-secondary education.[9] Fast-forward to today, where the majority of the net job growth in developed nations has been created by positions that require at least some post-secondary education.[10] The picture is certainly grim for the less educated, especially the less educated male. After adjusting for inflation, the median earnings for men without a high school diploma have actually declined 66 per cent since 1969.[11]

From 1969 to 2009 the median annual earnings dropped 38 per cent for male high school dropouts, 26 per cent for men with just a high school diploma and 2 per cent for men with a college degree – keep in mind those numbers only include the men who have jobs. The average earnings at every education level surpass median earnings, indicating a concentrated wage increase for those at the top of the distribution.[12] Yet, in 2010, the average cost of a new house was $272,900 and the median household income was $49,445. The average cost of tuition at a public four-year institution was $16,384.[13] Now it costs more to send kids to private elementary school than it used to cost to go to a prestigious university such as Harvard, Yale, or Stanford; proportions have grown out of control.

The UK is faring similarly. In 1998, when tuition fees were introduced in the UK, they were capped at £1,000, at the time when the average house cost £81,774[14] and the average wage was £17,414.[15] Later, in 2004, tuition was capped at £3,000, but the cap has tripled in the last ten years to £9,000! Today, UK households spend an average of 24 per cent of their disposable income on rent or mortgage.[16] The average wage in 2014 was £26,500[17] while the cost of a house was £265,000[18] and the average annual tuition fee for undergraduates during the 2013–14 year was £8,610.[19]

United States

1970:   Tuition: 5.5 per cent of annual household income
         House: 305 per cent of annual household income
1991:   Tuition: 19 per cent of annual household income
         House: 500 per cent of annual household income
2010:   Tuition: 33 per cent of annual household income
         House: 552 per cent of annual household income

United Kingdom

1971:   House: 282 per cent of annual wage
1998:   Tuition: 6 per cent of annual wage
         House: 470 per cent of annual wage
2014:   Tuition: 33 per cent of annual wage
         House: 1,000 per cent of annual wage

In sum, a high school diploma is no longer a passport to 'living the dream'. Now many people – even those with higher education – have little hope of getting ahead as their lives begin to resemble the drudgery of Sisyphus, endlessly pushing a boulder up a hill only for it to roll back down after it has been moved to the top.

The escalating cost of living is driving down personal and social values

In this recession era, three men have lost their jobs for every woman who has lost hers.[20] Has the cost of living combined with fewer prospects caused men to see the idea of family not as the reward of one's hard work but, rather, as a burden and the cause of now having to work harder? To many young men, the future looks bleak, and they wonder how they will ever be able to afford a wife, children, house and a reasonable lifestyle when they retire – assuming they had a job with benefits.

We can no longer buy the myth that the good life can be provided by a single pay cheque. Nor can we pretend that upward mobility is equally accessible to everyone, as Sir Ferdinand Mount, columnist for the *Sunday Times*, pointed out in his book, *Mind the Gap: The New Class Divide in Britain*:

> Over the course of the 20th century foreign competition demanded that we give up the old nepotism and promotion by seniority. In order to survive, we needed to reward and advance merit wherever it was found. As a result, a new elite was formed, and the lower classes were drained of their most talented members...Now that people are classified by ability, the gap between the classes has inevitably become wider...Less alluring still is the tendency of capitalism to de-skill workers, especially those at the bottom...capitalism is continually finding efficiency gains by simplifying tasks for humans, while it complicates them for machines, so that all the business of calculating, measuring, estimating and combining is done by the computer, while the human is required only to press a small selection of buttons.[21]

The new nature of physically undemanding work means women can participate in the jobs they never could before, he explains, but: 'it has a downside too, in that physical strength and endurance, once the principal selling qualities for lower-class men, find fewer takers now. Male pride and sense of usefulness diminish correspondingly. We are uncomfortably aware that a job for life in a steel mill or even a coal mine is more a man's life than a series of impermanent engagements to stack shelves in a supermarket.'[22]

This simplifying of previously complex tasks can partly explain why wages have not increased. 'We are the generation living through an information revolution every bit as profound as the industrial revolution of the past,' says psychologist Mary Ragan,[23] but the information revolution is leaving far too many behind without a sense of purpose. As one 26-year-old male from our survey said, millennials have 'struggled with higher unemployment rates due to…lack of opportunities in this volatile economy. We feel lost and abandoned, for as much talk as there is of …social programmes and getting the older generation back to work in the media, there is very little to no attention given to us 20- and 30-somethings that have been left behind.'

Mount references a 2003 education report that stated 'academic success in Britain is more determined by social class than in any other country', as those with unskilled backgrounds are five times less likely than those from professional backgrounds to enrol in higher education.[24] In the present day, there is still improvement to be made as the number of disadvantaged students who passed their GCSEs ranged from 60 per cent in some schools down to just 20 per cent in others.[25]

Even for the young men who have the desire to get additional education and fully apply themselves, the high price of schooling is sure to break their back.

Man maths
This amusing equation is all over the Internet. Sadly, many young men draw the same conclusion.

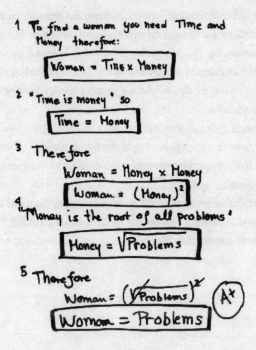

1 To find a woman you need Time and Money therefore:

$$\boxed{\text{Woman} = \text{Time} \times \text{Money}}$$

2 "Time is money" so

$$\boxed{\text{Time} = \text{Money}}$$

3 Therefore

Woman = Money × Money

$$\boxed{\text{Woman} = (\text{Money})^2}$$

4 "Money is the root of all problems"

$$\boxed{\text{Money} = \sqrt{\text{Problems}}}$$

5 Therefore

Woman $= (\sqrt{\text{Problems}})^2$ (A⁺)

$$\boxed{\text{Woman} = \text{Problems}}$$

Many students who go into serious debt for low-value degrees grasp the realities of employment only upon graduation: that there isn't a real job awaiting them and their diploma isn't an assured route for success. A whole generation of young people, who were told they could be anything they put their minds to, are being thrown into a junkyard of mass unemployment, settling for some 'cube farm' job just to make ends meet.

The pressure can be too much. We see extremes in Japan, where, in addition to the *soshoku danshi* – herbivorous men – there is another set of male shut-ins called *hikikomori*, who never leave their homes, or, in most cases, their parents' homes. China has its own version of this category of men, *diaosi*, which literally translates to 'male pubic hair'. The *diaosi* are working-class men, many in the tech industry, who lack social skills and spend much of their free time gaming. Although their wages are often considered middle class, they feel deprived relative to the *gao fu shuai* – tall, rich and handsome men – and are not optimistic about ever moving up the hierarchy. These self-labelled groupings of guys reflect the powerlessness many of them feel in the tough economy; all over the world it's getting harder for the ordinary male to succeed.

Without the real possibility of ever becoming the family bread-winner, young men are having to deal with feelings of anticipated failure. If they can't be the alpha male, what new roles are available for them?

If we don't figure this out soon, employing national as well as individual solutions, it's going to be a lonely, lonely world for many young men globally.

Part III

Solutions

16

What the Government
Can Do

Worldwide, people now trust social media more than they trust their government, in which confidence is at an all-time low.[1] More and more, people are counting on businesses and NGOs to invent, connect and take action in ways that governments are incapable, unwilling or too slow to do. The government has not utilized the Internet effectively in engaging citizens; for example, on Twitter Gov.uk has less than a quarter of a million followers while business magnate Sir Richard Branson has almost 5 million and Microsoft founder and entrepreneur Bill Gates has over 18 million.[2] In the US, Bill and Melinda Gates are even funding education reform through their foundation, with programmes such as 'Postsecondary Success',[3] because the government is failing to deliver positive results.

The following set of suggestions is aimed at saving costs, increasing social cohesion, and improving public safety and health. They can be accomplished through individual action and support from outside organizations, but would be accomplished much more quickly through policy changes. We urge more 'barrel makers' to get involved with raising public awareness of these issues and applying long-term solutions.

Support the father's role

In a 2012 poll by the Centre for Social Justice, 89 per cent of people agreed – 52 per cent strongly agreed – that 'if we want to have any hope of mending our broken society, family and parenting is where we've got to start'. Eighty-one per cent of people thought that children needed to grow up with both their parents, and 95 per cent believed that fathers are important to a child's well-being. Creating policies that emphasize a father's right to be present in his children's lives during divorce and custody battle situations, eliminating perverse welfare incentives for parents to live apart, offering men paternity leave that is equal to maternity leave, and encouraging family members to visit male inmates, would surely be steps in the right direction.[4]

Sponsoring a nationwide male mentorship programme would also bring more positive male figures into children's lives, especially given the rising number of single mothers. Separately, the large number of unemployed single mothers needs to be addressed. Matthew Tinsley of Policy Exchange, a think tank that compiled a report on unemployed single parents, suggested that 'policymakers must do more to assist unemployed single parents in finding a job'. Though 'it is right that the government extended free childcare ... it is also right to ask more from people to find a job'.[5] Helping reduce unemployment would not only boost the UK economy, it would increase savings in the welfare budget.

Limit the use of endocrine-disruptors

Despite the Food Standards Agency (FSA) recognizing that evidence relating to the long-term health effects of endocrine-disruptors is not conclusive, the agency still states that exposure to Bisphenol A (BPA), a known endocrine-disruptor, is 'not considered to be harmful'.[6] The European Food Safety Authority (EFSA), however, recently recognized BPA's adverse effects on liver, kidney and mammary glands and recommended that the tolerable daily intake be reduced to 5 µg/kg bw/day – one-tenth what it used to be![7]

Given the growing amount of research showing the damaging effects of these chemicals, some of which was discussed in Chapter 10, it is alarming that the government is not doing more to limit their use. Elsewhere, action is taking place. In San Francisco, for example, one-time-use plastic water bottles have recently been banned.[8] Legislators decided to reduce the amount of pollution caused by the plastic bottles and protect the health of its citizens. We recommend similar bans be put in place. Consumers can also take charge by reading labels and avoiding products that contain these chemicals.

Get more men into grade school teaching positions

Fewer than one in five schoolteachers in the UK is a man. Many people talk of changing the ratio to encourage more women to choose careers in science and technology and be present in greater numbers at higher-level positions within politics and private companies, which is terrific, but there should be similar efforts put into changing the gender-imbalanced ratio so that more men are represented in education and social sciences. The Teaching Agency (TA) has made progress in encouraging more men to join the profession in the last couple of years,[9] but more efforts are needed to attract quality male and female teachers.

Get junk food out of schools

Obesity-related conditions such as heart disease, stroke, type II diabetes and certain types of cancer are a few of the leading causes of preventable death – especially for men, who die from these illnesses in greater numbers. The estimated annual medical costs for people who are obese are much higher than that of normal-weight people.[10] It's clear that childhood habits tend to stick with people for the rest of their lives, so one obvious solution to reversing obesity trends is by improving food and beverage options in schools.

A good model already in existence is the 5210 programme, within the Let's Go! organization, which is part of the Kids CO-OP at the Barbara Bush Children's Hospital in Maine. 5210 is a nationally recognized obesity prevention programme that has proven to be effective with its 5-2-1-0 formula of five servings of fruits and vegetables a day, two hours or less of recreational screen time, one hour or more of physical activity a day, and zero sugary drinks (letsgo.org).

Some UK schools have made healthier foods more accessible by swapping regular vending machines for 'Green Machines' that are filled with organic, low-sugar and additive-free options,[11] but wide-scale efforts need to be made to ensure that healthier choices are made.

The government should consider requiring schools to install more water fountains and support city projects to connect bicycling and walking paths to schools from residential communities. By making it convenient to be physically fit and choose healthy options, cities can keep their rates of obesity low. When there are obvious social norms to encourage behaviour change in particular ways, that is, when there are supportive situational and systemic elements present, individuals almost always benefit.

Improve how schools prepare students for their lives ahead

> The logic is quite clear from an economic standpoint. We can invest early to close disparities and prevent achievement gaps, or we can pay to remediate disparities when they are harder and more expensive to close. Either way we are going to pay. And, we'll have to do both for a while. But, there is an important difference between the two approaches. Investing early allows us to shape the future; investing later chains us to fixing the missed opportunities of the past.
>
> – James J. Heckman, Henry Schultz Distinguished Service Professor of Economics at the University of Chicago and Nobel Memorial Prize winner in economics[12]

Children's life chances are strongly influenced by the quality of their education... The highest performing education systems across OECD countries are those that combine high quality and equity. In such education systems, the vast majority of students can attain high level skills and knowledge that depend on their ability and drive, more than on their socio-economic background... the benefits of investing in equity in education outweigh the costs for both individuals and societies... in particular if investments are made early on.

– Organisation for Economic Co-operation and Development (OECD),
Equity and Quality in Education[13]

In order to keep students interested and engaged through high school and post-secondary education, schools themselves need to be improved from the primary level upwards so students can take full advantage of education and training regardless of their background.

The OECD stated that the quality of a school depends on the quality of a school's teachers and administrators. Nations such as Brazil, Japan and Poland, which all had improved scores on the PISA (an international aptitude test), have created policies aimed at bettering the quality of their teachers, such as adding to the requirements needed in order to obtain a teacher's licence, increasing teacher's salaries to retain high-quality teachers and make the profession more appealing, offering incentives for promising students to go into the teaching profession, and providing incentives for teachers to attend teacher-training programmes. Higher salaries, however, must be complemented by placing teachers in schools where their presence and skills can make the most impact.[14]

What happens after high school could be used as a measure of success for high schools. If schools or individual teachers could be rewarded for increasing the number of students who complete high school and go on to finish a certificate or degree programme, it could change what and how well lessons get taught as well as ensure quality teachers get hired and remain for the long term. At present, few if any schools reward teaching excellence based on future outcome performances of their students.

The same model needs to be applied in prisons where guards get rewards, salary bonuses or additional vacation time for prisoners in their unit who have good behavioural records, do not get into trouble, get paroled early and then also for having a 'clean' record when they are back in the free world.

Along with blending school with work situations or mentorship programmes (discussed in the next chapter), the government could implement a career-counselling programme for high school students. Many universities have such programmes, but students need more information about their future options before they are confronted head-on with their future. There is no way the current ratio of counsellors to students (500 to 1 in middle and high schools[15]) can make much of an impact on student well-being – present or future. Providing students with more guidance during this crucial period of their lives can be an effective way to help them overcome future obstacles and stick with their education because they will have a better sense of their options and know what steps are necessary in order to achieve their goals.

Sex education also needs a major overhaul. Camille Paglia, professor of humanities and media studies at the University of the Arts in Philadelphia, said that the refusal of schools' sex-education programmes to recognize gender differences is 'betraying both boys and girls'. Due to the risk of pregnancy and undetectable sexually transmitted diseases that can compromise future fertility, the harsh reality is that girls have more to lose from casual sex than boys do. Paglia suggests that boys get lessons in basic ethics and moral reasoning about sex while girls learn how to tell the difference between sexual compliance and popularity.[16]

We agree with Ms Paglia. It makes no sense that we teach kids how to drive cars so they will be safe and responsible drivers, but we won't teach them anything useful about sex, even when it is just as vital to their health and safety.

Both kids and their parents are ready for change, and there is no excuse to avoid tackling this very important issue. Even communities that are pushing for abstinence-only programmes can still make improvements by talking realistically to young people about the risks and responsibilities of unprotected sex while still reinforcing the values parents are teaching at home.[17]

Schools need to employ certified health educators who can be objective and non-judgemental, covering such topics as:

- Communication around personal boundaries, safer sex, peer pressure and common relationship issues.

- How to know when you're ready to become sexually active.

- Abstinence, preventing pregnancy and how to use different kinds of contraception.

- Preventing sexual and relationship abuse.

- Questions to ask a prospective spouse before marriage.

- How to detect breast, ovarian and testicular cancers.

- Fertility and ageing.

- Reproduction and pregnancy.

- STI risks of various sexual acts.

- Legal and privacy issues around cybersex and sexting.

- How each sex goes through puberty.

- In-depth anatomy and biology.

- Positive aspects and health benefits of intimacy.

- Information about same-sex relationships and LGBTQ issues.

- Critical discussion around false representations of intimacy and romance in the media, television shows and in online porn.

- Relating basic life skills to intimacy and sexuality.

Students from around the UK who we spoke to suggested most of the above topics. The vast majority of them independently agreed that sex education should be taught yearly, starting at a younger age and continuing on into older year groups. They felt that too often sex education petered out right around the time when they were becoming sexually active and had the most questions. An especially critical time period for them was 14 to 15 years old. They thought sex education should be less formal and be taught in smaller groups because it would be easier for them to take the topics more seriously and to discuss issues openly. Some wanted to separate the sexes when sex education was being taught while others didn't. One great suggestion was to teach a co-ed group of students, then separate boys and girls for anonymous Q&A sessions with a trained health professional. The UK-based RAP (Raising Awareness and Prevention) Project is one programme to look at expanding. RAP offers a variety of presentations and workshops taught by professionals that discuss how porn and the media influence attitudes towards sex and body image. Visit therapproject. co.uk to learn more.

Leading up to this kind of comprehensive sex education can be lessons in even earlier years about respecting the boundaries of others and empathy. Miranda Horvath, a psychology professor at Middlesex University in London, suggests that young people would benefit from learning these types of lessons before they encounter online porn: 'If we start teaching kids about equality and respect when they are 5 or 6 years old, by the time they encounter porn in their teens, they will be able to pick out and see the lack of respect and emotion that porn gives us. They'll be better equipped to deal with what they are being presented with.'[18]

Other reasons for the government to support better sex education and family planning are the health care costs saved and to reduce the high unemployment rate of young single mothers. According to the Department of Health, 'for every £1 spent on contraception, £11 is saved in other healthcare costs'.[19] Over half of single mothers who had their first child as a teenager are not in work or looking for work versus 40 per cent who had their first child between 20 and 23 years old, and 19 per cent who had their first child in their early 30s.[20]

History books are never kind to those who stand idly by. Many a catastrophe could have been avoided if preventative action had been taken. In our view, it is worth investing and implementing these solutions because they will have positive and long-lasting impacts on current generations and future generations alike. We encourage both individuals and institutions to do their part to make them a reality.

17

What Schools Can Do

There is no question that the current education system is broken. The Pathways to Prosperity Project warns that a failure to reform the system will 'surely erode the fabric of our society'. As mentioned in earlier chapters, teens and young people in their early 20s – especially those from low-income families – are less likely to be employed and have job experience now than ten years ago. Economic inequality is increasing. If the young people of today are not better prepared to handle the challenges of the future, their animosity over their limited opportunities will only increase as their social status plummets with the high costs of living. The expense that they impose on society will also increase, and worse of all, many of their possible contributions to society will go unrealized.[1]

If we want our young people to develop effective skills that can be directly applied later in a career the most useful approach thus far has been to create and staff high-quality vocational and apprenticeship programmes that let students experience real-life workplace situations and problems that they can solve during their part-time schooling. Many countries throughout northern and central Europe enrol their students in these blended programmes after ages 14 or 15. The results from educators doing this have revealed that classrooms collaborating with local businesses and companies show students the *why* behind underlying theories

– which makes students become more engaged. Classrooms that did this were extremely effective in engaging students in learning and job training. This set-up also made the transition from adolescence to adulthood easier for students.[2]

Teach life skills

In our UK student survey, when we asked 'what class would you like at your school that doesn't already exist?' nearly a third of teens independently suggested a 'life skills' class that included guidance on personal finance, how to apply for a job properly and handle job interviews, and dealing with adult responsibilities and life changes, such as the death of a relative. Several students said they were embarrassed that they were as old as they were and didn't even know how to make a simple budget or keep track of the money in their bank accounts. One student even remarked, 'The lack of this class may be one of the reasons preventing young people from moving out of their parents' house.' It seems like common sense, let's teach it.

Incorporating practical life lessons into the classroom is not a pie-in-the-sky fantasy; these ideas are already in practice in many programmes with demonstrated effectiveness. The key is their national scalability. Montessori and Waldorf schools around the world similarly create exciting learning centres with well-rounded curriculums for students of all ages. Montessori schools, for example, emphasize independence, freedom within limits and respect for a child's natural psychological development, as well as technological advancements in society. Visit the websites for Montessori (montessori.edu) and Waldorf (whywaldorfworks. org) to learn more.

Some public schools, too, are making revolutionary changes in the way they teach. In the documentary film *Race to Nowhere*, when an Oregon high school banned homework, kids started learning more and doing better on tests. Other schools are starting to follow in its footsteps. Visit the film's website (racetonowhere. com) to learn more.

Another alternative is offering gender-specific, not gender-blind, class options and assignments – boys don't want to read the same books girls do. Girls can also benefit from single-sex classes since gender-related self-concepts become less accessible in single-sex classes. One randomized study that appeared in the *British Journal of Educational Psychology* found that girls who took a single-sex physics class were less likely than girls from the co-ed class to think 'physics is for boys'.[3]

National Association for Choice in Education (NACE), 4schoolchoice.org, is an excellent resource for information on single-sex schooling. Another great programme to check out is Project Lead the Way (PLTW), a non-profit organization that works with schools from the primary through high school level, engaging teachers in professional development that leads to project-based learning where students acquire relevant knowledge and skills in science and technology fields that help them succeed in future careers (pltw.org).

In addition to schools incorporating real-world challenges, teachers would also do well to take a page out of the video game industry – by making the process of learning enjoyable and rewarding.

Incorporate new technology for more interactive learning

Technology is dynamic and children are becoming accustomed to the fast pace at which information now travels. There's no question students today need to be stimulated in new ways that they didn't need before. 'Devices are catalysts,' says Harvard professor Chris Dede.[4] Many teachers are incorporating more technology into their lessons as a way to strengthen learning. Some professors take advantage of online forums to discuss topics from class or assign their lessons as homework (often in the form of a PowerPoint presentation) and use class time for clarity and discussion. These strategies have proven to be more effective and engaging for students than traditional or formal teaching methods.

If your school doesn't have its own internal network set up for classes, use existing social networks like Ning (ning.com), which cater to educators. Khan Academy is another great online resource that offers free tutorials and classes for anyone who wishes to bolster their knowledge in a particular topic (khanacademy.org).

Quash grade inflation

Grade inflation is another issue that must be addressed by educators. Not everyone deserves to get top marks, and telling students they're 'special' tends to backfire, especially in the long run. Psychologists have found that poor-performing students who were given self-esteem boosts in an effort to help improve their grades actually ended up performing much worse, though they remained confident and self-assured.[5] Students need to be taught how to study more effectively, how to deal with procrastination, how to manage their time efficiently, how to study and work well with others, and, finally, they need to see that focused, hard work pays off. Bring in inspirational speakers who can share their story and more importantly the path they took to complete their goals.

Schools have their work cut out for them, but they cannot accomplish everything they need to do without the support of policy-makers, administrators, parents and students. Parents especially can do their part by supporting teachers who are fair, and by doing their piece to ensure their children are better prepared for their lives as adults. More on that next…

18

What Parents Can Do

It is easier to build strong children than to repair broken men.
– Frederick Douglass, African-American social reformer and
a leader of the abolitionist movement

I f you don't raise your kids, who will? The bulk of change needs
to come from parents. It is time for parents to create more
boundaries and offer more guidance for their children. So turn
off the chronic digital stimulation and turn on your son's creativity.
If your son has been diagnosed with ADHD or similar, look at
alternatives to medication first. Try to find the right programme
for the boy instead of trying to fit the boy into a programme that's
not right for him. Consider enrolling him in school one year later
than usual, so he loves to learn rather than learns to hate school.
Encourage reading by giving him books with adventure stories or
topics he's actually interested in. Be a good role model or find good
male role models or mentors for your son. Teach him positive ways
to feel like a man but also ways to develop his unique character as
a human being.

Teach your daughters it's OK to ask out the boy they like and
inform your sons that it's all right to accept an invitation from a
girl who asks them on a date. A young man recently told us that,
'getting a sincere compliment from a girl just doesn't happen; if it
did I would be suspicious and assume that she either wanted
something from me or was attempting to sell me something'. It is

unfair that children are conditioned this way, because it sets them up for isolated frustration and distrust of the opposite sex. Allowing girls to feel confident by directly asking for what they want, and allowing boys to feel comfortable with girls taking the lead is a very simple way to build confidence, communication and trust between the sexes. In a similar vein, encourage your son to learn how to dance. It is a social skill that may offer some popularity in youth, but will prove to be fun and useful for him long into adulthood.

Responsibility and resiliency are twin pillars of strength for children

It is important to be fair, but not punish your son simply for being a boy. After gathering information and analysing the outcomes of bright young male Harvard students over decades, George Vaillant came to this conclusion: 'When you're just getting the hang of grief, rage, and joy, it makes all the difference in the world to have parents who can tolerate and "hold" your feelings rather than treating them as misbehaviour.'[1] One aspect of making space for kids is letting them experience and explore their feelings with minimal adult supervision. In her *Atlantic* article, 'The Overprotected Kid', Hanna Rosin visited an adventure playground in Wales called the Land, where kids jump on stacks of old mattresses, light fires, build forts out of wooden pallets and learn how to play with other children while resolving disagreements on their own. There are a couple of adults – professionally trained play-workers – at the Land but they rarely intervene. They don't have to. Despite the potential hazards, there have been no other injuries apart from a few scraped knees. It's not that the adults are lax, they keep an eye on the kids to prevent any serious accidents, it's that the children learn quickly when something doesn't work. Rosin argues that when parents stop organizing every aspect of their child's life, it is much easier for the child to develop self-confidence, courage, imagination and critical thinking. In an environment like the Land, kids organize their own play, which often revolves around them overcoming challenges that feel risky; so they get to see that they are resilient rather than fragile, and they learn how to overcome tricky physical or social situations – something they would not be able to discover on the sterile playgrounds with constant parent intervention.[2]

Resiliency goes hand in hand with responsibility. Greater responsibility was the most important thing men over 50 years old in our survey thought the younger generations of males were lacking. One older man said parents should be: 'Teaching sons about finance and politics when they become teenagers... Frequently give the son something important to do for a group (like family, sport teams, friends). Like buying equipment you will need for an activity. Also, teach kids to use public transportation and then let them take the bus or train home from school. Let them be responsible for something.'

At the same time, do not offer him empty praise when he does not follow through on his responsibilities or 'participation medals' just for showing up. Achievement feeds the motivation to learn, improve and succeed, and encourages a person to try new things and master new skills. When children get praised regardless of the quality of the work they do, they feel less motivated to do more. Same thing goes for when a child does exemplary work and they get similar approval as someone who didn't – they become sceptical of the feedback. What kids need is specific feedback about areas where they are doing well and areas where they can improve. They need what psychologist Carol Dweck calls a *growth mindset* that praises hard work and encourages them to develop their abilities, rather than a *fixed mindset* that tells them they are intrinsically talented and smart and therefore don't have to try.[3] Video games offer this kind of feedback; parents need to start offering it, too.

Many high-achievers, like former Secretary of Defense Robert M. Gates, specifically reference how this kind of encouragement combined with accountability shaped their character:

My parents told me repeatedly when I was a boy that there were no limits to what I might achieve if I worked hard, but they also routinely cautioned me never to think I was superior to anyone else... On those relatively infrequent occasions when I was disciplined, I'm confident I deserved it, though I felt deeply persecuted at the time. But their expectations and discipline taught me about consequences and taking responsibility for my actions. My parents shaped my character and therefore my life. I realized on the way to the Senate that day [being confirmed as the Secretary of Defense] that the human qualities they had imbued within me in those early years had brought me to this moment... [4]

It is critical that young people not only discover their passions but learn how to make their passions work for them, after they have graduated from school.

What about work?

If your son is in high school, chat with him about the job market. Encourage him to have a part-time job or volunteer in his community, to learn to be a bit more responsible and understand the rules and obligations of business. Talk to him about that job, what is good and bad about it. Obviously you want him to pursue his dreams, but you also want him to be aware of what opportunities will be available once he graduates so he doesn't enter a weak job market with no prospects and a huge student loan. Many parents aren't helping their kids develop realistic expectations or prepare for what awaits them beyond college. The world is changing; the general advice used to be to get a well-rounded liberal arts education in preparation for graduate school, but that advice is no longer relevant because the competition is high and the pay is dropping.

Encourage both your sons and daughters to look at vocational schools and associate degree programmes if they are not interested in going the science, technology, engineering or maths route.

Over one-quarter of people with post-secondary licences or certificates (credentials short of an associate's degree) make more money than the average person with a bachelor's degree.[5] Regardless of what direction they go, young people have to be tech savvy, and writing and communication skills are critical for success. Learning basic social interaction skills means others will want to be around them. Ask if they have friends who are girls as well as boys, and encourage both; open your home to them.

At the same time, encourage your son to take on babysitting or coaching roles while he is a teen so that he may learn how to directly nurture others. Some sports – such as European football – allow younger teens to earn a fair amount of money in the summertime and on weekends by refereeing the games of even younger players.

Getting out of your comfort zone and tackling taboo topics

Teach your son about sex. Whether or not you're OK with your son engaging in sexual behaviour now, surely you want him to have a healthy and shame-free sexual relationship with someone at some point in his adult life. Preparing him for that starts with supporting healthy, shame-free and realistic attitudes about sex when he is young.

Most people agree that sex is an important part of long-term relationships.[6] Along the way, though, many couples will struggle with a sexual issue, and it can sometimes distance partners from each other. Teaching young people to fear sex or not giving them any information at all does little to help their future relationships thrive. From the Harvard Grant study, Vaillant found that:

> overt fear of sex was a far more powerful predictor of poor mental health than sexual dissatisfaction in marriage was. After all, marital sexual adjustment depends heavily upon the partner, but fear of sex is closely linked with a personal

mistrust of the universe. The men who experienced lifelong poor marriages were six times as likely as men with excellent marriages, and twice as likely as men who divorced, to give evidence on questionnaires of being fearful or uncomfortable about sexual relations.[7]

Make yourself available for questions, be a good listener, don't back down on what you believe, admit when you don't know, and show unconditional love. Explain peer pressure, consent and boundaries, birth control, safer sex and STIs, the differences between porn and reality, or bring him to a trusted person who he might feel more comfortable discussing the challenges and risks of intimacy with (counsellor, sex educator, therapist, etc.). Just because 'everyone is doing it' that doesn't mean it's all right. If someone is trying to coerce or manipulate him into doing something, or something doesn't feel right, tell him how to get out of that situation safely.

However, it is equally important to go on to explain the positive sides of boundaries too. Emphasize the role of communication and help him start to understand that sex is about pleasure and connecting with his (eventual) partner. You might also think about adding some books about sex to your family library, or gifting your son a book when you think the time is right. *S.E.X. The All-You-Need-To-Know Progressive Sexuality Guide To Get You Through High School and College*, by Heather Corrina, and *The Good Vibrations Guide to Sex*, by Cathy Winks and Anne Semans, are comprehensive and informative selections we'd recommend. The Family Planning Association also offers up-to-date information and advice on their site (fpa.org.uk).

If the level of communication in your marriage needs a boost, check out John Gray's classic book, *Men Are From Mars, Women Are From Venus*. It is hands-down one of the best and simplest advice books that will improve the way you communicate with your partner. It's an appropriate book for older teenagers to read, too. We recommend excellent resource books such as John Gottman's

What Makes Love Last?: How to Build Trust and Avoid Betrayal and *Raising an Emotionally Intelligent Child*, along with Shefali Tsabary's *The Conscious Parent: Transforming Ourselves, Empowering Our Children*. If you are separated from your partner, be sure that both of you can spend quality time with your son. As much as you may not like the other parent of your child, do not lose sight of who they are to your child, and do your best not to speak badly about them in front of your kids. Live close enough to each other that your children don't have to sacrifice friendships or activities in order to spend time with the other parent.

Dads making fatherhood a priority

Fathers must make it a priority to be a part of their son's life. It is never too late to do so. If you have been a delinquent dad, working for success, travelling too much or being into your own thing, just press pause. Take time out from the old and familiar to tune into your son. Be willing to express regret for not being there earlier, and share a commitment to rectify that lack, to work at being a more diligent dad, a friend but also a source of both incentives and boundaries. Ask him about how such a new relationship can start out; seek advice, don't just give it.

Don't end up like so many people, who in old age look back on their life and feel empty despite their material success because they realize they have sacrificed too much for it – friends and family, or even fun. They did not take the time to be there for their wives, daughters or sons, and now they feel guilty. Sons need greater involvement from dads even more than daughters do because they will not get it from as many other sources as girls have available, such as friend networks and more expressive mums.

It is essential that dads, and uncles and grandpas, too, give top priority to mentoring the sons of this generation. They will value it if done honestly and openly in a constructive manner. You have to get past the awkwardness. Plan what you will say and maybe even practise it with your mate. Find a quiet, safe space to have a simple discussion about what is going on his life and in yours. You should know what his ambitions are – or are not. What is he concerned about, what are his fears? What does he feel are his strengths and what areas need finer tuning? Just make clear that he can talk to you anytime about anything, especially stuff that usually goes unsaid, such as sex or regrets or his uncertain future.

Time management activity

Another practical suggestion for all parents is to ask your kids to track how they spend their time for a week (don't include the porn for now). Here are key activities to include:

1. Sleeping.

2. Time at school/work.

3. Doing homework.

4. Doing chores.

5. Playing sports.

6. Hanging out with friends.

7. Being outdoors in natural environments.

8. Watching TV.

9. Texting, tweeting, emailing: sum of all electronic activities.

10. Playing video games.

Summarizing these behaviours is the place for starting a conversation about time management and creating a balanced time orientation for the best physical, mental and social success for them now as well as in their future. Give them an incentive for doing so, such as serving their favourite dinner, during which you can discuss the results. We expect both parents and kids will be surprised by what the data show: a huge number of hours devoted to gaming and Internet use. You can highlight any of this time spent with someone else in direct contact during the gaming or viewing to identify the extent of time in solitary confinement.

If your son is spending excessive amounts of time on his mobile phone, computer or gaming console, reduce access to those devices or make him earn the right to use them. A nationwide survey by Pew Research Center found that 75 per cent of teens are on a mobile phone plan that allows unlimited texting while only 13 per cent of teens pay per message. Those with the unlimited plan send and receive seven times the amount of texts per day than teens on more limited plans, and fourteen times the number of texts per day than teens who pay per message.[8] Consider getting a metered mobile phone plan that has limited voice and texting. Also consider keeping your son's computer or laptop in a main area of the house versus his bedroom. The National Sleep Foundation (NSF) found that when parents always enforce rules about how late smartphones and mobile phones can be used, their children got nearly an hour more sleep every night. The NSF also found that parents were two to three times more effective at enforcing those rules when they also removed electronic devices from their own bedrooms.[9]

For gaming consoles, it is important for parents not just to remove it or force their son to go cold turkey. 'If a game really is the only place where a teen can feel in control, rewarded, and happy, then simply taking all of that away could be devastating for him,' says Neils Clark.[10] A planned withdrawal programme must be made so that time playing video games is reduced over time while other rewarding activities are introduced.

Money goes wherever the ambition, innovation and resilience are. To keep financial interests and investment in North America and Europe, and to increase social trust, parents will need to instil strong values and a work ethic in today's youth. New York City recently overtook London as the world's financial centre, but by 2019 it is predicted that the centre will shift again to Shanghai.[11] Millennials will be the future leaders of tomorrow, but they won't be very good ones if they are overly medicated, obese, lack resilience and spend thousands of hours playing video games and watching porn. Parents need to step up to ensure that their children have the confidence and courage to succeed and cooperate with others in the real world.

19

What Men Can Do

Everyone must choose one of two pains: the pain of discipline or the pain of regret.

> – Jim Rohn, entrepreneur and motivational speaker

One can choose to go back toward safety or forward toward growth. Growth must be chosen again and again; fear must be overcome again and again.

> – Abraham Maslow, humanist psychologist

I f you are a young man and are looking for real life to be more rewarding or satisfying, you're going to have to make it happen. It's not going to happen while you're buried in a game or waiting on the sidelines. You are going to have to go outside and participate in it. When you're too busy looking down at your mobile phone or laptop, you aren't going to see the chances you miss. You may even start to develop the false belief that there are no opportunities to connect with others or get ahead in the world except for those found through technology. So turn off your digital identity and turn on yourself. Become the man that you would want to be friends with and do business with. Map out the steps to become that man.

Learn how to dance, rediscover nature, make a female friend, monitor social interactions to be sure others are being listened to adequately and sufficiently, and practise conversation openers. Practise the art of making others feel special by giving genuine compliments – one a day for the next week. Find people who possess traits you want to have and study their lives, find living role models or mentors, and find something in the real world that motivates you. Become resourceful, and realize that you may have to take one step back in order to take two steps forward.

Turn off the porn

Remember Gabe Deem, the recovering porn addict and public speaker we mentioned in Chapter 11? He suggests asking yourself whether the porn you are currently watching represents your actual desires. His advice to other young men is to stay away from porn completely: 'it will never satisfy you, and it will end up taking from you the one thing it promises to give you, the ability to feel pleasure'.[1] It's something for you to consider.

Sexologist and relationship therapist Veronica Monet agrees. In her experience, 'simply resolving to "cut back" rarely leads to anything but temporary results inevitably followed by yet more compulsive behaviours and ever increasing negative effects'. She wisely states that people should be 'careful when selecting a recovery resource', because 'shame can perpetuate addictive patterns... Many of those who seek relief from the oppression of addiction find themselves trading the suffering of an active addiction for the suffering created by needless shame. There is nothing inherently "wrong" with porn... The addictive behaviour is [the problem].'[2]

There's no question that if you desire intimacy with real people yet find you are having trouble getting turned on or climaxing with real people, you need to stop watching porn for at least a small period of time; there's really no way around it. During this downtime, you'll need to clarify your relationship with porn so you can avoid its downsides. Porn can be a part of your fantasy life, just not the whole thing – and hopefully not the best thing. If this is something you are struggling with the good news is your brain can heal.

The website YourBrainOnPorn.com states that turning off the porn will, in effect, 'reboot' the brain – allowing your dopamine receptors to recover and restore your reward circuit's sensitivity to normal and 'rewire' the brain – will weaken the porn pathways from disuse and will strengthen your executive control pathways. As your brain heals, you will become more easily aroused by real people and have more sensitivity in your penis. Your dopamine levels will most likely bounce back, too. Visit yourbrainonporn.com/tools-for-change for support and resources to help you make the change. We'd also recommend visiting the forums on RebootNation.org or Reddit (reddit.com/r/NoFap/) for extra tools and support.

For those who have a severe addiction to porn, the Internet itself is triggering. In these instances we've got very positive feedback from men who joined twelve-step programmes. One young man who is in the process of recovering from online porn addiction told us:

An Internet problem is typically not solved on the Internet. Trying to work on your online pornography problem online is like alcoholics hosting their AA [Alcoholics Anonymous] meetings at a bar. Just as they are an order and sip away from losing their sobriety, you are but four to five clicks away from your personal poison.

I feel like the first steps to getting the porn squid unglued from the back of your brain involves shutting that sucker down and connecting with people. Joining a support group will break some of the bonds of isolation and shame that are part of this disease. Sharing your darkest, dirtiest secrets with people, and finding that they will accept you with understanding and compassion, is a life-changing paradigm shift. We can't just go around blurting out our personal pornography struggles with just anyone. This is where a recovery community comes in!

There are a variety of resources available to those who are willing to go out of their comfort zone and seek the support of a group. Support groups can be an extremely valuable tool to those stuck in isolation who do not know how to approach their problem, or even ask for help. The therapy groups provide a clinically guided milieu where pornography addicts can provide support for each other, while adding in a dynamic of accountability, which creates healthy boundaries for the recovering individual.

Lastly (but CERTAINLY not least), twelve-step groups allow for individuals who are struggling with porn addiction to integrate themselves into a spiritually focused programme that will provide the recovering addict with a multitude of tools for staying sober, and addressing the aspects of their beliefs, character traits and personal histories that have been the underlying root of their addiction. Furthermore, they allow for one to connect with a community of recovery-focused individuals, and tap into the wealth of experience from its members. While I attend a twelve-step group regularly, I simultaneously visit a traditional therapist that specializes in sex/porn addiction. In the first session I told him, 'I had a pretty great childhood. I really don't think I have any trauma.' Unfortunately for me, this false belief kept me stuck in my recovery for quite a while. In fact, I could never piece together more than a month or two of sobriety, until I started really taking a look at the underlying network of issues. Being part of the group helped me delve deeper into these issues, and see that it was more than just an 'opportunity addiction'. I learned from the wisdom of their experiences.

It is important to remember that there are no quick fixes or magic bullets in overcoming excessive porn use – as in any addictions to drugs, alcohol, gambling or food.

Beyond porn, having sex on your mind all the time or as a big part of your identity is actually a good thing – a lot of very successful people have very high sex drives – but you need to learn how to redirect your sex energy out of lust and into the heart and mind, where it can serve your higher values instead of just your primal instincts. When transforming sexual energy into thoughts and actions of another nature, you have to use willpower to visualize and mindfully direct that energy.

One way to do this is to figure out what your arousal triggers are – for example, make a list of the traits you find sexually attractive in another person – and then seek goals that share those traits. Chances are the goals that will 'turn you on' the most will share the same qualities that turn you on the most in someone you're sexually attracted to (such as being creative, taking risks, etc.). An excellent resource for further reading on the topic is Napoleon Hill's classic text *Think and Grow Rich*, as well as the blog of personal development author Steve Pavlina. In his post, entitled 'Sex Energy', Pavlina suggests using sexual energy as fuel to achieve your goals. By learning your arousal triggers, he says, goals become more enjoyable because you can direct the path to get there:

> When you're sexually aroused, you feel a compulsion to take some kind of action. Your hormones take over, and you become incredibly focused and can't think about anything but the object of your desire. This is what it feels like to be driven by a goal that really inspires you...Pursuing your goals is like practicing the art of seduction...You may encounter some obstacles now and then that make you want to quit, but stop and ask yourself if the chemistry is still there. Momentarily forget about the path you're on, and just picture the goal itself. Imagine you're already there. Do you still really, really want it? ...Remember that the whole point of goal-setting is to get your thoughts and actions moving in a new direction. If you aren't driven to action, you've set lousy goals.[3]

Moral of the story: if you want more control over your life, acquire a better understanding of what motivates you. If your default behaviour involves frittering away your time with passive and semi-fulfilling distractions, guess what you're going to get? Semi-fulfilment.

Time Bandit – look at what else you could be doing

It's worth considering just how much time you spend engaged in various activities throughout the day. If you feel any resistance to doing this, chances are you need to cut the amount of time you spend playing video games, especially if you're doing it alone. People most vulnerable to addiction are usually socially or personally disadvantaged, so start playing games that involve interactions with others, preferably in person.

Consider transferring some hours spent gaming into accomplishing real-life passions. Below is a chart comparing the average number of hours spent playing video games with the average time it takes to complete other activities.

Average time for activity[4]

Annual average time a teen male plays video games	Learn the foundations of a new language with Rosetta Stone	Learn to play guitar with regular practice	Play a sport during an intramural season	Learn salsa dancing
676 hours	205 hours	260 hours	32 hours	40 hours

Play sports

As a boy, I (Phil) recall being less than capable physically because of a childhood medical problem that made me weak, uncoordinated and thus poor in sports. Determined to make the neighbourhood stickball team, I practised alone in the schoolyard hitting a Spalding (a pink rubber ball) with a sawed-off old broomstick for hours against the wall until I mastered the art. Hitting such a ball far was not so much a matter of muscles, but of wrist torque, of snapping the wrist properly at the moment of contact. In a matter of time, I became a legendary 'three sewer man', meaning I could reliably hit that Spalding over the length of three New York sewers. It's still one of my proudest achievements decades later.

Naturally my idol became Boston Red Sox baseball star, Ted Williams, nicknamed 'The Splendid Splinter', who was also a big skinny guy. That ability to hit a stickball carried over to softball and baseball, and I became a star centrefielder who could hit a softball over a 350-foot wall in the Kelly Street playground. With that athletic ability and a bit of charm, I became the captain of the team and used that authority to suggest to the other guys that they might also enjoy roller skating with the girls in the streets, and then persuaded the girlfriends of the older guys on the block to give the younger ones social dancing lessons at the local community centre to enhance their pick-up skills. In addition, the success from that dedicated practice also carried over to being conscientious in my schoolwork, and later being generous in my giving to others less fortunate. So the message is that practice may not always make perfect, but it surely will make you more competent at any activity that is important for you.

In this respect, the current times are no different. Many men who are able to conquer their fears and succeed physically among other men on any dimension find that instead of feeling the need to prove themselves to other males, they can now cultivate their 'feminine' core values, such as compassion, vulnerability and self-reflection. One parent from our survey commented on how her sons learn self-confidence through tae kwon do: 'They feel confident they can protect themselves against bullies. They can see their accomplishments through passing belt tests. They have older adult male and female mentors who teach discipline and mutual respect. Plus the kids get to see the older mentors sometimes try, fail and try again. Great life lessons!'

Few activities teach mental toughness and ownership like individual sports, or collaboration and resilience like team sports. No matter what your level of skill, there's a group of young men or even co-ed teams out there who want you on their team or to join their league. For adults who want to join or start a group, see if there's already one in your local area by looking up the sport on Google, Meetup (meetup.com), or join a gym or club where you can meet people who share your interests.

If sports aren't your thing, activities with rhythmic qualities, like singing, dancing or playing a musical instrument, are great alternatives. They also provide a powerful environment for social bonding. Another thing you can do to take a break from the constant bombardment of external stimuli is schedule a relaxing massage or fit in moments where you can go outside to a quiet park or hiking trail and allow your mind to free itself from distractions.

Make your bed: small accomplishments lead to bigger accomplishments

In 2014, when US Navy Admiral and US Special Operations Commander William H. McRaven delivered the commencement address at the University of Texas, the first piece of advice he gave to the new graduates was to make their bed. He explained that by doing so, a person will have just performed their first successful act of the day, which then sets the tone for accomplishing more tasks. When the day is over, that one small task can snowball into many finished tasks. Though the act of making one's own bed is simple and mundane, it reiterates that the little things in life can have a significant impact. 'If you can't do the little things right, you will never do the big things right,' he said. Plus, if the day didn't go as well as hoped, coming home to a made bed offers some encouragement that the next day will be better.[5]

This is how habits are formed. The more little things you do right on a regular basis, forming good habits, the easier it will be to move your life in a positive direction and reap the benefits that build on those habits.

Related advice comes from social psychologist Roy Baumeister. For years he researched self-esteem, but says he 'reluctantly advise[s] people to forget about it'. He believes that 'self-control plays a much more important role in personal success than self-esteem'.[6]

I (Phil) can also attest to the impact self-control has throughout one's life. In my research on time perspective, I found that the better a child understands causal sequences and the costs and benefits associated with their decisions, the more successful they will be in school and the better they will fare emotionally, financially and health-wise later in adulthood. In particular, children who are highly future-oriented are also highly conscientious, do not procrastinate and resist daily temptations when there is work to get done. (To learn more, and to discover your time perspective, visit thetimeparadox.com.)

Other basic things to get in the habit of doing are eating a balanced diet and getting enough sleep. Create a schedule for yourself that sets you up for success.

Discover your inner power

> A man's character is discernible in the mental or moral attitude in which, when it came upon him, he felt himself most deeply and intensely active and alive. At such moments there is a voice inside which speaks and says: 'This is the real me!'
>
> – William James, nineteenth-century American psychologist[7]

In her book *The Artist's Way*, writer and filmmaker Julia Cameron recommends an exercise called the 'morning pages', an 'apparently pointless' process of writing three pages of whatever comes to mind. When writing in the morning pages, there's no wrong way – the only requirement is that you do it every day, and do your best not to censor yourself. The morning pages will help you be less judgemental of yourself. It doesn't matter if you don't feel like writing or don't have anything to say, after a while you will come in contact with an unexpected inner power: your true self. You will become more honest with yourself, discovering not only who you are but also who you want to become. And with this knowledge you become motivated to go from where you are to where you want to be. It doesn't sound logical, but it works. Providing a space to contemplate sharpens the mind. And it's not just for creative types. Everyone benefits from doing the morning pages, including lawyers, politicians and entrepreneurs. If you dislike keeping a journal, try Penzu (penzu.com), a site that lets you store your thoughts online.[8]

At the very least, keep a small notebook or use the notes app in your mobile phone where you can jot down memorable phrases and quotes. Known in the seventeenth century as 'common-places', notebooks like these were seen as a vital means to nurture and inspire a capable mind as well as keep track of intellectual development.[9] It will force you to slow down, even just for a moment, to reflect on a stimulating thought and incorporate it into your own ideas and aspirations.

If you do such mindful exercises regularly, you will also develop wisdom, and be able to discern the difference between happiness and meaning. From psychologist and Holocaust survivor Viktor Frankl's book, *Man's Search for Meaning*, we can deduce that happiness is essentially about 'me' and meaning is about 'we'. Happiness can be found in the now while meaning is found in the past and in the future. Happy people enjoy receiving while people leading meaningful lives get satisfaction from giving to others. As much as happiness can be pursued, long-lasting happiness is actually derived from meaningful endeavours that allow you to discover your strengths and weaknesses, establish goals that can be achieved in the future and experience situations where you can bond and grow with others.

Make some female friends

Become friends with at least one young woman and make it clear that you just want to be friends – nothing more, nothing less. A lot of women never totally relax in their friendships with men because there is always the worry that one will develop more intense feelings for the other, and then it will become awkward, dealing a potentially fatal blow to the friendship. But if you put those fears to rest right from the get-go, it's much easier to really get to know someone and establish trust. You can even talk about how you'll handle the situation if one of you does develop a romantic interest. You can say, 'It might sound silly, but our friendship means a lot to me and I want to make sure we stay friends. If one of us develops romantic feelings for the other, let's talk about it right away.' By doing this, you set the standard for honest, open communication. And it's much less awkward to say that at the beginning of a relationship than risk losing a friend later down the road due to miscommunication. Find women with whom you have one or two activities or interests in common. If you don't know where to find these women, try using online clubs and forums or Meetup groups.

A note to shy men: just like mastering a video game takes a reasonable time commitment, with guided practice, even the most shy male can be trained to be 'socially fit'. If socializing is a challenge for you, start off slow. You want to make social goals for yourself and gradually work your way up to them; it could be as simple as smiling at the person checking you out at the supermarket, and then making some brief conversation. Don't get attached to the outcome of a social situation, socializing means another person with their own thoughts and emotions is involved, and the best we can all do is allow ourselves to be present and engaged in conversation. See shyness. com or visit the Shyness Research Institute (ius.edu/shyness) for more useful advice.

Don't call women 'sluts'

One point of contention that drives women away from men, as friends and especially as romantic partners, is when men call women 'sluts'. Assuming you are a heterosexual male, slut-shaming women isn't going to help you get the kind of sexual or romantic relationship that you really desire. 'The pseudo-scientific myth that all women are naturally predisposed toward sexual restraint and all men toward promiscuity isn't only inaccurate but dangerous, leading directly to the notion that women who differ from that norm are unacceptable, need to be corrected or deserve to be mistreated,' says Zhana Vrangalova, professor of human sexuality at New York University. 'What's more,' she adds, 'it creates a culture in which men who seek out many partners aren't just celebrated, but given permission to devalue women with a similar sexual appetite. Ironically, it's this negative attitude toward women who have casual sex that makes many women less likely to seek it out, which means less casual sex for the men who want it most.'[10]

Sexual shame is a huge barrier for a lot of women. Men's sexuality can be as intimidating as it is appealing. If you can communicate to a woman that she is safe with you and in the future you will treat her with the same respect you showed her today, it would make an enormous difference with a woman exploring her desire for you. When a male is indecisive romantically it ruins the chances of a woman really letting go with him. The most satisfying sexual relationships take place in an atmosphere where both people feel safe to express themselves and realize their turn-ons – and their turn-offs.

A lot of women would love to make the first move or take more sexual initiative, but hold back because they don't know what kind of reaction they are going to get. One way to communicate your interest in a woman taking more initiative is to say something like 'I love it when the woman makes the first move' when the conversation turns flirtatious. When you're in a relationship, tell her how much you like it when she surprises you, gets creative or takes the initiative.

If you're getting mixed messages, talk to her. Explain your observations and how it makes you feel. If it's not something you can work through together, move on to a woman who you are more compatible with. No one is perfect and the woman you're interested in may not know exactly what her needs and wants are, but she should have a sense of what she wants and be willing to examine how her expectations or fantasies may differ from reality and laugh at the contradictions. A woman who is strong will not consider you a chauvinist for voicing what you want or your intentions. She will be strong enough to say 'no', but also strong enough to say 'yes', and you'll be able to be yourself without over-analysing your actions.

Get a mentor, be a mentor

You will get some of the best relationship advice from older men who have been in your position. Not only will they be able to advise you on personal decisions, they will be able to help you make intelligent life and career choices. Those who have never had a mentor often underestimate the value of having one. Places where men and boys can gather together are more necessary than ever before. Older men should become mentors to younger men in their family, school or workplace. As mentioned earlier, dads have got to do it. Make mentoring part of who you are. Below are recommended organizations that support this kind of environment:

- Boy Scouts, scouts.org.uk.
- Chance UK, chanceuk.org.
- ManKind Project, mankindproject.org.
- Big Brothers Big Sisters International, bbbsi.org.
- Big Brothers Big Sisters of London and Area, bbbsola.org.
- Boys to Men Mentoring Network, boystomen.org.
- *Esquire* Magazine's Mentoring Initiative: mentoring. esquire.com

Vote

Catering to voters helps politicians get re-elected. As we mentioned earlier, between 1975 and 1980, women became the majority of undergraduate students. Since 1980, the proportion of female voters has also outnumbered the proportion of male voters; in the US, women have cast between 4 and 7 million more votes than men in recent presidential elections.[11] In the UK, women outvote men by 7 percentage points.[12] It follows that if men want policy-makers to pay more attention to men's issues such as workplace safety and paternity rights, they need to consider becoming more politically active, and, at the very least, voting. If men don't do this simple thing, we are going to see a lot more policies that leave them out.

There are a multitude of options for men that will put themselves in a better place, both as individuals and as a group. But they must act, just as generations before them have done. If men want to create more balanced lives, they must re-engage in exploring new social dynamics and realities (not just digital ones).

20

What Women Can Do

The current plight of boys and young men is, in fact, a
women's issue. Those boys are our sons; they are the people
with whom our daughters will build a future. If our boys are in
trouble, so are we all.

– Christina Hoff Sommers[1]

Sisters, mothers and friends

There is a need for hardened men, we will always need
rough men to 'stand the walls' – to protect and keep watch
– and tend the land, but we need to teach them from a
young age how to be affectionate in order for them to be connected emotionally in relationships. This means embracing and
encouraging the strength and hardness that are commonly associated with being a man, as well as developing the depth of character
and emotional insights that lend themselves to a viable interpersonal dynamic in a relationship later on.

Ultimately, women cannot teach men how to be men any more
than men can teach women how to be women, but they can
encourage them how to develop in appropriate directions. Around
8 to 12 years old – or just before puberty – boys start craving a
strong male role model, if they don't already have one. Mothers
showing approval and support for this process will enable a better
connection throughout a man's life between the seemingly

dichotic existence of male and female. Coincidentally, doing this can also garner more credibility for the mother with the man over his lifetime as she is seen as a positive part of this process rather than a detractor. A young man would benefit greatly from the women in his life respecting the time that he has with his father or mentor and encouraging him to discover manhood through age-appropriate activities with other young men.

Sisters, especially those close in age, are also crucial to the way a boy understands what women want in general as well as what they desire in a man. How a boy interacts with his sister and her friends can have a significant impact on his regard for women and the relationships he holds with them, both platonic and romantic. By lending their perspectives to their brothers in a direct but compassionate way, sisters can improve the level of communication and cooperation their brothers will have with women later on. It is also important for brothers and sisters, regardless of their age gap, to find fun things to do collectively and around those activities to help develop an ease of communicating their feelings and values. It can be the wellspring for both men and women to feeling comfortable relating to the opposite sex throughout their lives.

Gamer and porn 'widows'

To sum up the suggestions we heard from men, it is important for both men and women to discuss their feelings on how too much gaming or porn is affecting each person's life and the relationship. Be honest, patient and strong. If you are headed down the path to becoming a game or porn widow, bring to your partner's attention a clear set of options and consequences of what will happen if his behaviour doesn't change, and follow through on those words. It is OK to make suggestions to him, but don't assume you know why he is gaming or using porn so much. If either of you needs to see a counsellor or therapist, or better yet, couple's counselling, don't wait till the relationship is beyond repair or you have already decided in your mind that you are 'over it'. Whatever you do, don't offer to play video games or watch porn with him. In some relationships, it's perfectly all right if couples decide to play video games or watch porn together, but if your partner is doing either to excess, you're just enabling them. At the end of the day, you need to move on if your partner would rather live in a virtual world.

The effects of no-strings-attached (NSA) sex

> Whatever currency women are accepting is the currency men will carry.
>
> – Young man from our survey

Complaining about why there appears to be a shortage of decent men and tossing around the chauvinist label isn't going to get most women the kind of relationship that they want. When it comes to romantic commitments, women would benefit from approaching dating as if they are investing in the stock market: look for a man who is interesting, capable and appears to command a level of attention from other women (potential investors). As a relationship 'investor' – of your time, energy and emotions – you must learn how to identify the real deal when the majority of males you encounter either have 'swagger' (a good marketing strategy), don't make the time or space for a relationship, are indecisive or may be a good fit on some levels but are missing drive and emotional availability.

The substance (a solid business plan) that you want to look for in a man is whether or not he will use his skills to build a well-rounded, healthy and enduring relationship with meaning and mutual growth for both partners. The questions to ask and consider are: Does this man have true interpersonal skills, such as the ability to listen, empathize, communicate and work as a team to resolve issues? Does he have the wherewithal and desire to be in a relationship that is satisfying for both of you in the long term? You have to assess early on whether he is more of a giver than a taker. Is he full of gimmicks instead of possessing a well-balanced approach with the capability and inclination to be in a genuine relationship? These are important self-constructs that a man needs to bring to a relationship so that it will be sustainable over time.

These relationship skills cannot be forced or faked for very long so you need to pay close attention if you'd like to improve your selection choices. Years of women falling for the guy with the marketing strategy, not the man with real substance, have resulted in the significantly diminished dating pool with which women are now dealing. This choice in type of partner is relevant regardless of how long you want the relationship to last. Having flings and casual acquaintances can be a fun getaway from the weight of life sometimes, but after a while, the effect is that Mr Right becomes more elusive.

When you're out at the bar or club, and you are engaging in conversation with men, be aware that other men are watching, and they will replicate whatever strategy used by the man you're talking to if you appear to be responding positively to it. One of the most common shortcomings that men watch women fall prey to is when a guy can talk his way in, rather than prove his way to something. Men who can talk a good game rarely have to walk the walk, which is all the more reason for more males to learn and apply pick-up artist techniques and find women with a more open approach to sex. The benefits of this to men are multiplied: they get to practise their technique with a higher success rate, have more sex with a desirable woman, and most males don't have to worry about the 'messy' relationship entanglements that could follow.

When men see that quality women don't generally expect them to invest as much energy, time or commitment in return for sex and relationships as they formerly thought they would, they will adjust their behaviour accordingly – downwards. Speaking strictly in an economical sense, there is no reason for any person to invest more energy in acquiring something they already have the ability to possess. Just like someone wouldn't pay seven dollars for something that they know they can get for five dollars, a male won't put in 70 per cent effort when 50 per cent will get him exactly what he desires. Nobody would. This is a basic human condition proven everyday by consumers, stock traders and business negotiations: they are looking for the best value (mate) for their money (effort). If, instead of requiring the 70 per cent effort normally needed to initiate (and potentially maintain) a relationship with a quality woman, it only takes a man 50 per cent effort, that's the amount of work he'll put in. Every time. This benefits men in the short term but the consequence is that they are seldom forced or challenged to develop their more enduring relational skills.

Recently, there have been some articles published with unusual bits of advice. A young woman in New York proposed one, which sums up the main points of several. She suggested 'promiscuity is another way of saying "practice makes perfect"'.[2] Who would agree with such a formula? Any male who wanted to benefit from a bit of free sex would agree with that formula. However, any man who cares about the future of relational constructs will tell you that is the worst approach possible for long-term relationships and the women who want them. If you want a dog to learn a new trick do you give him his treat before you require him to perform it or after? If a male knows he can get access to sex indefinitely without committing anything for it, then why would he commit to something... ever? Seventy per cent versus 50 per cent...

Our contention is not with the approach but with the message it sends to young men; if this same process can be undertaken with a different message then we say go for it. Just realize that males, by and large, are paying attention to women's messages, which in general is: 'I will actively sleep with men until one of you takes me off the market.' This removes the potential moral issues that males may have with that approach. Your message, because you are a female, to males is that there will be a steady supply of desirable women who are actively sleeping with them. As long as a man knows he has access to new partners and hasn't already established a deeper relationship with a woman, it is in his best interests not to. And he knows this. Furthermore, it only perpetuates the access to random, no-strings-attached sex because desirable women are not being taken 'off the market' into long-term relationships.

One of the elements that feminism has brought about is greater sexual freedom for women; in turn this has brought an even greater sexual freedom for males. Males are motivated by sex with partners possessing desirable traits. Experience, quality and compatibility will determine the period of time that the male will want to repeat his experience with any one woman.

Additionally, most heterosexual men who had a loving mother have at least some desire to be a husband or a long-term primary partner in a female's life. While men have a significantly longer biological timeframe to find a long-term mate, beyond a certain point in their life they are not inclined to continue restarting the search after a certain number of dates once they believe that they have found the most desirable partner.

Choosing a good man

In 2013 the popular dating site OkCupid experimented with an app that set up people on blind dates. On launch day, they temporarily removed all user photos from the site, calling it 'Love Is Blind Day'. They kept track of user activity, however, and found that although there were fewer new conversations started per hour, people responded to first messages 44 per cent more often. Women were also more receptive to their dates when they used the blind date app. Women generally reported having a good time on their dates regardless of the attraction level of their partner. Interestingly, women reported having a slightly better time on dates with the less good-looking men. In contrast, online, those same men could not get their foot in the door – only 10 per cent of women rated as 'much hotter' than the men messaging them would reply back to a given message, versus 45 per cent of women who would reply when the men were more attractive than them.[3]

Although there is an imbalance of quality men to second-rate guys, there is still a cache of quality men who are being overlooked by women. They are the less flashy men with substance (a solid business plan). They are the ones who don't look the part even though they play it. They walk the walk but don't talk the talk – their marketing strategy is passive. While advances from well-rounded men looking for long-term relationships is not every woman's desire, women should still consider how their rejection will affect men's approaches to relationships. Sure, you can tell yourself that he will get over it and move on, but that is the message men are designed to exude. The reality is that these men will not stay that way for long. As the popular phrase goes, *insanity is doing the same thing over and over and expecting a different result*. Therefore males, as humans, will adjust their approach to meet their ends.

Why is this important? If there is no reinforcement incentive for those men who are trying hard and who do take relationships seriously, then women will remove the demand for these men and eventually the supply will dwindle. Women should find a way to reward the sincere attempts from men with something more than affable regard, such as helping him develop something he's lacking (confidence, style, etc.) or giving him more insight about women so he will be a better man for the next woman. We are suggesting some women teach men other ways to develop and sustain relationships. If you are going to have a friend with benefits (FWB) consider actually being their friend and not just someone to have sex with. If enough women whom a man desires tell him in one form or another that they do not want a long-term relationship with him – and more importantly the reasons why not – then he is more likely to adjust his approach to change that response.

The competitive nature of men who have made the conscious decision to pursue an honest relationship with a woman with the intent of growing a sustainable and enduring relationship is the very key to bringing the quality ratio of males and females back into balance. But men need to know the next steps to take. As women achieve higher levels of education, professional success and financial status, it should follow that they demand that men raise themselves as well. However, women must also encourage men to do more, to reach higher, to work harder in school and to make more time for people in the real world, rather than video games and porn. Women must therefore be willing to be supportive and collaborative, and recognize that men being men (responsibly) is a good thing.

21

What the Media Can Do

As mentioned in Chapter 8, young men spend on average forty-four hours in front of a screen for every half-hour they spend in one-on-one conversation with their fathers; so perhaps it's no wonder that in our survey, when we asked, 'What factors contribute to motivational problems in young men?' nearly two-thirds of participants said, 'Conflicting messages from media, institutions, parents and peers about acceptable male behaviour.'

It would be nice to think that the advertisement, press and entertainment industries would be willing to portray men in a more positive light, but it'll be hard for them to move away from the predictable stereotypes as long as they keep making good money from casting men as duds. Pressure to change will need to come from the outside, which will only happen when people are willing to recognize that gender biases affect men, too, and how desperately young men need more positive male role models to look up to in the media.

Raising public awareness will be tricky, but one of the simplest things to do is show the male versions of well-known feminist material and messages. For example, what if there was a reverse Bechdel Test that rated the portrayal of men in movies, such as a 'MacGyver Test', named after the popular television adventure series, that a film or television show passes if it meets *any* of these criteria regarding its male characters:

- Movie does not require the absence of the mother for the father to be portrayed as a competent dad.

- Honest hard-working man is in a successful or leadership position and/or is not a chump.

- Female protagonist shows interest in male protagonist before he is the hero.

- Male protagonist solves problems in creative ways, and only uses violence as a last resort to accomplish his goals or mission.

We imagine it would be a short list. The more men and women get a genuinely better understanding of what it's like to be in the other's position, the easier it will be for them to appreciate where the other is coming from.

Another way to do this is by swapping the male and female roles in movies and TV shows, and then re-examining the plots. For example, let's reverse the roles of the 'fearless' Princess Anna and the 'rugged' iceman Kristoff in the Academy Award-winning animated children's movie, *Frozen*. In the movie Anna's older sister, Elsa, banishes herself from their castle because she can't control her magical ability to produce ice and snow with her hands. Anna sets out to find her sister and bring her home. Initially Anna is offered assistance by the smooth talking Prince Hans, whom she immediately falls in love with. But who ends up helping her? The penniless iceman Kristoff, whose sled and reindeer Anna decides she can use for her own agenda – never mind if he needs it (she doesn't ask). After nearly getting him killed, destroying his sled, and finally rescuing Elsa, Anna and Kristoff go their separate ways. It is only after Prince Hans proves himself to be evil, and Olaf – the dopey snowman sidekick – says to Anna that Kristoff would be a good match that Anna even bothers to consider him.

Now imagine a movie where a prince felt entitled to use a hardworking woman whose only possessions are her sled and reindeer, which she uses to eke out a living, to go rescue his brother, and after she voluntarily busts her butt to help him he goes back to his life without a second thought. The politically correct folk would be horrified by Kristoff's behaviour, and audiences would be up in arms! We would think 'Why can't he get his act together?' Yet that thought doesn't even cross our minds while watching *Frozen*. Instead we think Anna is quirky and adventurous. By the way, *Frozen* does not pass the MacGyver Test.

Make better dating sites

Aside from poor grammar and lack of content in messages, the number one gripe women have when it comes to online dating is that their inboxes become filled with generic copy and paste messages from men they're just not that interested in. On the other hand, one of men's major issues with online dating beyond not getting dates is the number of messages they have to send in order to engage in conversation. It's a war of attrition. The solution? Make a woman-friendly dating app that lets women choose.

Of course, this app would cater towards heterosexual couples. Yet it would transform the way men and women approach each other. A Nielsen survey from 2014 found that men are twice as likely as women to use social media for dating (13 per cent for men versus 7 per cent for women[1]), yet they are half as likely as women to ask for assistance in creating or reviewing their profile.[2] It's not a coincidence that women spend more time on their profiles – they are the ones being pursued.

The main reason why young men use apps like Tinder (which uses GPS technology and matches users based on appearance) is because there's less to lose with regard to time and money spent to get a date, yet the amount of rejection is about the same as other dating sites. But if women had to make the first move, rejection for men would drop to zero, and they'd probably spend more time working on their profiles to make them more representative and interesting. It could be argued that men would then embellish their profiles in different ways to make them more appealing, but the people who are going to misrepresent themselves are going to do it no matter what dating site they're using. The point of having a new structure like this would be to allow women to have more control over the online dating process and not be so overwhelmed with random and aimless attempts. Plus, it would open up the opportunity for men to focus on stimulating discussion because they know that there is already some level of attraction to build upon.

People are just getting busier, and they have less time and patience to go out of their way to meet someone who may or may not be a good fit. Women especially are looking for middle ground in the dating arena. As attitudes become more positive towards online dating, there will need to be a greater variety of ways that people can meet and connect with each other. If only women were allowed to initiate first contact, it would change the entire dating game. But the big question is, would anyone use it? Are women willing to write the first message, and are men willing to receive it?

Another idea is to simply expand on already existing social networks. In the near future, Namisha Parthasarathy, a young British app designer and Stanford alumni, is set to release a new dating app called One Degree, which will create more meaningful connections by introducing people who have mutual friends. 'The concept,' she says, 'is that the likelihood of people treating each other poorly is lesser because there are extended friend circles involved and also . . . friends are a good vetting process.'[3]

What the porn industry can do

The average porn video is almost twenty minutes long. If you run an online porn website, especially a free one, consider running a fifteen-second ad on safer sex practices before every video; it would take up only about 1 per cent of the entire video's length. Then, if users want to skip ads, ask them to pay a fee, which would potentially generate revenue for you from those who choose to go straight to the video.

Another idea is to disrupt the porn industry as Cindy Gallop has done with MakeLoveNotPorn.tv (MLNP.tv). Cindy applied her philosophy of 'Pro sex. Pro porn. Pro knowing the difference' to the site. MLNP is unique. It's all user-submitted content, and the videos must follow a set of guidelines ensuring that the material is original and realistic. Gallop separated MLNP from amateur porn, saying her site reflects real-world sex.

> One of the issues here is the way our society uses the word 'porn' – often to describe anything involving naked people and/or sex. I get equally frustrated by the tendency for the term 'porn' to be used as if porn was all one big homogeneous mass. That's like using the term 'literature' as if all literature were the same. The landscape of porn is as varied and full of genres, sub-genres and numerous different forms as the landscape of literature. Just as a lot of things classified as 'porn,' strictly speaking aren't...Language matters – which is why one of the things we're doing is creating a new vocabulary for [real-world sex]. And why we draw a distinction between porn in the generally-used sense (professionally-produced – this applies to a lot of the so-called 'amateur' as well – performative, specifically-created entertainment) and [real-world sex].[4]

Probably the best distinction a viewer made was that when he watched regular porn he wanted to jerk off, but when he watched the MLNP stars he wanted to have sex. Another viewer wrote in: 'I just came across (no pun intended) your website and thought it's just spot on. I'm a typical 24-year-old guy who's heard (and seen) enough crap about sex from the prudes on one side and copious amounts of online porno on the other. What the subject was always lacking was a view from the middle ground; someone who doesn't think sex is inherently bad or shameful but also is not blind to the possible negative effects.'[5]

Something else porn sites could do is to challenge users to revolutionize the industry. Just as entrepreneur Bill Gates put forth a multimillion-dollar challenge for inventors to create a condom people would actually want to use,[6] major porn sites could do something similar, challenging users to change the way people consume porn to make it more satisfying, therapeutic, or even educational.

At the very least, porn sites should clearly post resources that users can easily refer to if they suffer from porn addiction – much the same way casinos offer resources for people who have gambling addictions.

What the gaming industry can do

In her 2012 TED Talk, cognitive researcher Daphne Bavelier said that game developers need to harness the 'nutritious' aspects of gaming and create a new kind of game that is irresistible but has elements that stimulate and develop the brain in positive ways.[7] The biggest challenge will be convincing companies to take the risk by deviating from a profitable formula.

Game companies currently make a lot of money by keeping up with the subscription base while changing the content as little as possible, so it would be surprising to see game developers go outside sports, violence and first-person shooter games. Yet it would be a welcome change to see games that bridged the gap between fantasy and reality so that users can enjoy playing the games while improving real-life abilities or contributing to something beyond themselves. Right now the industry is poised to make these changes; they have the tools and ability to apply the game mindset to real-world problems and create generations of real-life heroes.

In *Reality Is Broken: Why Games Make Us Better and How They Can Change the World*, Jane McGonigal discusses the power of crowdsourcing, making the observation that successful crowdsourcing projects are structured like a good multiplayer game. One example she uses is the parliamentary expenses scandal of 2009. Essentially, many members of the British Parliament, or MPs, had been filing illegal expense claims that added up to millions of pounds sterling, including frivolous charges like £32,000 (more than $50,000 at today's rates) for personal gardening expenses and £1,645 (nearly $2,600) for a 'floating duck island'.

The government released the expense forms in an unsorted collection of more than a million electronically scanned documents. The *Guardian*, which had been covering the scandal, knew it didn't have enough manpower to sort through the mess, so it hired Simon Willison, a software developer, to design a website where anyone could examine the documents for incriminating details. With his help, the *Guardian* launched a site called Investigate Your MP's Expenses, the world's first massive multiplayer investigative journalism project. After just three days, more than 20,000 people had sifted through 170,000 documents. Investigate Your MP's Expenses also had a remarkable 56 per cent visitor participation rate.

The investigation prompted the resignation of dozens of MPs, plus legal action, including suspensions and prosecutions. Ultimately, it led to widespread political reform.[8]

Though it may appear to be a suggestion not unlike Tom Sawyer persuading the neighbourhood boys that whitewashing a fence is fun, imagine the kind of force gamers would become if every gamer dedicated just 1 per cent of his gaming time – 30 million collective hours a week – to make a real-world impact like Investigate Your MP's Expenses. Considering Wikipedia represents roughly 100 million hours of human thought, hypothetically 15.6 Wikipedia-size projects could be accomplished every year if each gamer invested that 1 per cent into a crowdsourcing project. Who wouldn't want to get in on that?

Conclusion

> Our life, like the harmony of the world, is composed of contrast, also of varying tones, sweet and harsh, sharp and flat, soft and loud. If a musician liked one sort only, what effect would he make? He must be able to employ them together and blend them. And we too must accept the good and bad that coexist in our life. Our existence is impossible without this mixture, and one side is no less necessary to us than the other.
>
> – Michel de Montaigne, sixteenth-century French writer

Several nineteenth-century experiments showed that if a frog is put in a pot of boiling water, it will immediately leap out, but if it is placed in cold water that is heated gradually, it will not realize the danger and will be cooked to death.[1] Our future depends on the decisions made today, and this book is about checking the 'temperature' of our environment, observing the effects it has on individuals, and the implications it has for the future.

If the trends we've discussed in this book continue, what will happen is unclear, but our culture loses something important when we, as a population, are less able to think critically, delay gratification, or define and achieve meaningful personal and social goals. Technology especially needs to be embraced, but how we embrace it will make the difference between healthy and unhealthy human interaction.

In our increasingly fluid and interconnected world, one has to wonder who the game-changers and industry disruptors will be twenty years from now. Going forward, the question we should be asking ourselves is, will the tech and entertainment geniuses who shaped our world today still be the heroes of tomorrow? Will technological developments be used to make us better people or the world a better place, or, as Sherry Turkle says, will these things 'take us places that we don't want to go?'.[2]

It's just as important to understand the consequences as well as the potentials of technology so the following generations will have more personal responsibility in using them and companies will have a better professional understanding in producing them. Our worldwide obsession with technology is gaining speed, and we need to learn how to coexist with it so that we do not lose our autonomy or humanness.

Most people will agree that there's something missing in young men's worlds, and just by sheer numbers it is clear there are many activities young men are not pursuing and skills they are not developing in lieu of living their lives in virtual reality. When a person spends the vast majority of their time on any one thing they run the risk of becoming one-dimensional. Perhaps the young men whose parents are willing to support their son's addictive screen habits will end up like Japan's 'herbivorous' *hikikomori* males, who isolate themselves from the world and life's pleasures, but for the less financially insulated we may see fewer getting degrees, and a rise in fatherlessness and unemployment not unlike the gender imbalances minority and poorer communities have experienced for the last few decades. Additionally, the trajectory of low-income males will worsen if they are unable to find work. Their chances of ending up in trouble with the law may increase, as will the likelihood of their female counterparts ending up as single mothers.

We must provide real hope and inspiration for young men by creating new social expectations that are more productive for men and for society. We don't need to chuck the old system entirely – taking away certain concepts of masculinity could also take away from what makes a man push himself for something bigger than himself. The very concept of what exists today is because of that sentiment 'be a man', therefore we need to refine it and support it as a community. A more articulate and communicative man, who is confident, secure and comfortable showing and receiving respect is what we should be striving for. We must show men that they are lovable, not disposable.

If we can make these changes, we may see less of the emotionally detached breadwinner, and start to see men living more integrated lives within themselves, their families and their communities. The challenge for improving the situation for men without disadvantaging another group of people, such as girls and women, will require a combination of effort from individuals and institutions alike. The challenge for women will be to create enough economic independence so they do not compromise their values in exchange for a financial safety net, while men's challenge will be to understand how his traditional role of protector sets him up for detachment from intimacy with his wife and closeness with his children. Men must give themselves and each other permission to be more involved.

Progress is a bumpy road, but the destination cannot be reached if we only pay attention to one side of the equation – otherwise we'll just be going in circles. We cannot call it progress if, as women gain momentum, they are not any more empathetic to men's issues than the men who they had felt oppressed by were to their issues. Traditional career paths are changing, traditional gender roles are changing, the notion of marriage is changing. Navigating this changing landscape is not easy.

We must applaud the efforts of those wise men and women who have got us where we are today, but we must also continue moving forward and build on those foundations as a team. It's not about putting our differences aside; it's about recognizing the differences so we can utilize every individual's strengths for our shared future. The only way we can make things better is if we are willing to look at both sides, are proactive about providing support to everyone who needs it and are willing to cultivate balanced roles for both sexes.

We hope we have been able to highlight not only the *why* behind many young men's distressing academic, social and sexual symptoms but *how* to implement larger solutions that will guide them to a better place. Despite being endemic, these problems can be solved or ameliorated only if many people and institutions are willing to change the game plan. Finally, though the problems we have described are now global, we remain optimistic that solutions can be enacted, so that the only sequel we might write to this book would be to announce that the alarm has been silenced!

Appendix I

TED Survey Results

Year conducted: 2011

Total number of participants: 20,000

Gender: 75.7 male, 23.9 female, 0.4 other/prefer not to answer

Age: 0.1 per cent were 0 to 12 years old

4.3 per cent were 13 to 17 years old

35.5 per cent were 18 to 25 years old

28.7 per cent were 26 to 34 years old

20.4 per cent were 35 to 50 years old

10.9 per cent were 51+ years old

In all the questions we asked, participants were allowed to select multiple answers, so percentages will add up to more than 100 per cent.

What factors contribute to motivational problems in young men?

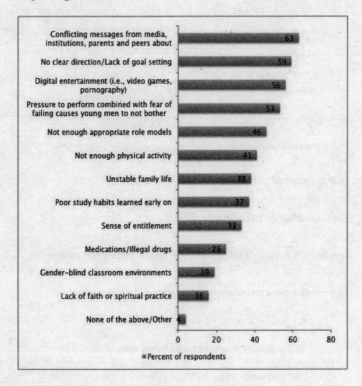

■ Percent of respondents

Survey highlights

- 64 per cent of boys aged 12 and younger chose 'Pressure to perform combined with fear of failing causes young men to not bother trying in the first place.'

- 62 per cent of young men aged 13 through 17 chose 'Digital entertainment (i.e., video games, pornography).'

- 66 per cent of young men aged 18 through 25, and 63 per cent of men aged 26 through 34, chose 'No clear direction/Lack of goal setting.'

How would you change the school environment to engage young men?

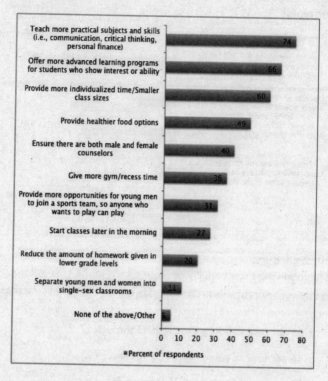

Teach more practical subjects and skills (i.e., communication, critical thinking, personal finance) — 74

Offer more advanced learning programs for students who show interest or ability — 66

Provide more individualized time/Smaller class sizes — 60

Provide healthier food options — 49

Ensure there are both male and female counselors — 40

Give more gym/recess time — 36

Provide more opportunities for young men to join a sports team, so anyone who wants to play can play — 31

Start classes later in the morning — 27

Reduce the amount of homework given in lower grade levels — 20

Separate young men and women into single-sex classrooms — 11

None of the above/Other — 5

0 10 20 30 40 50 60 70 80

■ Percent of respondents

Survey highlights

- 64 per cent of boys aged 12 and younger chose 'Ensure there are both male and female counselors.'

- 73 per cent of young men aged 13 through 17 chose 'Offer more advanced learning programs for students who show interest or ability.'

- 75 per cent of men aged 18 through 34 chose 'Teach more practical subjects and skills.'

How will the increased dropout rates and slipping test scores of young men affect the United States' success?

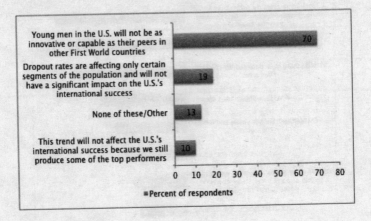

■ Percent of respondents

Survey highlights

The following groups all chose 'Young men in the U.S. will not be as innovative or capable as their peers in other First World countries':

- 65 per cent of young men aged 13 through 17.

- 66 per cent of young men aged 18 through 25.

- 75 per cent of men aged 26 through 34.

- 74 per cent of all participants aged 35 and older.

How can we empower young men in safe, pro-social ways?

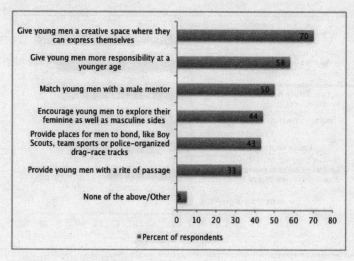

Give young men a creative space where they can express themselves — 70

Give young men more responsibility at a younger age — 58

Match young men with a male mentor — 50

Encourage young men to explore their feminine as well as masculine sides — 44

Provide places for men to bond, like Boy Scouts, team sports or police-organized drag-race tracks — 43

Provide young men with a rite of passage — 33

None of the above/Other — 5

0 10 20 30 40 50 60 70 80

■ Percent of respondents

Survey highlights

The following groups all chose 'Give young men a creative space where they can express themselves':

- 89 per cent of boys aged 12 and younger.

- 72 per cent of young men aged 13 through 17.

- 74 per cent of young men aged 18 through 25.

- 68 per cent of men aged 26 through 34.

Why are video games and porn so popular among young men?

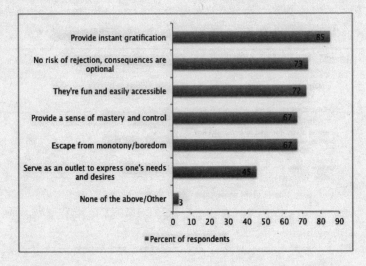

	Percent of respondents
Provide instant gratification	85
No risk of rejection, consequences are optional	73
They're fun and easily accessible	72
Provide a sense of mastery and control	67
Escape from monotony/boredom	67
Serve as an outlet to express one's needs and desires	45
None of the above/Other	3

■ Percent of respondents

Survey highlights

- 78 per cent of boys aged 12 and younger chose 'Provide a sense of mastery and control'.

- 84 per cent of young men aged 13 through 17 chose 'They're fun and easily accessible.'

- 85 per cent of young men aged 18 through 25, and 84 per cent of men aged 26 through 34, chose 'Provide instant gratification.'

How do young men benefit from playing video games?

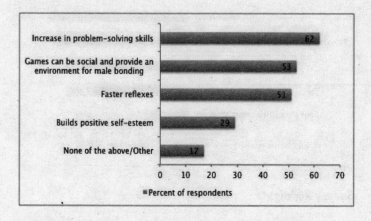

Percent of respondents

- Increase in problem-solving skills: 62
- Games can be social and provide an environment for male bonding: 53
- Faster reflexes: 51
- Builds positive self-esteem: 29
- None of the above/Other: 17

Survey highlights

- 63 per cent of young men aged 13 through 17 chose 'Games can be social and provide an environment for male bonding.'

- 67 per cent of young men aged 18 through 25, and 69 per cent of men aged 26 through 34, chose 'Increase in problem-solving skills.'

How do young men benefit from watching porn?

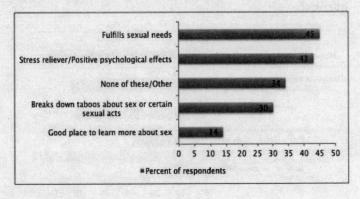

Fulfills sexual needs — 45
Stress reliever/Positive psychological effects — 43
None of these/Other — 34
Breaks down taboos about sex or certain sexual acts — 30
Good place to learn more about sex — 14

0 5 10 15 20 25 30 35 40 45 50

■ Percent of respondents

Survey highlights

- 58 per cent of young men aged 13 through 17, and
  60 per cent of young men aged 18 through 25,
  chose 'Stress reliever/Positive psychological effects.'

- 51 per cent of men aged 26 through 34 chose
  'Fulfills sexual needs.'

- 51 per cent of all participants aged 35 and older did not
  agree with any of the statements, often writing in the
  comments that they believed there were no benefits at
  all, and chose 'None of these/Other'.

Do you think there is a strong relationship between excessive video game playing and/or porn watching (2 or more hours per day [later defined as 4 or more hours a week of gaming or 2 or more hours per week of porn use]) and any of these areas of a romantic relationship?

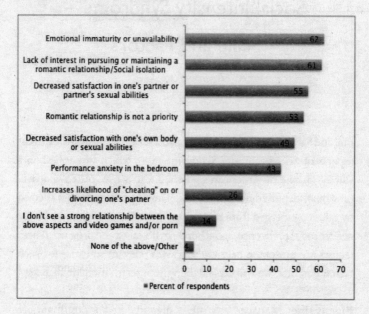

Survey highlights

- 76 per cent of young women aged 18 through 25, and 78 per cent of women aged 26 through 34, chose 'Emotional immaturity or unavailability.'

- 57 per cent of young men aged 13 through 17, 59 per cent of young men aged 18 through 25, and 58 per cent of men aged 26 through 34 chose 'Lack of interest in pursuing or maintaining a romantic relationship/Social isolation.'

Appendix II

Social Intensity Syndrome –

Scale and Factors

Phil and Sarah Brunskill have developed a scale that measures different aspects of Social Intensity Syndrome (SIS), which was tested on a survey sample of American soldiers, some active, others inactive, previously deployed overseas or not. The six primary factors affected by SIS that emerged from their research are: military friends, family, gender social preference, social bonding, nostalgia and drug use. These factors are presented below, along with relevant statistics for each factor, but, first, we will explain the various terms used for analysis:

Eigenvalue: Matrices are often diagonalized in multivariate analyses. In that process, eigenvalues are used to consolidate the variance. In factor analysis, eigenvalues are used to condense the variance in a correlation matrix. 'The factor with the largest eigenvalue has the most variance and so on, down to factors with small or negative eigenvalues that are usually omitted from solutions' (Tabachnick and Fidell, 1996, p. 646). From the analyst's perspective, only variables with eigenvalues of 1.00 or higher are traditionally considered worth analysing.

    Cronbach's (alpha): A coefficient of internal consistency. It is commonly used as an estimate of the reliability of a survey for a sample of test or assessment measures. Cronbach's alpha will generally increase as the intercorrelations among test items increase, and is thus known as an internal consistency estimate of reliability of test scores.

Mean: The terms arithmetic mean and sometimes average are used synonymously to refer to a central value of a discrete set of numbers: specifically, the sum of the values divided by the number of values. The arithmetic mean of a set of numbers $x_1, x_2, ..., x_n$ is typically denoted by M= or $\mathcal{X}$.

Variance: The variance is the expected value of the squared deviation from the mean. It measures how far a set of numbers is spread out. A variance of zero indicates that all the values are identical. Variance is always non-negative: a small variance indicates that the data points tend to be very close to the mean (expected value) and hence to each other, while a high variance indicates that the data points are very spread out around the mean and from each other. An equivalent measure is the square root of the variance, called the standard deviation. The standard deviation has the same dimension as the data, and hence is comparable to deviations from the mean.

Standard Deviation (SD): Measures the amount of variation or dispersion from the average. A low standard deviation indicates that the data points tend to be very close to the mean (also called expected value); a high standard deviation indicates that the data points are spread out over a large range of values.

Factor loading: Defined by how many unique groups of items/questions group together from the survey. Loadings represent degree to which each of the variables 'correlates' with each of the factors.

Social Intensity Syndrome – factors

Military friends: This 16-item factor describes an irreplaceable bond among those who have also served in the United States military (eigenvalue=9.04; 15.58% of variance explained; $M=3.32$, $SD=.95$). Examples: 'I like spending more time with my military friends than my non-military friends', 'I can be myself when with my military friends' and 'I spend time in places where other active and inactive military personnel tend to be.' Average factor loading was .69 (α=.95).

Family: This 11-item factor reflects an overall negative disposition towards one's family (eigenvalue=6.65; 11.47% of variance explained; M=2.23, SD=1.03). Examples: 'I feel down when with my significant other', 'I feel bored when with my family' and 'It is easier to trust my military friends than my significant other.' Average factor loading was .69 (α=.92).

Gender social preference: This 7-item factor outlines a distinct male preference for social gatherings and camaraderie rather than female (eigenvalue=5.12; 8.82% of variance explained; M=2.69, SD=1.10). Examples: 'Women just don't know how to have fun like guys do', 'I feel less comfortable around female friends than male friends' and 'It is not as fun if there are women in the group.' Average factor loading was .77 (α=.92).

Social bonding: This 11-item factor focuses on the general need for social bonding and to be around others (eigenvalue=5.05; 8.71% of variance explained; M=2.68, SD=.81). Examples: 'I often need to be around others', 'I feel an intense need to be around friends' and 'I would rather hangout with a group than hangout with just one friend.' Average factor loading was .66 (α=.87).

Nostalgia: This 9-item factor echoes a theme of positive memories and reminiscence about one's time in the service (eigenvalue=4.96; 8.55% of variance explained; M=3.63, SD=1.01). Examples: 'I often thought about seeking redeployment/ reenlisting', 'I have more good memories with my military friends than bad' and 'I wanted to redeploy/reenlist because I missed the excitement.' Average factor loading was .69 (α=.89).

Drug use: This 4-item factor focused on recreational drug use (eigenvalue=3.11; 5.36% of variance explained: M=1.34, SD=0.79). Examples: 'I enjoy doing illegal drugs (marijuana, cocaine, crack, speed, etc.)' and 'I often get high.' Average factor loading was .85 (α=.88).

Notes

Introduction

1 Fry, R. (2013, October 18), *Millennials Still Lag in Forming their own Households*. Retrieved May 9, 2014, from Pew Research Center: http://www.pewresearch.org/fact-tank/2013/10/18/ millennials-still-lag-in-forming-their-own-households/.

2 Fry, R. (2013, August 1), *A Rising Share of Young Adults Live in Their Parents' Home*. Retrieved May 9, 2014, from Pew Research Center: http://www.pewsocialtrends. org/2013/08/01/a-rising-share-of-young-adults-live-in-their-parents-home/.

3 Miller, C.C. (2014, November 7), 'Paternity Leave: The Rewards and the Remaining Stigma'. Retrieved November 7, 2014, from the *New York Times*: http://www.nytimes.com/2014/11/09/upshot/paternity-leave-the-rewards-and-the-remaining-stigma.html.

4 Budnikov, M., personal communication, May 28, 2012 and June 19, 2012.

5 Robinson, M., personal communication, November 13, 2014; and Wilson, G. (2014), *Your Brain on Porn: Internet Pornography and the Emerging Science of Addiction*. Kent, England: Commonwealth Publishing.

6 Liew, J. (2009, December 2), 'All Men Watch Porn, Scientists Find'. Retrieved October 10, 2014, from the *Telegraph*: http://www.telegraph. co.uk/women/sex/6709646/All-men-watch-porn-scientists-find.html.

7 Abel, I. (2013, January 12), 'Did Porn Warp me Forever?' Retrieved June 24, 2014, from Salon: http://www.salon.com/2013/01/13/did_porn_ warp_me_forever/; and Sanghani, R. (2013, September 30), 'Teenage Boys Addicted to "Extreme" Porn and Want Help'. Retrieved June 24, 2014, from the *Telegraph*: http://www.telegraph.co.uk/women/sex/ better-sex-education/10339424/Teenage-boys-addicted-to-extreme-porn-and-want-help.html.

8 Ogas, O. and Gaddam, S. (2011), *A Billion Wicked Thoughts: What the World's Largest Experiment Reveals About Human Desire* (pp. 14, 19, 23–34). New York, NY: Penguin Group (USA), Inc.

9 Ibid. (pp. 74, 123–6).

10 Hebert, E. (n.d.), 'Busy NYC Restaurant Solves Major Mystery by Reviewing Old Surveillance'. Retrieved July 22, 2014, from DineAbility: http://dineability.com/busy-nyc-restaurant-solves-major-mystery-reviewing-old-surveillance/.

11 Thompson, C. (2007, September 25), 'Your Outboard Brain Knows All'. Retrieved May 9, 2014, from *Wired*: http://archive.wired.com/techbiz/people/magazine/15-10/st_thompson.

12 American Academy of Pediatrics (2013), 'Children, Adolescents, and the Media', *Pediatrics*, *132(5)* (pp. 958–9). Retrieved June 7, 2014, from http://pediatrics.aappublications.org/content/early/2013/10/24/peds.2013-2656.full.pdf+html.

13 Turkle, S. (2012, February), 'Connected, but Alone?' Retrieved April 21, 2014, from TED: http://www.ted.com/talks/sherry_turkle_alone_together.

Part I

1. Disenchantment with Education

1 Brooks, D. (2007, October 26), 'The Outsourced Brain'. Retrieved May 17, 2014, from the *New York Times*: http://www.nytimes.com/2007/10/26/opinion/26brooks.html.

2 Turk, G. (2014, April 25), 'Look Up'. Retrieved May 7, 2014, from YouTube: https://www.youtube.com/watch?v=Z7dLU6fk9QY.

3 Carr, N.G. (2010), *The Shallows: What the Internet Is Doing to Our Brains* (p. 162). New York: W.W. Norton.

4 'The Personal News Cycle' (2014, March). Retrieved June 5, 2014, from the Media Insight Project, American Press Institute: http://www.americanpressinstitute.org/wp-content/uploads/2014/03/The_Media_Insight_Project_The_Personal_News_Cycle_Final.pdf.

5 Voyer, D. (2014, April 9), 'April 29, 2014 Girls Make Higher Grades than Boys in All School Subjects, Analysis Finds'. Retrieved July 22, 2014, from American Psychological Assocation: http://www.apa.org/news/press/releases/2014/04/girls-grades.aspx; also see Voyer, D. and Voyer, S.D. (2014), 'Gender Differences in Scholastic Achievement: A Meta-Analysis', *Psychological Bulletin*, *140(4)*. Retrieved July 22, 2014, from http://www.apa.org/pubs/journals/releases/bul-a0036620.pdf.

6 Cribb, R. (2011, November 25), 'The Grim Evidence That Men Have Fallen Behind Women'. Retrieved November 26, 2011, from *Toronto*

Star: http://www.thestar.com/life/2011/11/25/rob_cribb_the_grim_
evidence_that_men_have_fallen_behind_women.html.

7 Salahu-Din, D., Persky, H., and Miller, J. (2008), *The Nation's Report Card:
Writing 2007* (p. 68). Retrieved November 11, 2011, from National Center
for Education Statistics, Institute of Education Sciences, US Department
of Education (NCES 2008-468): http://nces.ed.gov/nationsreportcard/
pdf/main2007/2008468.pdf; and Lee, J., Grigg, W., and Donahue, P.
(2007), *The Nation's Report Card: Reading 2007* (p. 64). Retrieved
November 11, 2011, from National Center for Education Statistics,
Institute of Education Sciences, US Department of Education (NCES
2007-496): http://nces.ed.gov/nationsreportcard/pdf/
main2007/2007496.pdf.

8 Strauss, V. (2011, September 14), 'What the Decline in SAT Scores
Really Means'. Retrieved December 8, 2011, from the *Washington Post*:
http://www.washingtonpost.com/blogs/answer-sheet/post/what-the-
decline-in-sat-scores-really-means/2011/09/14/gIQAdUzdSK_blog.
html; and Steinberg, K. (2011, September 14), '43% of 2011 College-
Bound Seniors Met SAT College and Career Readiness Benchmark'.
Retrieved December 8, 2011, from the College Board: http://media.
collegeboard.com/pdf/cbs_2011_nat_release_091411.pdf.

9 Stern, P. (Director) (2006), *Raising Cain: Boys in Focus* [documentary].
United States: PBS Films.

10 *Equity and Quality in Education: Supporting Disadvantaged Students and
Schools* (p. 22) (2012). Retrieved June 8, 2014, from Organisation for
Economic Co-operation and Development: http://www.oecd.org/
education/school/50293148.pdf.

11 *PISA 2009 at a Glance* (p. 22) (2010). Retrieved June 8, 2014, from
Organisation for Economic Co-operation and Development: http://
www.oecd-ilibrary.org/docserver/download/9810131ec008.
pdf?expires=1402278232&id=id&accname=guest&check-
sum=BDB231357DFDA0AEA929A60B339F737C.

12 *United Kingdom* (n.d.). Retrieved September 23, 2014, from OECD Better
Life Index: http://www.oecdbetterlifeindex.org/countries/
united-kingdom/.

13 Sommers, C.H. (2013), *The War Against Boys: How Misguided Policies Are
Harming Our Young Men* (p. 14). New York, NY: Simon & Schuster.

14 Planty, M., et al. (2007, June), *The Condition of Education 2007* (NCES
2007-064). Retrieved June 5, 2014, from National Center for Education
Statistics, Institute of Education Sciences, US Department of Education:
http://nces.ed.gov/pubs2007/2007064.pdf.

15 *Attention-Deficit / Hyperactivity Disorder (ADHD)* (n.d.). Retrieved June 8,
2014, from Division of Human Development, National Center on Birth
Defects and Developmental Disabilities, Centers for Disease Control
and Prevention: http://www.cdc.gov/ncbddd/adhd/data.html.

16 Note: According to NCES, in the US between 2008 and 2009, boys were about 22 per cent more likely than girls to have dropped out of high school. Average percentage taken between these two sources (13 per cent and 30 per cent, respectively).

See: Chapman, C., Laird, J., and KewalRamani, A. (2010, December), *Trends in High School Dropout and Completion Rates in the United States: 1972–2008* (NCES 2011-012) (p. 24). Retrieved June 5, 2014, from National Center for Education Statistics, Institute of Education Sciences, US Department of Education: http://nces.ed.gov/pubs2011/2011012.pdf; and Chapman, C., Laird, N., Ifill, N., and KewalRamani, A. (2011, October), *Trends in High School Dropout and Completion Rates in the United States: 1972–2009* (IES 2012-006) (p. 22). Retrieved June 5, 2014, from National Center for Education Statistics, Institute of Education Sciences, US Department of Education: http://nces.ed.gov/pubs2012/2012006.pdf.

Note: In Canada, five boys drop out for every three girls who do.

See: Richards, J. (2011, January 6), 'School Dropouts: Who Are They and What Can Be Done?' (p. 1). Retrieved December 26, 2011, from C.D. Howe Institute: http://www.cdhowe.org/pdf/ebrief_109.pdf.

17 Chapman, C., Laird, J., and KewalRamani, A. (2010, December), *Trends in High School Dropout and Completion Rates in the United States: 1972–2008* (NCES 2011-012) (p. 1). Retrieved June 5, 2014, from National Center for Education Statistics, Institute of Education Sciences, US Department of Education: http://nces.ed.gov/pubs2011/2011012.pdf.

18 *America's Young Adults at 27: Labor Market Activity, Education, and Household Composition: Results From a Longitudinal Survey Summary* (2014, March 26). Retrieved May 7, 2014, from Bureau of Labor Statistics, US Department of Labor (USDL-14-0491): http://www.bls.gov/news.release/nlsyth.nr0.htm.

19 Hussar, W.J. and Bailey, T.M. (2013, January), *Projections of Education Statistics to 2021* (NCES 2013-008) (pp. 75–7). Retrieved May 9, 2014, from National Center for Education Statistics, Institute of Education Sciences, US Department of Education: http://nces.ed.gov/pubs2013/2013008.pdf.

20 Frenette, M. and Zeman, K. (2008, December 1), *Why Are Most University Students Women? Evidence Based on Academic Performance, Study Habits and Parental Influences*. Retrieved September 22, 2014, from Statistics Canada: http://www.statcan.gc.ca/pub/81-004-x/2008001/article/10561-eng.htm; and Maslen, G. (2013, November 25), 'Degrees of Separation: More Women Enrolling at Universities'. Retrieved September 22, 2014, from the *Sydney Morning Herald*: http://www.smh.com.au/national/education/degrees-of-separation-more-women-enrolling-at-universities-20131124-2y46e.html.

21 Griffiths, S. (2013, August 18), 'Girls Crowd the Campus as Boys Lose Taste for Uni'. Retrieved June 20, 2014, from the *Sunday Times*: http://www.thesundaytimes.co.uk/sto/news/uk_news/Education/article1302079.ece.

22 Kirkup, J. (2014, January 31), 'Boys being Left Behind as University Gender Gap Widens'. Retrieved October 10, 2014, from the *Telegraph*: http://www.telegraph.co.uk/education/educationnews/10608739/Boys-being-left-behind-as-university-gender-gap-widens.html.

23 *Degrees Conferred by Sex and Race* (2012). Retrieved June 5, 2014, from National Center for Education Statistics, Institute of Education Sciences, US Department of Education: http://nces.ed.gov/fastfacts/display.asp?id=72.

2. Men Opting Out of the Workforce

1 Symonds, W.C., Schwartz, R.B., and Ferguson, R. (2011, February), 'Pathways to Prosperity: Meeting the Challenge of Preparing Young Americans for the 21st Century' (pp. 4–5). Retrieved May 30, 2014, from Report issued by the Pathways to Prosperity Project, Harvard Graduate School of Education: http://www.gse.harvard.edu/news_events/features/2011/Pathways_to_Prosperity_Feb2011.pdf.

2 *United Kingdom* (n.d.). Retrieved September 23, 2014, from OECD Better Life Index: http://www.oecdbetterlifeindex.org/countries/united-kingdom/.

3 *Labour Force Statistics by Sex and Age – Indicators* (n.d.). Retrieved May 12, 2014, from Organisation for Economic Co-operation and Development: http://stats.oecd.org/.

4 Coombes, A. (2009, July 16), '*Men Suffer Brunt of Job Losses in Recession*'. Retrieved May 10, 2014, from the Wall Street Journal: http://online.wsj.com/news/articles/SB10001424052970203577304574272570149153010.

5 Hartmann, H., Shaw, E., and Pandya, E. (2013, November), *Women and Men in the Recovery: Where the Jobs Are* (p. 12). Retrieved November 17, 2014, from Institute for Women's Policy Research: www.iwpr.org.

3. Excessive Maleness: Social Intensity Syndrome (SIS)

1 Carducci, B., personal communication, December 4, 2014.

2 Ibid.

3 Loewe, F. and Lerner, A.J., 'A Hymn to Him' *[originally released in 1956 by Sony BMG Music Entertainment]* (n.d.). Retrieved February 21, 2012, from ST Lyrics: http://www.stlyrics.com/lyrics/myfairlady/ahymntohim.htm.

4 'Pornhub Traffic Change During Super Bowl XLVIII' (2014, February 4). Retrieved May 12, 2014, from PornHub: http://www.pornhub.com/insights/pornhub-super-bowl/.

5 'Frequently Asked Questions' (n.d.). Retrieved May 12, 2014, from BroApp: http://broapp.net/faq.html.

6 Martin, A. (2011, January 14), 'Young Men, Couples Shunning Sex'. Retrieved January 14, 2011, from the Japan Times: http://www.japantimes.co.jp/news/2011/01/14/national/young-men-couples-shunning-sex/#.U27MwV6JUwI.

4. Excessive Gaming: Mastering the Universe from Your Bedroom

1 The U.S. Digital Consumer Report (2014, February 10). Retrieved April 28, 2014, from Neilsen: http://www.nielsen.com/us/en/reports/2014/the-us-digital-consumer-report.html.

2 McGonigal, J. (2011), Reality Is Broken: Why Games Make Us Better and How They Can Change The World (Inside cover, pp. 4, 6). New York, NY: Penguin Press.

3 Note: This calculation is based on the average university requirement of 120 credit hours, with each credit hour involving 2.5 hours of homework and class time. Take an average of 15 hours of actual class time and 22.5 hours of homework outside class each week – 37.5 hours – multiplied by 16 weeks per semester, multiplied by 8 semesters, and you've got 4,800 hours. See also the table 'Time Bandit' in Chapter 19.

4 Gentile, D.A. (2004), 'The Effects of Violent Video Game Habits on Adolescent Hostility, Aggressive Behaviours, and School Performance', Journal of Adolescence, 27, 6.

5 Albanesius, C. (2010, December 27), '"Call of Duty: Black Ops" Gamers Log 600M Hours of Play Time'. Retrieved June 20, 2014, from PC Mag: http://www.pcmag.com/article2/0,2817,2374762,00.asp.

6 Thier, D. (2013, September 18), '"GTA 5" Sells $800 Million in One Day'. Retrieved April 20, 2014, from Forbes: http://www.forbes.com/sites/davidthier/2013/09/18/gta-5-sells-800-million-in-one-day/.

7 Erik, K. (2013, September 20), '"Grand Theft Auto V" Crosses $1B in Sales, Biggest Entertainment Launch in History'. Retrieved April 20, 2014, from Forbes: http://www.forbes.com/sites/erikkain/2013/09/20/grand-theft-auto-v-crosses-1b-in-sales-biggest-entertainment-launch-in-history/.

8 Nayak, M. (2013, June 10), 'FACTBOX – A Look at the $66 billion Video-games Industry'. Retrieved April 29, 2014, from Reuters: http://in.reuters.com/article/2013/06/10/gameshow-e-idINDEE9590DW20130610.

9 *Education Department Budget History Table* (2013, October 30). Retrieved May 17, 2014, from US Department of Education: https://www2. ed.gov/about/overview/budget/history/edhistory.pdf.

10 *BookStats Overall Highlights* (n.d.). Retrieved November 11, 2011, from Association of American Publishers: http://www.publishers.org/ bookstats/highlights/.

11 *Total Circ: Consumer Magazines* (n.d.). Retrieved April 30, 2014, from Alliance for Audited Media: http://abcas3.auditedmedia.com/ecirc/ magtitlesearch.asp.

12 Retrieved November 17, 2014, from Alexa: http://www.alexa.com.

13 Kent, S. (2001), *The Ultimate History of Video Games: The Story behind the Craze that Touched our Lives and Changed the World* (p. 152). Roseville, CA: Prima Publishing/Random House.

14 Bai, M. (2013, December 31), 'Master of His Virtual Domain'. Retrieved June 25, 2014, from the *New York Times*: http://www.nytimes. com/2013/12/22/technology/master-of-his-virtual-domain. html?pagewanted=1&ref=video-games.

15 *Free to Play: The Movie* (2014). Retrieved June 30, 2014, from YouTube: https://www.youtube.com/watch?v=UjZYMI1zB9s.

16 Davis, N. (2014, July/August), 'Game Changers', *Playboy: Entertainment For Men*, *61(6)*, 18.

17 American Academy of Pediatrics (2013), 'Children, Adolescents, and the Media', *Pediatrics*, 132(5) (p. 959). Retrieved June 7, 2014, from http:// pediatrics.aappublications.org/content/early/2013/10/24/peds.2013- 2656.full.pdf+html.

18 *Children and Parents: Media Use and Attitudes Report* (2014, October) (p. 9). Retrieved November 17, 2014, from Ofcom: http://stakeholders.ofcom. org.uk/binaries/research/media-literacy/media-use-attitudes-14/ Childrens_2014_Report.pdf.

19 *Sleep and Teens* (n.d.). Retrieved June 17, 2014, from UCLA Sleep Disorders Center, University of California, Los Angeles: http:// sleepcenter.ucla.edu/body.cfm?id=63.

20 National Sleep Foundation, *2014 Sleep In America Poll Finds Children Sleep Better When Parents Establish Rules, Limit Technology and Set a Good Example* (2014, March 3). Retrieved June 17, 2014, from National Sleep Foundation: http://sleepfoundation.org/media-center/press-release/ national-sleep-foundation-2014-sleep-america-poll-finds-children-sleep.

21 *Sleep and Teens* (n.d.). Retrieved June 17, 2014, from UCLA Sleep Disorders Center, University of California, Los Angeles: http:// sleepcenter.ucla.edu/body.cfm?id=63.

22 National Sleep Foundation, *2014 Sleep In America Poll Finds Children Sleep Better When Parents Establish Rules, Limit Technology and Set a Good*

Example (2014, March 3). Retrieved June 17, 2014, from National Sleep Foundation: http://sleepfoundation.org/media-center/press-release/national-sleep-foundation-2014-sleep-america-poll-finds-children-sleep.

23 *Children and Parents: Media Use and Attitudes Report* (2014, October) (p. 5). Retrieved November 17, 2014, from Ofcom: http://stakeholders.ofcom.org.uk/binaries/research/media-literacy/media-use-attitudes-14/Childrens_2014_Report.pdf.

24 Paton, G. (2014, April 15), 'Infants "unable to use toy building blocks" due to iPad addiction'. Retrieved April 15, 2014, from the *Telegraph*: http://www.telegraph.co.uk/education/educationnews/10767878/Infants-unable-to-use-toy-building-blocks-due-to-iPad-addiction.html.

25 Ahlstrom, M., Lundberg, N.R., Zabriskie, R., Eggett, D., and Lindsay, G.B. (2012), 'Me, My Spouse, and My Avatar: The Relationship between Marital Satisfaction and Playing Massively Multiplayer Online Role-Playing Games (MMORPGs)', *Journal of Leisure Research*, 44(1). Retrieved June 20, 2014, from http://js.sagamorepub.com/jlr/article/view/2507.

26 (1982, September 10), 'Marriage Vows May Conquer Space Invaders', Reuters, *San Francisco Chronicle*.

27 Liu, M. (2008, October 19), 'Former "Game Widow" Shares her Heartache and How she got her Husband Back'. Retrieved May 11, 2014, from the *Seattle Times*: http://seattletimes.com/html/living/2008275940_gamewidow19.html; also see the site www.gamewidow.com.

5. Becoming Obese Banana Slugs

1 *Overweight and Obesity Rates for Adults by Gender, 2010* (n.d.). Retrieved April 29, 2014, from Henry J. Kaiser Family Foundation: http://kff.org/other/state-indicator/adult-overweightobesity-rate-by-gender/.

2 Ogden, C.L., Lamb, M.M., Carroll, M.D., and Flegal, K.M. (2010, December), *Obesity and Socioeconomic Status in Adults: Unites States, 2005–2008* (p. 1). Retrieved June 5, 2014, from National Center for Health Statistics, Centers for Disease Control and Prevention, US Department of Health and Human Services: http://www.cdc.gov/nchs/data/databriefs/db50.pdf.

3 *Adult Risk Factors: Obesity, Blood Sugar, Blood Pressure Data by Country* (2013). Retrieved May 30, 2014, from World Health Organization: http://apps.who.int/gho/data/node.main.NCD56?lang=en.

4 Painter, K. (2014, May 28), 'The Whole World has a Weight Problem, New Report Says'. Retrieved May 29, 2014, from *USA Today*: http://www.usatoday.com/story/news/nation/2014/05/28/world-obesity-report/9675267/.

5 Christeson, W., et al. (2012), *Still Too Fat to Fight*. Retrieved May 16, 2014, from Mission: Readiness: http://missionreadiness.s3.amazonaws.com/wp-content/uploads/Still-Too-Fat-To-Fight-Report.pdf.

6 Christeson, W., et al. (2010), *Too Fat to Fight*. Retrieved May 16, 2014, from Mission: Readiness: http://www.missionreadiness.org/wp-content/uploads/MR_Too_Fat_to_Fight-11.pdf.

7 Campbell, D. (2014, April 24), 'Jamie Oliver Calls for Crackdown on Junk Food being Sold Near Schools'. Retrieved October 10, 2014, from the *Guardian*: http://www.theguardian.com/lifeandstyle/2014/apr/25/jamie-oliver-crackdown-junk-food-schools.

8 *School Land: Decisions about Disposals* (2014, October 31). Retrieved November 17, 2014, from Gov.uk: https://www.gov.uk/government/publications/school-land-decisions-about-disposals.

9 Christeson, W., et al. (2010), *Too Fat to Fight*. Retrieved May 15, 2014, from Mission: Readiness: http://www.missionreadiness.org/wp-content/uploads/MR_Too_Fat_to_Fight-11.pdf.

10 Crawford, P.B. (2007), 'Key Partners Working Together to Stem Obesity Epidemic', *California Agriculture*, 61(3). Retrieved May 16, 2014, from http://ucce.ucdavis.edu/files/repository/calag/fullissues/CAv061n03.pdf.

11 Ogden, C.L. (n.d.), *Childhood Obesity in the United States: The Magnitude of the Problem*. Retrieved May 16, 2014, from Division of Health and Nutrition Examination Surveys, National Center for Health Statistics, Centers for Disease Control and Prevention: http://www.cdc.gov/cdcgrandrounds/pdf/gr-062010.pdf.

12 McMichael, W.H. (2009, November 3), 'Most U.S. Youths Unfit to Serve, Data Show'. Retrieved May 15, 2014, from *Army Times*: http://www.armytimes.com/article/20091103/NEWS/911030311/Most-U-S-youths-unfit-serve-data-show.

13 Ibid.

14 Ogas, O. and Gaddam, S. (2011), *A Billion Wicked Thoughts: What the World's Largest Experiment Reveals About Human Desire* (p. 198). New York, NY: Penguin Group (USA), Inc.

15 Golokhov, D. (n.d.), 'Weight Loss and Sex'. Retrieved December 31, 2011, from AskMen: http://www.askmen.com/daily/sex_tips_400/421_lose-weight-for-better-sex.html; and University of Buffalo study described in 'Male Obesity Linked to Low Testosterone Levels, Study Shows' (2010, May 5). Retrieved February 21, 2012, from *ScienceDaily*: http://www.sciencedaily.com/releases/2010/05/100503135659.htm.

16 Tremblay, L. (2011, March 28), 'High Oestrogen Signs and Symptoms in Men'. Retrieved January 10, 2012, from *Livestrong*: http://www.livestrong.com/article/127328-high-oestrogen-symptoms-men/.

17 Fulton, A. (2010, May 4), 'Some Teens Who Sleep Less Gain More Weight'. Retrieved January 10, 2012, from National Public Radio: http://www.npr.org/blogs/health/2010/05/some_teens_who_sleep_less_gain.html?ps=rs.

18 Ogden, C.L. (n.d.), *Childhood Obesity in the United States: The Magnitude of the Problem*. Retrieved May 16, 2014, from Division of Health and Nutrition Examination Surveys, National Center for Health Statistics, Centers for Disease Control and Prevention: http://www.cdc.gov/cdcgrandrounds/pdf/gr-062010.pdf.

19 *Why People Become Overweight* (n.d.). Retrieved January 10, 2012, from Harvard Medical School: http://www.health.harvard.edu/newsweek/Why-people-become-overweight.htm.

20 Bellows, L. and Moore, R. (2013, March), *Childhood Overweight*. Retrieved June 27, 2014, from Colorado State University: http://www.ext.colostate.edu/pubs/foodnut/09317.html.

6. Excessive Porn Use: Orgasms on Demand

1 Stein, J. (2014, May), 'The Great Porn Hunt', *Playboy: Entertainment For Men*, 61(4), 34.

2 Rumbelow, H. (2014, November 17), 'The Boys Want to Know – "What can I Get Away With?"', *The Times*, p. 3.

3 Ogas, O. and Gaddam, S. (2011), *A Billion Wicked Thoughts: What the World's Largest Experiment Reveals About Human Desire* (pp. 6–7). New York, NY: Penguin Group (USA), Inc. Also see: Morley-Souter, P. (2007, June 25). 'Rule 34: There is Porn of It. No Exceptions', *Blogspot*: http://rule34.blogspot.com/2007/06/first-post.html.

4 Mazléres, A., Trachman, M., Cointet, J., Coulmont, B., and Prieur, C. (2014, March 21), 'Deep Tags: Toward a Quantitative Analysis of Online Pornography', *Porn Studies*, 1(1–2). Retrieved June 27, 2014, from http://www.tandfonline.com/doi/abs/10.1080/23268743.2014.888214?journalCode=rprn20#.U64XnF5tswI.

5 Ogas, O. and Gaddam, S. (2011), *A Billion Wicked Thoughts: What the World's Largest Experiment Reveals About Human Desire* (p. 8). New York, NY: Penguin Group (USA), Inc.

6 Ropelato, J. (n.d.), *Internet Pornography Statistics*. Retrieved November 17, 2011, from Top Ten Reviews, TechMediaNetwork: http://internet-filter-review.toptenreviews.com/internet-pornography-statistics.html.

7 *PornHub 2013 Year in Review* (2013, December 17). Retrieved June 25, 2014, from PornHub Insights: http://www.pornhub.com/insights/pornhub-2013-year-in-review/.

8 Ropelato, J. (n.d.), *Internet Pornography Statistics*. Retrieved November 17, 2011, from Top Ten Reviews, TechMediaNetwork: http://internet-filter-review.toptenreviews.com/internet-pornography-statistics.html.

9 'Introducing the Future of Pornography Viewing: PornIQ' (2013, October 5). Retrieved June 25, 2014, from PornHub Insights: http://www.pornhub.com/insights/introducing-the-future-of-pornography-viewing-porniq/.

10 *Children and Parents: Media Use and Attitudes Report* (2014, October) (p. 232). Retrieved November 17, 2014, from Ofcom: http://stakeholders.ofcom.org.uk/binaries/research/media-literacy/media-use-attitudes-14/Childrens_2014_Report.pdf.

11 Betkowski, B. (2007, March 2), *Study Finds Teen Boys Most Likely to Access Pornography*. Retrieved June 16, 2014, from University of Alberta: http://www.ualberta.ca/~publicas/folio/44/13/09.html.

12 *Daily Mail* Reporter (2011, April 22), 'Young Men Watch TWO HOURS of Porn Online Each Week ... and One in Three have Missed a Deadline Because of It'. Retrieved June 16, 2014, from *Daily Mail*: http://www.dailymail.co.uk/news/article-1379464/Porn-Young-men-watch-2-HOURS-week-missed-deadline-it.html.

13 Beyens, I., Vandenbosch, L., and Eggermont, S. (2015), 'Early Adolescent Boys' Exposure to Internet Pornography: Relationships to Pubertal Timing, Sensation Seeking, and Academic Performance', *Journal of Early Adolescence* (in-press). Retrieved September 29, 2014, from https://lirias.kuleuven.be/handle/123456789/458526.

14 Marshall, P. (2010, March 8), 'Teenage Boys Watching Hours of Internet Pornography Every Week Are Treating Their Girlfriends Like Sex Objects'. Retrieved November 22, 2011, from *Daily Mail*: http://www.dailymail.co.uk/news/article-1255856/Teenage-boys-watching-hours-internet-pornography-week-treating-girlfriends-like-sex-objects.html.

15 Trost, M. (2009, December 2), 'Cindy Gallop: Make Love Not Porn'. Retrieved February 18, 2015, from TEDblog: http://blog.ted.com/2009/12/02/cindy-gallop_ma/.

16 Sanghani, R. (2013, September 30), 'Teenage Boys Addicted to "Extreme" Porn and Want Help'. Retrieved June 24, 2014, from the *Telegraph*: http://www.telegraph.co.uk/women/sex/better-sex-education/10339424/Teenage-boys-addicted-to-extreme-porn-and-want-help.html.

17 *500 Online Interviews amongst UK Adults aged 18* (2014, June). Retrieved October 8, 2014, from Institute for Public Policy Research: http://www.ippr.org/assets/media/publications/attachments/OP4391-IPPR-Data-Tables.pdf.

18 'Burnet Studies Shed Light on Sexual Behaviour of Teenagers' (2014, October 9). Retrieved October 9, 2014, from Burnet Institute: http://www.burnet.edu.au/news/435_burnet_studies_shed_light_on_sexual_behaviour_of_teenagers.

19 Saletan, W. (n.d.), 'The Ass Man Cometh'. Retrieved October 8, 2014, from Slate: http://www.slate.com/articles/health_and_science/human_nature/2010/10/the_ass_man_cometh.html; also see Reece, M,. et al. (2010). Special Issue: Findings from the National Survey of Sexual Health and Behaviour (NSSHB), Center for Sexual Health Promotion, Indiana University. *The Journal of Sexual Medicine, 7(s5)*. http://onlinelibrary.wiley.com/doi/10.1111/jsm.2010.7.issue-s5/issuetoc.

20 James, S.D. (2008, December 10), 'Study Reports Anal Sex on Rise Among Teens'. Retrieved October 8, 2014, from ABC News: http://abcnews.go.com/Health/story?id=6428003.

21 Cates, J.R., Herndon, N.L., Schulz, S.L., and Darroch, J.E. (2004, February), *Our Lives, Our Futures: Youth and Sexually Transmitted Diseases* (p. 1). Retrieved July 22, 2014, from School of Journalism and Mass Communication, University of North Carolina at Chapel Hill: http://joancates.web.unc.edu/files/2010/11/Our-Voices-Our-Lives-Our-Futures-Youth-and-Sexually-Transmitted-Diseases.pdf.

7. High on Life, or High on Anything: Over-reliance on Medications and Illegal Drugs

1 Sax, L. (2009), *Boys Adrift: The Five Factors Driving the Growing Epidemic of Unmotivated Boys and Underachieving Young Men* (p. 88). New York, NY: Basic Books.

2 Ibid. (pp. 89–91).

3 Stern, P. (Director) (2006), *Raising Cain: Boys in Focus* [documentary]. United States: PBS Films.

Note: Since 2010 in the US, the Affordable Care Act (ACA) has allowed under-26-year-olds to remain on their parents' health insurance. The following year, 19- to 25-year-olds were the only age group whose number of prescriptions increased. ADHD medications were 28 per cent of all the newly prescribed medications for the group, followed by antidepressants, which made up 16 per cent of new medications.

See: *The Use of Medicines in the United States: Review of 2011* (2012, April) (pp. 11–12, 29). Retrieved May 30, 2014, from IMS Institute for Healthcare Informatics: http://www.imshealth.com/ims/Global/Content/Insights/IMS%20Institute%20for%20Healthcare%20Informatics/IHII_Medicines_in_U.S_Report_2011.pdf.

4 Meserve, J. and Ahlers, M.M. (2009, May 14), 'Marijuana Potency Surpasses 10 per cent, U.S. Says'. Retrieved November 22, 2011, from CNN: http://articles.cnn.com/2009-05-14/health/marijuana.potency_1_average-thc-potent-marijuana-marijuana-users?_s=PM:HEALTH.

5 Sterling, T. (2011, October 8), 'Dutch Classify High-Potency Marijuana as Hard Drug'. Retrieved November 22, 2011, from SF Gate: http://www.sfgate.com/cgi-bin/article.cgi?f=/c/a/2011/10/07/MNQO1LES53.DTL.

6 Ramaekers J.G., et al. (2006), 'High-Potency Marijuana Impairs Executive Function and Inhibitory Motor Control', *Neuropsychopharmacology,* 10, 2296–303.

7 Zimbardo, P.G. and Boyd, J. (2009), *The Time Paradox: The New Psychology of Time That Will Change Your Life.* New York, NY: Atria Books.

Part II

8. Rudderless Families, Absent Dads

1 Table 8. *Average Class Size for Public School Teachers in Elementary Schools, Secondary Schools, and Schools with Combined Grades, by Classroom Type and State: 2007–08* (n.d.). Retrieved June 30, 2014, from US Department of Education, National Center for Education Statistics, Schools and Staffing Survey (SASS): http://nces.ed.gov/surveys/sass/tables/sass0708_2009324_t1s_08.asp.

2 Salcedo, A., Schoellman, T., and Tertilt, M. (2009, October), *Families as Roommates: Changes in U.S. Household Size from 1850 to 2000.* Retrieved February 21, 2012, from Stanford Institute for Economic Policy Research: http://www.stanford.edu/group/siepr/cgi-bin/siepr/?q=system/files/shared/pubs/papers/pdf/09-01.pdf.

3 O'Grady, S. (2013, March 8), 'Rise of the Single-parent Family'. Retrieved October 10, 2014, from *Express*: http://www.express.co.uk/news/uk/382706/Rise-of-the-single-parent-family.

4 Szalavitz, M. and Perry, B.D. (2010), *Born for Love: Why Empathy Is Essential – and Endangered* (p. 16). New York, NY: HarperCollins.

5 Martin, J.A., Hamilton, B.E., Osterman, M.J., Curtin, S.C., and Mathews, T.J. (2013, December 30), *Births: Final Data for 2012.* Retrieved May 19, 2014, from National Vital Statistics Reports, Centers for Disease Control and Prevention: http://www.cdc.gov/nchs/data/nvsr/nvsr62/nvsr62_09.pdf#table02.

6 Note: US birth rates by race for women under 30 – Blacks: 73 per cent; Hispanics: 53 per cent; Whites: 29 per cent.

See: DeParle, J. and Tavernise, S. (2012, February 17), 'For Women Under 30, Most Births Occur Outside Marriage'. Retrieved February 21, 2012, from the *New York Times*: http://www.nytimes.com/2012/02/18/us/for-women-under-30-most-births-occur-outside-marriage.html.

7 Cribb, R. (2011, November 25), 'The Grim Evidence That Men Have Fallen Behind Women'. Retrieved November 26, 2011, from *Toronto Star*: http://www.thestar.com/life/2011/11/25/rob_cribb_the_grim_evidence_that_men_have_fallen_behind_women.html.

8 *Families and Households, 2013* (2013, October 31) (p. 4). Retrieved October 10, 2014, from Office for National Statistics: http://www.ons.gov.uk/ons/dcp171778_332633.pdf.

9 O'Grady, S. (2013, March 8), 'Rise of the Single-parent Family'. Retrieved October 10, 2014, from *Express*: http://www.express.co.uk/news/uk/382706/Rise-of-the-single-parent-family.

10 Lawlor, J. (1987, August 17), 'The Time Crunch; Poll: We Zoom through Life in Fast Forward', *USA Today*, p. 1A.

11 Saad, L. (2013, December 26), *Most U.S. Families Still Routinely Dine Together at Home*. Retrieved July 26, 2014, from Gallup: http://www.gallup.com/poll/166628/families-routinely-dine-together-home.aspx.

12 *The Importance of Family Dinners VII* (Figure 1.A., 2.A.) (2011, September). Retrieved November 22, 2011, from the National Center on Addiction and Substance Abuse at Columbia University: http://www.casacolumbia.org/upload/2011/2011922familydinnersVII.pdf.

13 Shteynberg, C. (2009, June 16), 'How Many Stamps Does it Take to Mail a Baby?'. Retrieved May 11, 2014, from Smithsonian Institution Archives: http://siarchives.si.edu/blog/how-many-stamps-does-it-take-mail-baby.

14 Retrieved June 9, 2014, from NannyCam: http://www.nannycam.com/.

15 For 1960, Larsen, C.A. (2013), *The Rise and Fall of Social Cohesion: The Construction and De-construction of Social Trust in the US, UK, Sweden and Denmark* (p. 12). United Kingdom: Oxford University Press; and for 2009, Hampton, K., Goulet, L.S., Rainie, L., and Purcell, K. (2011, June 16), *Part 4: Trust, Support, Perspective Taking, and Democratic Engagement*. Retrieved October 10, 2014, from Pew Research Center: http://www.pewinternet.org/2011/06/16/part-4-trust-support-perspective-taking-and-democratic-engagement/.

16 *Millennials in Adulthood* (2014, March 7). Retrieved October 10, 2014, from Pew Research Center: http://www.pewsocialtrends.org/2014/03/07/millennials-in-adulthood/.

17 Larsen, C.A. (2013), *The Rise and Fall of Social Cohesion: The Construction and De-construction of Social Trust in the US, UK, Sweden and Denmark* (p. 12). United Kingdom: Oxford University Press.

18 Putnam, R.D. (2001), *Bowling Alone: The Collapse and Revival of American Community* (p. 138). New York, NY: Touchstone Books.

19 Gottman, J.M. and Silver, N. (2000), *The Seven Principles for Making Marriage Work: A Practical Guide from the Country's Foremost Relationship Expert* (pp. 5–6). New York, NY: Harmony.

20 'Divorce Rates' (1999, October 8). Retrieved May 7, 2014, from University of Maryland: http://www.vanneman.umd.edu/socy441/trends/divorce.html.

21 Gottman, J.M. and Silver, N. (2000). *The Seven Principles for Making Marriage Work: A Practical Guide from the Country's Foremost Relationship Expert* (p. 4). New York, NY: Harmony.

22 Chapman, J. (2011, April 18), *The Collapse of Family Life: Half of Children See Parents Split by 16 as Births outside Marriage Hit Highest Level for Two Centuries*. Retrieved May 7, 2014, from *Daily Mail*: http://www.dailymail.co.uk/news/article-1377940/Half-parents-split-16-births-outside-marriage-hit-highest-level-200-years.html#ixzz1wOdPJZTo.

23 FlorCruz, M. (2013, February 27), 'China's Divorce Rate Rises for Seventh Consecutive Year'. Retrieved May 9, 2014, from *International Business Times*: http://www.ibtimes.com/chinas-divorce-rate-rises-seventh-consecutive-year-1105053.

24 'Poland: The Soaring Divorce Rate' (2010, January 14). Retrieved May 7, 2014, from *European Journal*, DW: http://www.dw.de/european-journal-the-magazine-from-brussels-2010-01-14/e-5094566-9798.

25 Rosen, R. (2001), *The World Split Open: How the Modern Women's Movement Changed America* (p. 43). New York, NY: Penguin Books.

26 Parker, K. and Wang, W. (2013, March 14), *Modern Parenthood*. Retrieved June 7, 2014, from Pew Research Center: http://www.pewsocialtrends.org/2013/03/14/modern-parenthood-roles-of-moms-and-dads-converge-as-they-balance-work-and-family/.

27 Saad, G. (2013, November 14), *Do Men or Women File for Divorce More Often?* Retrieved December 4, 2014, from Psychology Today: http://www.psychologytoday.com/blog/homo-consumericus/201311/do-men-or-women-file-divorce-more-often.

28 'Why Do Women Win Most Custody Battles?' (n.d.). Retrieved May 17, 2014, from Attorneys.com: http://www.attorneys.com/child-custody/why-do-women-win-most-custody-battles/.

29 Farrell, W. (2001), *The Myth of Male Power: Why Men are the Disposable Sex* (p. 21). New York: Berkeley Books.

30 Vaillant, G.E. (2012), *Triumphs of Experience: The Men of the Harvard Grant Study* (p. 4). Cambridge, MA: Belknap Press.

31 Ibid. (p. 143).

32 Ibid. (p. 113).

33 Ibid. (pp. 118–19).

34 Glenn, N. and Whitehead, B.D. (2009), *MAMA SAYS: A National Survey of Mothers' Attitudes on Fathering* (p. 9). Retrieved June 26, 2014, from National Fatherhood Institute: http://www.fatherhood.org/mama-says-survey.

35 Zak, P. (2011), *Paul Zak: Trust, Morality — and Oxytocin?* Retrieved November 22, 2011, from TED Conferences: http://www.ted.com/talks/paul_zak_trust_morality_and_oxytocin.html; and Zak, P.J. and Knack, S. (2001). Trust and growth. *The Economic Journal*, 111, 295-321.

36 Larsen, C.A. (2013), *The Rise and Fall of Social Cohesion: The Construction and De-construction of Social Trust in the US, UK, Sweden and Denmark* (p. 12). United Kingdom: Oxford University Press.

37 Fukuyama, F. (1996). *Trust: The Social Virtues and the Creation of Prosperity* (p. 4). Free Press.

38 Murray, C. (2013), *Coming Apart: The State of White America, 1960–2010* (p. 169). New York, NY: Crown Forum.

39 Notes: The US National Longitudinal Survey of Youth reported married men spent the most time – 82 per cent of weeks – between 18 and 26 years old in the labour force while single men spent only 70 per cent of weeks and cohabiting men spent 75 per cent of weeks working. For women, there were no significant differences found in the number of weeks worked and partner status, but when a child was present, women worked only 65 per cent of weeks compared with 76 per cent of weeks for women with no child in the home. By 27 years old, 41 per cent of single women have a child living in their household, compared with 5 per cent of single men. Overall, single black women were the most likely group to have a child in their home while single Hispanic men were the least likely; single white men were nearly tied for least likely. For cohabiting couples, Hispanics and blacks were more than twice as likely as whites to have a child in the home. For married couples, black couples were the most likely to have a child while whites were the least likely. Only 15 per cent of blacks were married while 39 per cent of whites were. For those aged 35 and over, 25 per cent of black women, 26 per cent of black men, 8 per cent of white women and 12 per cent of white men were never married. More educated people were less likely to be cohabiting and more likely to be married. Regardless of ethnicity and partner status, having a bachelor's degree or higher also led to a significant drop in the likelihood of having a child in the home at 27 years old. By that age, just over one in four blacks and Hispanics who enrolled in university had received a bachelor's degree, compared to nearly half of whites.

See: *America's Young Adults at 27: Labor Market Activity, Education, and Household Composition: Results From a Longitudinal Survey Summary* (2014,

March 26). Retrieved May 7, 2014, from Bureau of Labor Statistics, US Department of Labor (USDL-14-0491): http://www.bls.gov/news. release/nlsyth.nr0.htm.

Note: see table 7 for ethnicity and the likelihood of having a child; and for never-married rates by ethnicity.

See: Elliott, D.B., Krivickas, K., Brault, M.W., and Kreider, R.M. (2012, May), *Historical Marriage Trends from 1890–2010: A Focus on Race Differences*. Retrieved May 9, 2014, from US Census Bureau: http:// www.census.gov/hhes/socdemo/marriage/data/acs/ ElliottetalPAA2012presentation.pdf; and for increase in never-married rates: Lofquist, D., Lugaila, T., O'Connell, M., and Feliz, S. (2012, April), *Households and Families: 2010* (C2010BR-14) (p. 3). Retrieved May 9, 2014, from US Census Bureau: https://www.census.gov/prod/ cen2010/briefs/c2010br-14.pdf.

40 *UK Labour Market, September 2014* (2014, September 17) (p. 9).Retrieved October 10, 2014, from Office for National Statistics: http://www.ons. gov.uk/ons/dcp171778_374770.pdf.

41 O'Grady, S. (2013, March 8), 'Rise of the Single-parent Family'. Retrieved October 10, 2014, from *Express*: http://www.express.co.uk/ news/uk/382706/Rise-of-the-single-parent-family.

42 *Families and Households, 2013* (2013, October 31) (p. 5). Retrieved October 10, 2014, from Office for National Statistics: http://www.ons. gov.uk/ons/dcp171778_332633.pdf.

43 Wilcox, W.B. (2011, August 30), 'A Shaky Foundation for Families'. Retrieved May 8, 2014, from the *New York Times*: http://www.nytimes. com/roomfordebate/2011/08/30/shotgun-weddings-vs-cohabitating-parents/cohabitation-is-a-shaky-foundation.

44 Szalavitz, M. and Perry, B.D. (2010), *Born for Love: Why Empathy Is Essential – and Endangered* (pp. 163, 167). New York, NY: HarperCollins.

45 Sandnes, H.E. (2014, February 9), *Dad is Important for His Children's Development*. Retrieved November 30, 2014, from Kilden Information Centre for Gender Research in Norway: http://eng.kilden. forskningsradet.no/c52778/nyhet/vis.html?tid=88722.

46 Vaillant, G.E. (2012), *Triumphs of Experience: The Men of the Harvard Grant Study* (p. 357). Cambridge, MA: Belknap Press.

47 Ibid. (p. 115).

48 Bolick, K. (2011, November), 'All the Single Ladies', *Atlantic* magazine, 120.

49 Stern, P. (Director) (2006), *Raising Cain: Boys in Focus* [documentary]. United States: PBS Films.

50 *Fractured Families: Why Stability Matters* (2013, June) (p. 20). Retrieved October 10, 2014, from the Centre for Social Justice: http://www. centreforsocialjustice.org.uk/UserStorage/pdf/Pdf%20reports/ CSJ_Fractured_Families_Report_WEB_13.06.13.pdf.

51 Borden, C. and Obsatz, K. (Directors) (2007), *Journeyman* [documentary]. United States: MirrorMan Films.

52 Perera, J. (2013, October 5), 'What I Like and Don't Like About Being a Boy: Thoughts from a Group of Grade 4 Boys'. Retrieved May 15, 2014, from Higher Unlearning: http://higherunlearning.com/2013/10/05/what-i-like-and-dont-like-about-being-a-boy-thoughts-from-a-group-of-grade-4-boys/.

53 Co, P., Maggiore, N., and Unay, J. (Cinematographers) (2014), *Free to Play* [documentary]. United States: Valve.

54 Hjern, A., Weitoft, G.R., and Lindblad, F. (2010, June), 'Social Adversity Predicts ADHD-Medication in School Children – A National Cohort Study'. Retrieved November 22, 2011, from *Acta Paediatrica*: http://onlinelibrary.wiley.com/doi/10.1111/j.1651-2227.2009.01638.x/pdf.

55 Dawson, D.A. (1991, June), *Family Structure and Children's Health: United States, 1988* (Table 13). Retrieved November 22, 2011, from US Department of Health and Human Services, Centers for Disease Control and Prevention, National Center for Health Statistics: http://www.cdc.gov/nchs/data/series/sr_10/sr10_178.pdf.

56 Borden, C. and Obsatz, K. (Directors) (2007), *Journeyman* [documentary]. United States: MirrorMan Films.

57 Ibid.

58 Guidubaldi, J. (1987), 'Growing Up in a Divorced Family: Initial and Long Term Perspectives on Children's Adjustment', *Applied Social Psychology*, 7, 230.

59 Christoffersen, M.N. (1995), *An Investigation of Fathers with 3 to 5-Year old Children*. Social Research Institute Ministerratskonferenz, Stockholm, Sweden (Chart 3).

60 Guidubaldi, J. (1987), 'Growing Up in a Divorced Family: Initial and Long Term Perspectives on Children's Adjustment', *Applied Social Psychology*, 7, 212.

61 Borden, C. and Obsatz, K. (Directors) (2007), *Journeyman* [documentary]. United States: MirrorMan Films.

62 Farrell, W., personal communication, January 5, 2012.

63 Tickner, N. (2008, November 14), 'Unhappy People Watch TV, Happy People Read/Socialize'. Retrieved January 10, 2012, from *Newsdesk*, University of Maryland: http://www.newsdesk.umd.edu/sociss/release.cfm?ArticleID=1789.

64 Tolstoy, L., Pevear, R., and Volokhonsky, L. (2002), *Anna Karenina* (p. 1). New York, NY: Penguin Group (USA), Inc.

65 Stern, P. (Director) (2006), *Raising Cain: Boys in Focus* [documentary]. United States: PBS Films.

66 Farrell, W., personal communication, January 10, 2012.

67 Notes: The main federal assistance programme for American families in
    need, or 'welfare', in the US today is the Temporary Assistance for
    Needy Families (TANF). President Clinton initiated it in 1997 after the
    Personal Responsibility and Work Opportunity Reconciliation Act
    (PRWORA) was passed in 1996, succeeding Aid to Families with
    Dependent Children (AFDC), which had been in effect since 1935.
    TANF transitioned the cost-sharing model, where the federal
    government's stipend for state welfare programmes went up as the need
    for assistance grew, to block grants where states were given a set
    amount and had greater control over their programmes and how
    assistance is distributed. In 2013 an average of 4.1 million people
    received TANF or State Supplemental Programme (SSP) benefits each
    month during the fiscal year, most were children:

>   Children: 3,091,888 (75 per cent)
>
>   Adults: 1,007,243 (25 per cent)
>
>   Families (total): 1,751,351
>
>   Zero-parent families: 760,293
>
>   One-parent families: 908,443
>
>   Two-parent families: 82,615

See: *Caseload Data 2014* (2014, January 23). Retrieved May 17, 2014, from
the Office of Family Assistance, US Department of Health and Human
Services: http://www.acf.hhs.gov/programmes/ofa/resource/
caseload-data-2013.

68 Notes: Regardless of ethnicity, women were about twice as likely as
    men (23 per cent vs 12 per cent), and minorities were twice as likely as
    whites, to have received food stamps:

>   39 per cent of black women
>
>   31 per cent of Hispanic women
>
>   21 per cent of black men
>
>   19 per cent of white women
>
>   14 per cent of Hispanic men
>
>   11 per cent of white men

See: Morin, R. (2013, July 12), *The Politics and Demographics of Food
Stamp Recipients*. Retrieved May 17, 2014, from Pew Research Center:
http://www.pewresearch.org/fact-tank/2013/07/12/
the-politics-and-demographics-of-food-stamp-recipients/.

69 Notes: Despite the significant rising costs of living, basic assistance is
    now only a relatively small share and TANF and maintenance of effort
    (MOE) spending has decreased from 70 per cent at the beginning of the
    programme to 29 per cent in 2011 – with nine states spending less than

15 per cent. The Center on Budget and Policy Priorities (CBPP) says some states shifted resources 'from cash assistance to activities designed to promote or support work, but those investments leveled off nearly a decade ago . . . States are using a significant and growing share of TANF and MOE funds to support *other* state services, including child welfare; states also have diverted substantial funds formerly used to assist poor families to other purposes,' such as 'filling state budget holes'.

See: Schott, L., Pavetti, L., and Finch, I. (2012, August 7), 'How States Have Spent Federal and State Funds Under the TANF Block Grant'. Retrieved May 19, 2014, from Center on Budget and Policy Priorities: http://www.cbpp.org/cms/index.cfm?fa=view&id=3808.

70 Moffitt, R.A., Reville, R.T., Winkler, A.E., and Burstain, J.M. (2008, August revised 2009, February), *Cohabitation and Marriage Rules in State TANF Programs*. Retrieved May 19, 2014, from Office of the Assistant Secretary for Planning and Evaluation, US Department of Health and Human Services: http://www.aspe.hhs.gov/hsp/09/CohabitationMarriageRules/index.shtml.

71 Ibid.

72 Hardisty, J. and Williams, L.A. (n.d.), *The Right's Campaign Against Welfare*. Retrieved May 17, 2014, from Jean Hardisty: http://www.jeanhardisty.com/writing/articles-chapters-and-reports/the-rights-campaign-against-welfare/.

73 *UK Labour Market, September 2014* (2014, September 17) (p. 38). Retrieved October 10, 2014, from Office for National Statistics: http://www.ons.gov.uk/ons/dcp171778_374770.pdf.

74 Martin, D. (2014, January 16), 'A Quarter of British Children are being Raised by a Single Parent, New Figures Reveal'. Retrieved October 10, 2014, from Mail Online: http://www.dailymail.co.uk/news/article-2540974/Britain-fourth-highest-number-single-parents-EU.html.

75 *Fractured Families: Why Stability Matters* (2013, June) (p. 14). Retrieved October 10, 2014, from the Centre for Social Justice: http://www.centreforsocialjustice.org.uk/UserStorage/pdf/Pdf%20reports/CSJ_Fractured_Families_Report_WEB_13.06.13.pdf.

76 Ibid. (pp. 13, 22).

77 Ibid. (p. 15).

78 Gottlieb, L. (2011, July/August), 'How to Land Your Kids in Therapy'. Retrieved November 11, 2011, from *Atlantic* magazine: http://www.theatlantic.com/magazine/archive/2011/07/how-to-land-your-kid-in-therapy/8555.

79 *National Visitor Use Monitoring Results USDA Forest Service National Summary Report* (2013, May 20) (p. 8). Retrieved May 15, 2014, from National Visitor Use Monitoring (NVUM), US Forest Service: http://www.fs.fed.us/recreation/programmes/nvum/2012%20National_Summary_Report_061413.pdf.

80 Regnerus, M. (2012), 'How Different are the Adult Children of Parents who have Same-sex Relationships? Findings from the New Family Structures Study', *Social Science Research*, 41 (2012). Retrieved June 18, 2014, from http://www.sciencedirect.com/science/article/pii/S0049089X12000610.

81 Mcpherson, G. (2013, March 6), 'Children as Happy with Gay Parents – Research'. Retrieved June 18, 2014, from *Cambridge News*: http://www.cambridge-news.co.uk/Health/Family/Children-as-happy-with-gay-parents-research-06032013.htm; and van Gelderen, L., et al. (2012), 'Quality of Life of Adolescents Raised from Birth by Lesbian Mothers: The US National Longitudinal Family Study', *Journal of Developmental & Behavioural Pediatrics*, 33(1), 5.

82 Chadwick, V. (2013, June 5), 'Tick for Same-sex Families'. Retrieved June 18, 2014, from the *Age Victoria*: http://www.theage.com.au/victoria/tick-for-samesex-families-20130605-2npxf.html.

83 Mcpherson, G. (2013, March 6), 'Children as Happy with Gay Parents – Research'. Retrieved June 18, 2014, from *Cambridge News*: http://www.cambridge-news.co.uk/Health/Family/Children-as-happy-with-gay-parents-research-06032013.htm; and van Gelderen, L., et al. (2012), 'Quality of Life of Adolescents Raised from Birth by Lesbian Mothers: The US National Longitudinal Family Study', *Journal of Developmental & Behavioural Pediatrics*, 33(1), 5.

84 *Lesbian & Gay Parenting* (2005). Retrieved June 18, 2014, from American Psychological Association: http://www.apa.org/pi/lgbt/resources/parenting-full.pdf.

85 White, R.R. (2011, October 3), 'The Role Non-Monogamy Will Play in the Future of Marriage'. Retrieved November 18, 2014, from the *Atlantic*: http://www.theatlantic.com/health/archive/2011/10/the-role-non-monogamy-will-play-in-the-future-of-marriage/245960/.

86 Guttentag, M. and Secord, P.F. (1983), *Too Many Women?: The Sex Ratio Question* (pp. 20–21). Thousand Oaks, CA: Sage Publications.

9. Failing Schools

1 *Education at a Glance 2013: OECD Indicators* (Indicator B1.1) (2013). Retrieved June 30, 2014, from Organisation for Economic Co-operation and Development: http://dx.doi.org/10.1787/eag-2013-en.

2 Corcoran S.P., Evans, W.N., and Schwab, R.M. (2004), 'Women, the Labor Market, and the Declining Relative Quality of Teachers', *Journal of Policy Analysis and Management*, 23(3), 449–70.

3 Ibid.; and Vance, V.S. and Schlechty, P.C. (1982), 'The Distribution of Academic Ability in the Teaching Force', *Phi Delta Kappan*, 64(1), 22–7.

4 Chetty, R., Friedman, J., and Rockoff, J. (n.d.), *The Long-Term Impacts of Teachers: Teacher Value-Added and Student Outcomes in Adulthood*.

Retrieved January 12, 2012, from Harvard University: http://obs.rc.fas. harvard.edu/chetty/value_added.html.

5 Richardson, H. (2013, February 13), '"Not Enough Strenuous Activity" in School PE'. Retrieved November 18, 2014, from BBC News: http:// www.bbc.com/news/education-21449610.

6 Freeman, C.E. (2004, November), *Trends in Educational Equity of Girls and Women: 2004* (p. 45). Retrieved December 26, 2011, from National Center for Education Statistics, Institute of Education Sciences, US Department of Education (NCES 2005-016): http://nces.ed.gov/ pubs2005/2005016.pdf.

7 C, K.N., K, P., and W, P.J. (2013, December 3). 'Diligent Asia, Indolent West'. Retrieved June 26, 2014, from the *Economist*: http://www. economist.com/blogs/graphicdetail/2013/12/daily-chart-1.

8 Sax, L. (2009), *Boys Adrift: The Five Factors Driving the Growing Epidemic of Unmotivated Boys and Underachieving Young Men* (p. 21). New York, NY: Basic Books.

9 Steinberg, K. (2011, September 14), '43% of 2011 College-Bound Seniors Met SAT College and Career Readiness Benchmark' (p. 12). Retrieved December 8, 2011, from the College Board: http://media.collegeboard. com/pdf/cbs_2011_nat_release_091411.pdf.

10 'GCSE Results 2013: The Complete Breakdown' (2013, August 22). Retrieved October 10, 2014, from the *Guardian*: http://www. theguardian.com/news/datablog/2013/aug/22/ gcse-results-2013-the-complete-breakdown.

11 Szalavitz, M. and Perry, B.D. (2010), *Born for Love: Why Empathy Is Essential – and Endangered* (pp. 95, 231, 295). New York, NY: HarperCollins.

12 Stern, P. (Director) (2006), *Raising Cain: Boys in Focus* [documentary]. United States: PBS Films.

13 'Record Numbers of Men Teaching in Primary Schools – But More Still Needed' (2012, July 6). Retrieved October 10, 2014, from Gov.uk: https://www.gov.uk/government/news/ record-numbers-of-men-teaching-in-primary-schools-but-more-still-needed.

14 *What's the Problem with School?* (n.d.). Retrieved December 26, 2011, from PBS: http://www.pbs.org/parents/raisingboys/school02.html.

15 Dretzin, R. (Director) (2010), *Digital Nation: Life on the Virtual Frontier* [documentary]. United States: PBS Films [Frontline].

16 Notes: 82 per cent of US libraries reduced operating hours in the 2011–12 year and 65 per cent cut hours in the 2012–13 year.

See: Rosa, K., *Research and Statistics on Libraries and Librarianship in 2012* (n.d.) (p. 352). Retrieved May 10, 2014, from Office for Research and

Statistics, American Library Association: http://www.ala.org/research/
sites/ala.org.research/files/content/librarystats/LBTA-research2013.pdf.

17 C, K.N., K, P., and W, P.J. (2013, December 3), 'Diligent Asia, Indolent
    West'. Retrieved June 26, 2014, from the *Economist*: http://www.
    economist.com/blogs/graphicdetail/2013/12/daily-chart-1.

18 'Finn-ished' (2013, December 7). Retrieved June 26, 2014, from the
    Economist: http://www.economist.com/news/
    international/21591195-fall-former-nordic-education-star-latest-pisa-
    tests-focusing-interest.

19 *Suicide and Attempted Suicide – China, 1990–2002* (2004, June 11).
    Retrieved June 26, 2014, from Centers for Disease Control and
    Prevention: http://www.cdc.gov/mmwr/preview/mmwrhtml/
    mm5322a6.htm.

20 'China's Young People at Increasing Risk of Suicide' (2013, September
    11). Retrieved June 26, 2014, from Radio Free Asia: http://www.rfa.
    org/english/news/china/suicide-09112013114030.html.

21 Shlam, S. and Medalia, H. (2014, January 19), 'China's Web Junkies'.
    Retrieved June 26, 2014, from the *New York Times*: http://www.nytimes.
    com/2014/01/20/opinion/chinas-web-junkies.
    html?ref=opinion&_r=1.

22 Steinberg, K. (2011, September 14), '43% of 2011 College-Bound Seniors
    Met SAT College and Career Readiness Benchmark' (p. 9). Retrieved
    December 8, 2011, from the College Board: http://media.collegeboard.
    com/pdf/cbs_2011_nat_release_091411.pdf.

23 Hornig, D. and Daley, A. (2011, December 1), 'Not Enough New
    Scientists: How America's Obsession with Liberal Arts Is Making Us Less
    Competitive'. Retrieved January 4, 2012, from *Casey Daily Dispatch*: http://
    www.caseyresearch.com/cdd/friends-dont-let-friends-major-liberal-arts.

24 Ibid.

25 Hirschman, C., personal communication, January 19, 2012.

26 Ogas, O. and Gaddam, S. (2011), *A Billion Wicked Thoughts: What the
    World's Largest Experiment Reveals About Human Desire* (p. 50). New York,
    NY: Penguin Group (USA), Inc.

27 'Italian Men Suffer "Sexual Anorexia" after Internet Porn Use' (2011,
    March 4). Retrieved January 9, 2012, from ANSA English: http://www.
    ansa.it/web/notizie/rubriche/english/2011/02/24/visualizza_new.
    html_1583160579.html.

28 Ropelato, J. *Internet Pornography Statistics* (n.d.). Retrieved November 17,
    2011, from Top Ten Reviews, TechMediaNetwork: http://internet-
    filter-review.toptenreviews.com/internet-pornography-statistics.html.

29 *Vital Signs: Teen Pregnancy – United States, 1991–2009* (2011, April 8).
    Retrieved November 17, 2011, from Centers for Disease Control and

Prevention: http://www.cdc.gov/mmwr/preview/mmwrhtml/mm6013a5.htm?s_cid=mm6013a5_w.

30 'State Policies in Brief, Sex and HIV Education' (2014, June 1). Retrieved June 17, 2014, from Guttmacher Institute: https://www.guttmacher.org/statecenter/spibs/spib_SE.pdf.

31 *Sex and Relationships Education Factsheet* (2011, January). Retrieved October 13, 2014, from Family Planning Association Web: http://www.fpa.org.uk/factsheets/sex-and-relationships-education#aNh7.

32 Parker, I. (2014, August), *Young People, Sex and Relationships: The New Norm* (p. 10). Retrieved October 9, 2014, from Institute for Public Policy Research: http://www.ippr.org/assets/media/publications/pdf/young-people-sex-relationships_Aug2014.pdf.

33 *Estimated Median Age at First Marriage, by Sex: 1890 to the Present* (2011, November). Retrieved February 20, 2012, from US Census Bureau: http://www.census.gov/population/socdemo/hh-fam/ms2.xls.

34 *Marriages in England and Wales (Provisional), 2012* (p. 8) (2014, June 11). Retrieved October 9, 2014, from Office for National Statistics: http://www.ons.gov.uk/ons/dcp171778_366530.pdf.

35 Connor, S. (2013, November 26), 'The Truth about Women and Sex: They Start Younger and Have More Partners – and Those are not Necessarily Men'. Retrieved October 13, 2014, from the *Independent*: http://www.independent.co.uk/news/science/the-truth-about-women-and-sex--they-start-younger-and-have-more-partners--and-those-are-not-necessarily-men-8962997.html; also see *The Third National Survey of Sexual Attitudes and Lifestyles* (2013, November 26). Retrieved October 13, 2014, from the *Lancet*: http://www.thelancet.com/themed/natsal.

36 Brükner H. (2005), 'After the Promise: The STD Consequences of Adolescent Virginity Pledges', *Journal of Adolescent Health*, 36, 271–8.

37 Klein, M. (Kindle edition, 2008), *America's War on Sex: The Attack on Law, Lust, and Liberty*. Amazon.com: Praeger Paperback.

38 *Comprehensive Sex Education: Research and Results* (2009, September). Retrieved May 31, 2014, from Advocates for Youth: http://www.advocatesforyouth.org/storage/advfy/documents/fscse.pdf; and Darroch, J.E., Singh, S., and Frost, J.J. (2001, December), *Differences in Teenage Pregnancy Rates Among Five Developed Countries: The Roles of Sexual Activity and Contraceptive Use*. Retrieved May 31, 2014, from Guttmacher Institute: http://www.guttmacher.org/pubs/journals/3324401.html.

39 *2009 Sexually Transmitted Diseases Surveillance, STDs in Adolescents and Young Adults* (2010). Retrieved November 17, 2011, from Centers for Disease Control and Prevention: http://www.cdc.gov/std/stats09/adol.htm.

40 Notes: Compare the average US birth rate of 29.4 per 1,000 15- to 19-year-old women to the rate in Rwanda (34), India (33), Turkey (31),

Kazakhstan (30) and Vietnam (29). According to the CDC, these states have the highest teen birth rates:

> New Mexico (47.5) – most comparable to Peru (51), Yemen (47), Puerto Rico (47), Barbados (48) and Indonesia (48)
>
> Oklahoma (47.3)
>
> Mississippi (46.1)
>
> Arkansas (45.7)
>
> Texas (44.4)

States with the lowest teen birth rates per 1,000 teens aged 15–19:

> New Hampshire (13.8) – most comparable to Australia (12), Hungary (12), Poland (12), Portugal (13) and Canada (14)
>
> Massachusetts (14.1)
>
> Connecticut (15.1)
>
> Vermont (16.3)
>
> New Jersey (16.7)

If we go by ethnicity, there were 27.4 teen births per 1,000 white women, 44 for black women, 46.3 for Hispanic women, 34.9 for American Indian or Alaska Natives, and 9.7 for Asian or Pacific Islanders. The per cent changes for each ethnicity since 2000 are: white – 37 per cent reduction (from 43.2); black – 43 per cent reduction (from 77.4); Hispanic – 47 per cent reduction (from 87.3); American Indian or Alaska Native – 40 per cent reduction (from 58.3); and Asian or Pacific Islander – 53 per cent reduction (from 20.5).

See: Martin, J.A., Hamilton, B.E., Osterman, M.J., Curtin, S.C., and Mathews, T.J. (2013, December 30), *Births: Final Data for 2012*. Retrieved May 19, 2014, from National Vital Statistics Reports, Centers for Disease Control and Prevention: http://www.cdc.gov/nchs/data/nvsr/nvsr62/nvsr62_09.pdf#table02; and world statistics: *Adolescent Fertility Rate (Births per 1,000 Women ages 15–19)* (n.d.). Retrieved May 19, 2014, from United Nations Population Division, World Population Prospects. The World Bank: http://data.worldbank.org/indicator/SP.ADO.TFRT?order=wbapi_data_value_2012+wbapi_data_value+wbapi_data_value-last&sort=desc.

41 Notes: Abortion rates for US teens in 2008 were: 22 per cent of white pregnancies, 65 per cent of black pregnancies and 19 per cent of Hispanic pregnancies.

See: Ventura, S.J., Curtin, S.C., Abma, J.C., and Henshaw, S.K. (2012, June 20), *Estimated Pregnancy Rates and Rates of Pregnancy Outcomes for the United States, 1990–2008*. Retrieved May 19, 2014, from National Vital Statistics System, US Department of Health and Human Services, Centers for Disease Control and Prevention: http://www.cdc.gov/nchs/data/nvsr/nvsr60/nvsr60_07.pdf.

42 *Conceptions in England and Wales, 2012* (2014, February 25). Retrieved May 19, 2014, from Office for National Statistics: http://www.ons.gov.uk/ons/dcp171778_353922.pdf.

43 Doughty, S., 'UK Tops League of Teenage Pregnancy' (n.d.). Retrieved October 10, 2014, from Daily Mail Online: http://www.dailymail.co.uk/news/article-28860/UK-tops-league-teenage-pregnancy.html.

44 Ventura, S.J., Curtin, S.C., and Mathews, T.J. (1998), *Teenage Births in the United States: National and State Trends, 1990–96*. Retrieved May 19, 2014, from National Vital Statistics System, US Department of Health and Human Services, Centers for Disease Control and Prevention: http://www.cdc.gov/nchs/data/misc/teenbrth.pdf.

45 *Conceptions in England and Wales, 2012* (2014, February 25). Retrieved May 19, 2014, from Office for National Statistics: http://www.ons.gov.uk/ons/dcp171778_353922.pdf.

46 *Vital Signs: Teen Pregnancy – United States, 1991–2009* (2011, April 8). Retrieved November 17, 2011, from Centers for Disease Control and Prevention: http://www.cdc.gov/mmwr/preview/mmwrhtml/mm6013a5.htm?s_cid=mm6013a5_w.

47 Martinez, G., Copen, C.E., and Abma, J.C. (2011, October), *Teenagers in the United States: Sexual Activity, Contraceptives, and Child Bearing, 2006–2010 National Study of Family Growth* (p. 10). Retrieved October 8, 2014, from National Center for Health Statistics. Centers for Disease Control and Prevention: http://www.cdc.gov/nchs/data/series/sr_23/sr23_031.pdf.

48 *HHS Funding for Abstinence Education, Education for Teen Pregnancy and HIV/STD Prevention, and Other Programmes that Address Adolescent Sexual Activity* (n.d.). Retrieved November 17, 2011, from National Abstinence Education Association: http://gallery.mailchimp.com/e71e76ba0a0760415775e4352/files/funding_comparison_Sheet2.pdf?utm_source=General+Email+list+for+Weekly+Updates&utm_campaign=04e533396b-Day_on_the_hill&utm_medium=email.

49 Doughty, S. 'UK Tops League of Teenage Pregnancy' (n.d.). Retrieved October 10, 2014, from Daily Mail Online: http://www.dailymail.co.uk/news/article-28860/UK-tops-league-teenage-pregnancy.html.

10. Environmental Changes

1 Wang, S.S. (2013, July 15), 'The Decline in Male Fertility'. Retrieved May 28, 2014, from the *Wall Street Journal*: http://online.wsj.com/news/articles/SB10001424127887323394504578607641775723354; also see http://www.rainestudy.org.au.

2 *Low Sperm Count Causes* (2012, September 22). Retrieved May 30, 2014, from Mayo Clinic: http://www.mayoclinic.org/diseases-conditions/low-sperm-count/basics/causes/con-20033441.

3 *What Are Endocrine Disruptors?* (n.d.). Retrieved May 28, 2014, from Endocrine Disruptor Screening Programme, Office of Chemical Safety and Pollution Prevention, Environmental Protection Agency: http://www.epa.gov/endo/pubs/edspoverview/whatare.htm.

4 *Endocrine Disruptors* (n.d.). Retrieved May 28, 2014, from National Institute of Environmental Health Sciences, National Institute of Health: http://www.niehs.nih.gov/health/topics/agents/endocrine/.

5 Colborn, T., Dumanoski, D., and Myers, J.P. (1997), *Our Stolen Future: Are We Threatening Our Fertility, Intelligence, and Survival? A Scientific Detective Story* (p. xv). New York City: Plume.

6 Wakefield, J. (2002), 'Boys Won't Be Boys', *New Scientist*, 2349. Retrieved May 28, 2014, from http://www.newscientist.com/article/mg17423495.300;jsessionid=JGIKANPNOJPP.

7 Interlandi, J. (2013, December), 'The Toxins That Affected Your Great-Grandparents Could Be In Your Genes'. Retrieved May 29, 2014, from *Smithsonian*: http://www.smithsonianmag.com/innovation/the-toxins-that-affected-your-great-grandparents-could-be-in-your-genes-180947644/?device=iphone?no-ist&no-ist. Also see: http://skinner.wsu.edu.

8 *Testicular Cancer Incidence Statistics* (n.d.). Retrieved May 28, 2014, from Cancer Research UK: http://www.cancerresearchuk.org/cancer-info/cancerstats/types/testis/incidence/uk-testicular-cancer-incidence-statistics; and *Testicular Cancer Screening* (n.d.). Retrieved May 28, 2014, from National Cancer Institute, National Institutes of Health: http://www.cancer.gov/cancertopics/pdq/screening/testicular/HealthProfessional/page2; and Walschaerts, M. et al. (2008), 'Doubling of Testicular Cancer Incidence Rate over the last 20 Years in Southern France', *Cancer Causes Control*, 19(2). Retrieved May 28, 2014, from http://www.ncbi.nlm.nih.gov/pubmed/18236173.

9 Colborn, T., Dumanoski, D., and Myers, J.P. (1997), *Our Stolen Future: Are We Threatening Our Fertility, Intelligence, and Survival? A Scientific Detective Story* (p. 9). New York City: Plume.

10 Wakefield, J. (2002), 'Boys Won't be Boys', *New Scientist*, 2349. Retrieved May 28, 2014, from http://www.newscientist.com/article/mg17423495.300;jsessionid=JGIKANPNOJPP.

11 Crawford, T. (2014, May 28), 'SFU Study Finds Lower IQ in Kids Linked to Mom's Exposure to Flame Retardants in Pregnancy'. Retrieved May 29, 2014, from the *Vancouver Sun*: http://www.vancouversun.com/health/study+finds+flame+retardant+exposure+utero+lower+children+boost+hyperactivity/9884560/story.html.

12 Betts, K.S. (2002), 'Rapidly Rising PBDE Levels in North America', *Environmental Science and Technology, Science News*, 36(3), 50A–52A.

13 Bramwell, L., Fernandes, A., Rose, M., Harrad, M., and Pless-Mulloli, T. (2014), 'PBDEs and PBBs in Human Serum and Breast Milk from Cohabiting UK Couples', *Chemosphere*, 116. Retrieved October 13, 2014,

from http://www.sciencedirect.com/science/article/pii/S0045653514004093.

14 Crawford, T. (2014, May 28), 'SFU Study Finds Lower IQ in Kids Linked to Mom's Exposure to Flame Retardants in Pregnancy'. Retrieved May 29, 2014, from the *Vancouver Sun*: http://www.vancouversun.com/health/study+finds+flame+retardant+exposure+utero+lower+children+boost+hyperactivity/9884560/story.html.

15 Wakefield, J. (2002), 'Boys Won't Be Boys', *New Scientist*, 2349. Retrieved May 28, 2014, from http://www.newscientist.com/article/mg17423495.300;jsessionid=JGIKANPNOJPP.

11. Technology Enchantment and Arousal Addiction

1 Dretzin, R. (Director) (2010), *Digital Nation: Life on the Virtual Frontier* [documentary]. United States: PBS Films [Frontline].

2 J.R.R. Tolkien, *On Fairy Stories* (n.d.). Retrieved May 1, 2014, from California Lutheran University: http://public.callutheran.edu/~brint/Arts/Tolkien.pdf, 8.

3 Laier, C., Schulte, F.P., Brand, M., and Hahn, E.L. (2013), 'Pornographic Picture Processing Interferes with Working Memory Performance', *The Journal of Sex Research*, 50(7). Retrieved June 27, 2014, from http://dx.doi.org/10.1080/00224499.2012.716873.

4 Clark, N. and Scott, P.S. (2009), *Game Addiction: The Experience and the Effects* (p. 84). Jefferson, North Carolina: McFarland & Company.

5 Ibid. (p. 88).

6 Deem, G., personal communication, April 13, 2014.

7 Carr, N.G. (2010), *The Shallows: What the Internet Is Doing to Our Brains* (pp. 26–7). New York: W.W. Norton.

8 Ibid. (pp. 27–8, 33).

9 *The Diagnostic and Statistical Manual for Mental Disorders, Fifth Edition* (DSM-5) offers a tentative list of criteria for Internet Gaming Disorder (IGD), of which at least five out of nine points must be met in a year-long period. See also: Voss A., et al. (2015), 'Case Report: Internet Gaming Disorder Associated With Pornography Use', *Yale Journal of Biology and Medicine*. 88, 319–24.

10 See Brunborg, G., Hanss, D., Mentzoni, R., and Palleson, S. (2015), 'Core and Peripheral Criteria of Video Game Addiction in the Game Addiction Scale for Adolescents,' *Cyberpsychology, Behavior, and Social Networking*, 18(5), 280–5.

11 Doan, A. (2011, October 4), 'The Lure of Sex in Video Games'. Retrieved November 11, 2011 from Hooked on Games: http://www.hooked-on-games.com/blog/33-the-lure-of-sex-in-video-games.html; also see Doan, A., Strickland, B., and Gentile, D. (2012), *Hooked on*

Games: The Lure and Cost of Video Game and Internet Addiction (pp. 87-88). Iowa: FEP International.

12 'So, Uh, You Can Have Virtual Sex, Now' (2012, December 18). Retrieved June 26, 2014, from SourceFed: http://sourcefed.com/so-uh-you-can-have-virtual-sex-now/.

13 Van den Bosch, J. (2013), 'Sinful Robot: Creating the World's Most Immersive Virtual Reality Erotic Encounters (with Oculus Rift)'. Retrieved June 26, 2014, from Reddit: http://www.reddit.com/r/technology/comments/1a2tev/sinful_robot_creating_the_worlds_most_immersive/c8trcpj.

14 Kaplan, E. and Purdum, J. (2001, May 13), 'I Dated A Robot', in M. Groening and D.X. Cohen, *Futurama*. Los Angeles, CA: 20th Century.

15 Yee, N., Bailenson, J.N., and Ducheneaut, N. (2009), 'The Proteus Effect: Implications of Transformed Digital Behaviour Self-Representation on Online and Offline Behaviour' (p. 294), *Communication Research*, 36(2). Retrieved June 12, 2014, from http://vhil.stanford.edu/pubs/2009/yee-proteus-implications.pdf.

16 Korolov, M. (2010, October 8), 'Treatment Center gets $865,000 for OpenSim Project'. Retrieved June 12, 2014, from Hypergrid Business: http://www.hypergridbusiness.com/2010/10/treatment-center-gets-865000-for-second-opensim-project/.

17 Yee, N., Bailenson, J.N., and Ducheneaut, N. (2009), 'The Proteus Effect: Implications of Transformed Digital Behaviour Self-Representation on Online and Offline Behaviour' (p.287), *Communication Research*, 36(2). Retrieved June 12, 2014, from http://vhil.stanford.edu/pubs/2009/yee-proteus-implications.pdf.

18 Dretzin, R. (Director) (2010), *Digital Nation: Life on the Virtual Frontier* [documentary]. United States: PBS Films [Frontline].

19 Ibid.

20 Sipress, D. (2011, December 19), 'When I was your age, I had to hike ten miles through the ice and snow to …' – *New Yorker* cartoon. Retrieved June 16, 2014, from Condé Nast Collection: http://www.condenaststore.com/-sp/When-I-was-your-age-I-had-to-hike-ten-miles-through-the-ice-and-snow-to-New-Yorker-Cartoon-Prints_i8638277_.htm.

21 'Porn: Business of Pleasure' (2007, July 9). Retrieved November 17, 2011, from CNBC: http://www.cnbc.com/id/31586577/?slide=4.

22 Macfarlane, J. (2008, June 14), 'Men Aged 18 to 30 on Viagra to Keep Up with Sex and the City Generation'. Retrieved January 10, 2012, from *Daily Mail*: http://www.dailymail.co.uk/health/article-1026523/Men-aged-18-30-Viagra-Sex-And-The-City-generation.html.

23 (2011, July/August). *Men's Health*, 30.

24 Retrieved June 8, 2011, from Alexa: http://www.alexa.com UK statistics were retrieved November 17, 2014.

25 Schonfeld, E. (2011, April 25), 'Netflix Q1 Earnings Up 88%, Adds 3.M Subscribers'. Retrieved November 11, 2011, from Seeking Alpha: http://seekingalpha.com/article/265310-netflix-q1-earnings-up-88-adds-3-m-subscribers.

26 *Daily Mail* Reporter (2011, April 22), 'Young Men Watch TWO HOURS of Porn Online Each Week ... and One in Three have Missed a Deadline Because of It'. Retrieved June 16, 2014, from *Daily Mail*: http://www.dailymail.co.uk/news/article-1379464/Porn-Young-men-watch-2-HOURS-week-missed-deadline-it.html.

27 Wilson, G., personal communication.

28 Kühn, S. and Gallinat, J. (2014), 'Brain Structure and Functional Connectivity Associated With Pornography Consumption', *JAMA Psychiatry*, 71(7). Retrieved November 29, 2014, from http://archpsyc.jamanetwork.com/article.aspx?articleid=1874574.

29 Osterath, B. (2014, June 5), *Pea brain: watching porn online will wear out your brain and make it shrivel*. Retrieved November 29, 2014, from Deutsche Welle: http://www.dw.de/pea-brain- watching-porn-online-will-wear-out-your-brain-and-make-it-shrivel/a-17681654.

30 Wilson, G. (2011, June 17), *Start Here: Porn-Induced Sexual Dysfunction*. Retrieved February 21, 2012 from Your Brain on Porn: http://yourbrainonporn.com/porn-induced-ed-start-here; and Wilson, G. (2011, February 10). *Erectile Dysfunction and Porn*. Retrieved February 21, 2012 from Your Brain on Porn: http://yourbrainonporn.com/erectile-dysfunction-and-porn.

31 Carr, N.G. (2010), *The Shallows: What the Internet Is Doing to Our Brains* (p. 210). New York: W.W. Norton.

32 O'Donohue, W.T. and Geer, J.H. (1985), 'The Habituation of Sexual Arousal', *Archives of Sexual Behaviour*, 14(3). Retrieved June 16, 2014, from http://www.ncbi.nlm.nih.gov/pubmed/4004547.

33 Ogas, O. and Gaddam, S. (2011), *A Billion Wicked Thoughts: What the World's Largest Experiment Reveals About Human Desire* (p. 193). New York, NY: Penguin Group (USA), Inc.

34 Max, T. *The Date Application* (n.d.). Retrieved November 22, 2011, from Tucker Max: http://www.tuckermax.com/stories/the-date-application/.

35 Martin, D. (2012, April 10), 'Jack Tramiel, a Pioneer in Computers, Dies at 83'. Retrieved April 24, 2014, from the *New York Times*: http://www.nytimes.com/2012/04/11/technology/jack-tramiel-a-pioneer-in-computers-dies-at-83.html?_r=0.

36 Rose, G.L. (2011, October 6), 'Steve Jobs – Here's to the Crazy Ones'. Retrieved April 16, 2014, from Virgin: http://www.virgin.com/news/steve-jobs-here's-crazy-ones.

37 *Great Male Survey* (2011, July). Retrieved August 21, 2011, from AskMen: http://www.askmen.com/specials/great_male_survey/men_in_2011.html.

38 'Study Examines Video Game Play Among Adolescents' (2007, July 4). Retrieved December 31, 2011, from ScienceDaily: http://www.sciencedaily.com/releases/2007/07/070702161141.htm.

39 Weis, R. and Cerankosky, B. (2010), 'Effects of Video-Game Ownership on Young Boys' Academic and Behavioural Functioning', *Psychological Science*, 21(4). Retrieved June 20, 2014, from http://pss.sagepub.com/content/21/4/463.

40 Gentile, D.A., et al. (2004), 'The Effects of Violent Video Game Habits on Adolescent Hostility, Aggressive Behaviours, and School Performance', *Journal of Adolescence*, 27, 6.

41 Deem, G., personal communication, April 13, 2014.

42 Clark, N. and Scott, P.S. (2009), *Game Addiction: The Experience and the Effects* (p. 14). Jefferson, North Carolina: McFarland & Company.

43 Sax, L. (2009), *Boys Adrift: The Five Factors Driving the Growing Epidemic of Unmotivated Boys and Underachieving Young Men* (p. 91). New York, NY: Basic Books.

44 Paton, G. (2014, April 15), 'Infants "unable to use toy building blocks" due to iPad addiction'. Retrieved April 15, 2014, from the *Telegraph*: http://www.telegraph.co.uk/education/educationnews/10767878/Infants-unable-to-use-toy-building-blocks-due-to-iPad-addiction.html.

45 Gentile, D.A. (2012), 'Video Game Playing, Attention Problems, and Impulsiveness: Evidence of Bidirectional Causality', *Psychology of Popular Media Culture*, 1(1), 62–70.

46 Brandt, M. (2008, February 4), 'Video Games Activate Reward Regions of Brain in Men More Than Women, Stanford Study Finds'. Retrieved June 12, 2014, from Stanford Medicine News Center: http://med.stanford.edu/news/all-news/2008/02/video-games-activate-reward-regions-of-brain-in-men-more-than-women-stanford-study-finds.html.

47 McGonigal, J. *About World Without Oil* (n.d). Retrieved February 18, 2015, from World Without Oil: http://worldwithoutoil.org/metaabout.htm.

48 Haberstroh, M. (2008, April 24), 'Wii Are Family – Two-Thirds of Parents Say Social Gaming Has a Positive Impact on Family Life'. Retrieved January 10, 2012, from TNS Technology: http://www.tnsglobal.com/news/news-185D8B66AE3F44C3B60E79E03A469E24.aspx.

49 Seaman, A.M. (2014, March 14), 'Exercise Video Games May Add to Kids' Activity: Study'. Retrieved June 26, 2014, from Reuters: http://uk.reuters.com/article/2014/03/14/us-exercise-video-games-kids-idUKBREA2D1AE20140314.

50 Loyola University Health System (2008, March 22), 'Virtual-reality Video Game to Help Burn Patients Play Their Way to Pain Relief'. Retrieved June 20, 2014, from *ScienceDaily*: http://www.sciencedaily.com/releases/2008/03/080319152744.htm.

51 Stilphen, S., *Bob Whitehead* (n.d.). Retrieved April 21, 2014, from DP Interviews, Digital Press: http://www.digitpress.com/library/interviews/interview_bob_Whitehead.html.

52 Kent, S. (2001), *The Ultimate History of Video Games: The Story behind the Craze that Touched our Lives and Changed the World* (pp. 550–51). Roseville, CA: Prima Publishing/Random House.

53 Parkin, S. (2012, April 22), 'Don't Blame Video Games for Anders Behring Breivik's Massacre'. Retrieved May 17, 2014, from the *Guardian*: http://www.theguardian.com/commentisfree/2012/apr/22/video-games-anders-breivik-massacre.

54 Twenge, J.M. and Campbell, W.K. (2009), *The Narcissism Epidemic: Living in the Age of Entitlement* (pp. 199–200). New York: NY: Free Press; also see Twenge, J.M. and Campbell, W.K. (2003), '"Isn't it Fun to get the Respect that we're Going to Deserve?" Narcissism, Social Rejection, and Aggression', *Personality and Social Psychology Bulletin*, 29(2). Retrieved June 23, 2014, from http://www.ncbi.nlm.nih.gov/pubmed/15272953.

55 Von Drehle, D. (2007, April 19), 'It's All About Him'. Retrieved June 23, 2014, from *Time*: http://content.time.com/time/magazine/article/0,9171,1612688,00.html.

56 (1982, November 10), 'Video Game Warning From Surgeon General', *San Francisco Chronicle*, p. 7.

57 Chomik, A., 'Top 10: Most Violent Video Games' (n.d.). Retrieved December 31, 2011, from AskMen Web Site: http://www.askmen.com/top_10/videogame/top-10-most-violent-video-games.html.

58 Huesmann L.R. (2006), 'The Role of Media Violence in Violent Behaviour', *Annual Review of Public Health*, 27, 393–415. Retrieved from: http://bscw-app1.let.ethz.ch/pub/bscw.cgi/d5907573/HuesmannTaylor-The%20Role%20of%20Media%20Violence%20in%20Violent%20Behavio.pdf.

59 Carr, N.G. (2010), *The Shallows: What the Internet Is Doing to Our Brains* (p. 213). New York: W.W. Norton.

60 Kent, S. (2001), *The Ultimate History of Video Games: The Story behind the Craze that Touched our Lives and Changed the World* (pp. 4–6, 116, 166). Roseville, CA: Prima Publishing/Random House.

61 Dretzin, R. (Director) (2010), *Digital Nation: Life on the Virtual Frontier* [documentary]. United States: PBS Films [Frontline].

62 Barcott, R., personal communication, January 26, 2012.

63 Dretzin, R. (Director) (2010), *Digital Nation: Life on the Virtual Frontier* [documentary]. United States: PBS Films [Frontline].

64 Card, O.S. (1994), *Ender's Game*. New York: Tor Science Fiction.

65 *Digital Nation: Life on the Virtual Frontier*, op. cit.

12. Sour Grapes: Entitlement vs Reality

1 Ashliman, D.L. (2003), *Aesop's Fables* (introduction). New York: Barnes & Noble Books.

2 Sherman, D. K. and Cohen, G. L. (2006), 'The Psychology of Self-defense: Self-affirmation Theory, *Advances in Experimental Psychology* (38), 183–242.

3 Carlin, G. (1990), 'Euphemisms', on *Parental Advisory: Explicit Lyrics* [CD]. Tarzana, California: Atlantic/Laugh.

4 Twenge, J.M. and Campbell, W.K. (2009), *The Narcissism Epidemic: Living in the Age of Entitlement* (pp. 47, 83). New York, NY: Free Press.

5 Coughlan, S. (2014, January 21). 'University Grade Inflation Disputed'. Retrieved October 13, 2014, from BBC News: http://www.bbc.com/news/education-25811702.

6 Erikson, E.H. (1994), *Identity: Youth and Crisis*. New York, NY: W.W. Norton & Company.

7 Sax, L. (2010), *Girls on the Edge: The Four Factors Driving the New Crisis for Girls* (pp. 189–90). New York: Basic Books; and Bly, R. and Woodman, M. (1998), *The Maiden King* (p. 20). New York: Henry Holt & Co.; and as the source of this idea, Pearce, J.C. (1992), *Evolution's End: Claiming the Potential of Our Intelligence* (p. 190). New York: HarperCollins.

8 Yahr, E. (2014, May 5), 'Five Times Louis C.K. got Really Philosophical on Late-night Talk Shows'. Retrieved May 23, 2014, from the *Washington Post*: http://www.washingtonpost.com/blogs/style-blog/wp/2014/05/05/five-times-louis-c-k-got-really-philosophical-on-late-night-talk-shows/.

9 Twenge, J.M., Campbell, W.K., and Gentile, B. (2012), 'Changes in Pronoun Use in American Books and the Rise of Individualism, 1960–2008' (p. 406), *Journal of Cross-Cultural Psychology*, 44(3). Retrieved June 12, 2014, from http://web.natur.cuni.cz/~houdek3/papers/Twenge%20et%20al%202013.pdf.

10 Eagan, K., Lozano, J.B., Hurtado, S., and Case, M.H., *The American Freshman: National Norms Fall 2013* (2014, March) (p. 4). Retrieved June 11, 2014, from The Higher Education Research Institute, The Cooperative Institutional Research Programme, University of California, Los Angeles: http://www.heri.ucla.edu/briefs/TheAmericanFreshman2013-Brief.pdf.

11 '2012 Report Card on the Ethics of American Youth' (2012, November 20) (pp. 12, 18). Retrieved June 5, 2014, from Character Counts: http://

charactercounts.org/pdf/reportcard/2012/ReportCard-2012-
DataTables-HonestyIntegrityCheating.pdf.

12 Hvistendahl, M. (2011), *Unnatural Selection Choosing Boys Over Girls, and the Consequences of a World Full of Men* (p. xiii). New York, NY: PublicAffairs.

13 Tierney, J. (2007, August 20), 'Is There Anything Good About Men? And Other Tricky Questions'. Retrieved June 16, 2014, from the *New York Times*: http://tierneylab.blogs.nytimes.com/2007/08/20/ is-there-anything-good-about-men-and-other-tricky-questions/?_ php=true&_type=blogs&_r=0.

14 Baumeister, R. (2010), *Is There Anything Good About Men?: How Cultures Flourish by Exploiting Men* (p. 63). New York, NY: Oxford University Press; also see Wilder, J.A., Mobasher, Z., and Hammer, M.F. (2004), 'Genetic Evidence for Unequal Effective Population Sizes of Human Females and Males', *Molecular Biology and Evolution*, 21(11). Retrieved June 16, 2014, from http://mbe.oxfordjournals.org/ content/21/11/2047.full.pdf+html.

15 Maywell, H. (2003, February 14), 'Genghis Khan a Prolific Lover, DNA Data Implies'. Retrieved November 20, 2014, from *National Geographic*: http://news.nationalgeographic.com/news/2003/02/0214_030214_ genghis.html.

16 Gurwitz, J.H. (2005), 'The Age/Gender Interface in Geriatric Pharmacotherapy', *Journal of Women's Health*, 12(1). Retrieved June 18, 2014, from http://www.ncbi.nlm.nih.gov/pubmed/15692280.

17 *Statistics and Indicators on Women and Men, Table 1a*. (2012). Retrieved June 17, 2014, from Demographics and Social Statistics, United Nations: http://unstats.un.org/unsd/Demographic/products/ indwm/.

18 Ibid., *Table 1b*; and *The World Factbook, Age Structure* (2013). Retrieved June 17, 2014, from Central Intelligence Agency: https://www.cia.gov/ library/publications/the-world-factbook/fields/2010.html.

19 Bolick, K. (2011, November), 'All the Single Ladies', *Atlantic* magazine, 124.

20 *Statistics and Indicators on Women and Men, Table 1c* (2012). Retrieved June 17, 2014, from Demographics and Social Statistics, United Nations: http://unstats.un.org/unsd/Demographic/products/indwm/.

21 Sax, L. (2010), *Girls on the Edge: The Four Factors Driving the New Crisis for Girls* (pp. 34–5). New York: Basic Books.

22 Weiss, R. (2014, July 10), 'Narcissism, Porn Use, and Addiction'. Retrieved July 26, 2014, from PsychCentral: http://blogs.psychcentral. com/sex/2014/07/narcissism-porn-use-and-addiction/; also see Kasper, T.E., Short, M.B., and Milam, A.C. (2014), 'Narcissism and Internet Pornography Use', *Journal of Sex and Marital Therapy*.

13. The Rise of Women?

1 Bolick, K. (2011, November), 'All the Single Ladies', *Atlantic* magazine, 120, 126; and 4 per cent to 23 per cent statistic: Wang, W., Parker, K., and Taylor, P. (2013, May 29), 'Chapter 3: Married Mothers Who Out-Earn Their Husbands'. Retrieved September 28, 2014, from Pew Research Center: http://www.pewsocialtrends.org/2013/05/29/chapter-3-married-mothers-who-out-earn-their-husbands/.

2 (2014, September 6), 'Women Beat Men to High-skilled Jobs', *The Times*, pp. 28, 2G.

3 Rosen, R. (2001), *The World Split Open: How the Modern Women's Movement Changed America* (pp. xxiv–xxv, xxix, xxxi, xxxiv). New York, NY: Penguin Books.

4 Equal Pay Act 1970 (1970, May 29). Retrieved October 13, 2014, from Legislation.gov.uk: http://www.legislation.gov.uk/ukpga/1970/41.

5 Sex Discrimination Act 1975 (1975, November 12). Retrieved October 13, 2014, from Legislation.gov.uk: http://www.legislation.gov.uk/ukpga/1975/65.

6 *A History of Family Planning Services Factsheet* (2011, October 8). Retrieved October 13, 2014, from Family Planning Assocation: http://www.fpa.org.uk/factsheets/history-family-planning-services.

7 *Valentina Tereshkova* (n.d.). Retrieved May 27, 2014, from StarChild, NASA: http://starchild.gsfc.nasa.gov/docs/StarChild/whos_who_level2/tereshkova.html.

8 *About UNiTE* (n.d.). Retrieved May 27, 2014, from UNiTE to End Violence Against Women, United Nations: http://www.un.org/en/women/endviolence/about.shtml.

9 *FAQs* (n.d.). Retrieved May 27, 2014, from Olympic.org: http://registration.olympic.org/en/faq/detail/id/135.

10 *Current Numbers of Women Officeholders* (n.d.). Retrieved May 12, 2014, from Center for American Women and Politics: http://www.cawp.rutgers.edu/fast_facts/levels_of_office/Current_Numbers.php.

11 Goldsmith, B. (2014, March 26), 'Women Struggling to Crack Glass Ceiling in Top UK Companies – Report'. Retrieved October 13, 2014, from Reuters: http://uk.reuters.com/article/2014/03/26/uk-britain-boardroom-women-idUKBREA2P00320140326.

12 *MPs* (n.d.). Retrieved October 13, 2014, from Parliament.uk: http://www.parliament.uk/mps-lords-and-offices/mps/?sort=4&type=0.

13 Williams, Z., Adewunmi, B., Khaleeli, H., and Bates, L. (2014, October 28), 'How Life for Women in Britain is Getting Tougher'. Retrieved November 2, 2014, from the *Guardian*: http://www.theguardian.com/lifeandstyle/2014/oct/28/how-life-for-women-britain-getting-tougher.

14 Muñoz, C. (2014, April 8), 'Here's What the President is Doing to Close the Pay Gap'. Retrieved April 8, 2014, from The White House, Newsletter. Also see: www.wh.gov/equalpay.

15 (2014, April 19–24), 'The Return of the Stay-at-home Mother', the *Economist*, 411(8883), 24. Also see: http://www.economist.com/news/united-states/21600998-after-falling-years-proportion-mums-who-stay-home-rising-return.

16 *United Kingdom* (n.d.). Retrieved September 23, 2014, from OECD Better Life Index: http://www.oecdbetterlifeindex.org/countries/united-kingdom/.

17 (2014, April 19–24), 'The Return of the Stay-at-home Mother', the *Economist*, 411(8883), 24. Also see: http://www.economist.com/news/united-states/21600998-after-falling-years-proportion-mums-who-stay-home-rising-return.

18 Rosen, R. (2001), *The World Split Open: How the Modern Women's Movement Changed America* (p. 78). New York, NY: Penguin Books.

19 Parker, K. and Wang, W. (2013, March 14), *Modern Parenthood*. Retrieved June 7, 2014, from Pew Research Center: http://www.pewsocialtrends.org/2013/03/14/modern-parenthood-roles-of-moms-and-dads-converge-as-they-balance-work-and-family/.

20 *Anne-Marie Slaughter* (n.d.). Retrieved May 27, 2014, from Princeton University: http://www.princeton.edu/~slaughtr/.

21 Slaughter, A. (2012, June 13), 'Why Women Still Can't Have It All'. Retrieved May 23, 2014, from the *Atlantic*: http://www.theatlantic.com/magazine/archive/2012/07/why-women-still-cant-have-it-all/309020/?single_page=true.

22 *Paternity Pay and Leave* (2014, October 1). Retrieved October 2014, from Gov.uk: https://www.gov.uk/paternity-pay-leave/overview; and *Maternity Pay and Leave* (2014, July 29). Retrieved October 9, 2014, from Gov.uk: https://www.gov.uk/maternity-pay-leave.

23 *Adult Risk Factors: Obesity, Blood Sugar, Blood Pressure Data by Country* (2013). Retrieved May 30, 2014, from World Health Organization: http://apps.who.int/gho/data/node.main.NCD56?lang=en.

24 Twenge, J.M. and Campbell, W.K. (2009), *The Narcissism Epidemic: Living in the Age of Entitlement* (pp. 2, 31). New York, NY: Free Press.

25 'Gender Divide Reaching Male vs. Female Millenials' (2012, September 14). Retrieved April 28, 2014, from Nielsen: http://www.nielsen.com/us/en/newswire/2012/gender-divide-reaching-male-vs-female-millennials.html.

26 *Bechdel Test Movie List* (2014). Retrieved May 27, 2014, from Bechdel Test: http://bechdeltest.com.

27 Agnello, A.J., Keiser, J., Nelson, S., Sanskrit, D., and Teti, J. (2012, July 18), 'Something Other than a Man: 15 Games that Pass the Bechdel

Test'. Retrieved May 27, 2014, from The Gameological Society: http://gameological.com/2012/07/something-other-than-a-man-15-games-that-pass-the-bechdel-test/.

28 *Stats* (2014). Retrieved May 27, 2014, from Bechdel Test: http://bechdeltest.com/statistics/.

29 'Swedish Cinemas Take Aim at Gender Bias with Bechdel Test Rating' (2013, November 6). Retrieved May 27, 2014, from the *Guardian*: http://www.theguardian.com/world/2013/nov/06/swedish-cinemas-bechdel-test-films-gender-bias.

30 Lenhart, A., Ling, R., Campbell, S., and Purcell, K. (2010, April 20), *Teens and Mobile Phones*. Retrieved June 7, 2014, from Pew Research Center: http://www.pewinternet.org/2010/04/20/teens-and-mobile-phones/.

31 Crocker, L. (2013, November 13), *Why Women Don't Like Lady Bosses*. Retrieved September 28, 2014, from the Daily Beast: http://www.thedailybeast.com/witw/articles/2013/11/13/why-do-women-say-they-don-t-like-working-for-female-bosses.html.

32 Haworth, A. (2013, October 19), 'Why Have Young People in Japan Stopped Having Sex?'. Retrieved April 27, 2014, from the *Guardian*: http://www.theguardian.com/world/2013/oct/20/young-people-japan-stopped-having-sex.

33 Pelletier, D. (2012, November 13), *Artificial Wombs: Is a Sexless Reproduction Society in our Future?*. Retrieved November 25, 2014, from Institute for Ethics & Emerging Technologies: http://ieet.org/index.php/IEET/more/pelletier20121113.

34 Antenucci, A. and Li, D.K. (2014, April 10), 'More Young Women Choosing Dogs over Motherhood'. Retrieved April 12, 2014 from *New York Post*: http://nypost.com/2014/04/10/more-young-women-choosing-dogs-over-motherhood/.

35 Wang, W. and Parker, K. (2014, September 24), *Record Share of Americans Have Never Married*. Retrieved September 28, 2014, from Pew Research Center: http://www.pewsocialtrends.org/2014/09/24/record-share-of-americans-have-never-married/.

36 Gentry, J. (2014, September 25), 'Who Pays for the First Date? Survey Says Men Should'. Retrieved September 28, 2014, from *USA Today*: http://www.usatoday.com/story/news/nation/2014/09/25/survey-who-pays-for-first-date/16195739/.

37 White, M.D. (2013, August 25), 'Why Men Find It So Hard to Understand What Women Want'. Retrieved April 25, 2014, from *Psychology Today*: http://www.psychologytoday.com/blog/maybe-its-just-me/201308/why-men-find-it-so-hard-understand-what-women-want.

38 'Why Men Find It So Hard to Understand What Women Want: Do Men Know What it's Like to be Desired–and Why Woman Value it so

Much?' (2014, March 19). Retrieved May 27, 2014, from Reddit: http://
www.reddit.com/r/sex/comments/20twqv/why_men_find_it_so_
hard_to_understand_what_women/cg837ak.

39 Retrieved June 9, 2014, from Candida Royalle: http://candidaroyalle.
com.

40 Retrieved June 9, 2014, from Annie Sprinkle: http://anniesprinkle.org.

41 Levy, A., 'The Prisoner of Sex' (n.d.). Retrieved June 9, 2014, from *New York Magazine*: http://nymag.com/nymetro/news/people/
features/11907/.

42 Levy, A. (2006), *Female Chauvinist Pigs: Women and the Rise of Raunch Culture* (p. 168–9). New York: Free Press.

43 Ibid. (pp. 162, 169, 199).

44 Ibid. (pp. 163–4).

45 Hastings, C. (2014, April 26), 'Germaine Greer: Twitter Trolls and Online Porn Mean We've Never Had it so Bad as Women'. Retrieved June 9, 2014, from *Daily Mail*: http://www.dailymail.co.uk/news/
article-2614067/Germaine-Greer-Twitter-trolls-online-porn-mean-weve-never-bad-women.html.

46 Cohen, N. (2014, April 7), 'You Sexist/Racist/Liberal/Elitist Bastard! How Dare You?'. Retrieved May 8, 2014, from the *Spectator*: http://
blogs.spectator.co.uk/nick-cohen/2014/04/
you-sexistracistliberalelitist-bastard-how-dare-you/.

47 Hess, A. (2014, April 3), 'Mississippi Sex Ed Class Compares Women to Dirty Pieces of Chocolate'. Retrieved May 8, 2014, from Slate: http://
www.slate.com/blogs/xx_factor/2014/04/03/mississippi_
sex_ed_class_compares_women_to_dirty_peppermint_patties.

48 Boardman, M. (2014, April 24), 'Beyonce Covers Time's 100 Most Influential People Issue'. Retrieved May 22, 2014, from *US Weekly*:
http://www.usmagazine.com/entertainment/news/beyonce-covers-times-100-most-influential-people-issue-2014244. See also: http://time.
com/time100-2014/.

49 Jones, R., 'Why Is Everyone Getting Naked? Rashida Jones on the Pornification of Everything' (n.d.). Retrieved April 30, 2014, from *Glamour*: http://www.glamour.com/entertainment/2013/12/
rashida-jones-major-dont-the-pornification-of-everything.

50 Moran, C. (2012), *How to Be a Woman* (p. 301). New York, NY: Harper Perennial.

51 Levy, A. (2006), *Female Chauvinist Pigs: Women and the Rise of Raunch Culture* (p. 200). New York: Free Press.

52 McFadden, C. and Whitman, J. (2014, March 10), 'Sheryl Sanberg Launches "Ban Bossy" Campaign to Empower Girls to Lead'. Retrieved

April 28, 2014, from *Good Morning America*, ABC News: http://abcnews.
go.com/US/sheryl-sandberg-launches-ban-bossy-campaign-empower-
girls/story?id=22819181.

53 Note: *Cosmopolitan, Glamour, Redbook, Seventeen, US Weekly, InStyle,
Shape, Self, Weight Watchers, Vogue, Vanity Fair, Allure, Elle, Lucky, Teen
Vogue* and *Marie Claire* all ranked higher than *Forbes*, the *Economist* and
Working Mother in magazine circulation.

See: *Total Circ: Consumer Magazines* (n.d.). Retrieved April 30, 2014, from
Alliance for Audited Media: http://abcas3.auditedmedia.com/ecirc/
magtitlesearch.asp.

54 Note: *Good Housekeeping, Woman & Home, OK! Magazine, Cosmopolitan,
HELLO!, Prima* and *Marie Claire* all had more subscribers than any
version of the *Economist* (the continental Europe edition had 246,451
subscribers and the UK edition had 217,265 subscribers).

See: *PPA Combined Circulation Chart (CCC)* (2013, February 14). Retrieved
October 10, 2014, from the Professional Publishers Association (PPA):
http://www.ppa.co.uk/marketing/abc/
abc-combined-circulation-chart/.

55 Gilbert, E. (2010), *Committed: A Skeptic Makes Peace With Marriage* (pp.
188–9). New York, NY: Penguin Group, Inc.

56 Pryor, J.H., et al. (2013, January), *The American Freshman: National Norms
Fall 2012* (pp. 14–15). Retrieved June 11, 2014, from the Higher
Education Research Institute, the Cooperative Institutional Research
Programme, University of California, Los Angeles: http://www.heri.
ucla.edu/monographs/TheAmericanFreshman2012.pdf.

14. Patriarchy Myths

1 Brand, N. (2013, July 18), 'Men Must Be Needed Because We Can't Be
Wanted'. Retrieved June 17, 2014, from the Good Men Project: http://
goodmenproject.com/ethics-values/
brand-men-must-be-needed-because-we-cant-be-wanted/.

2 Planty, M., et al., US Department of Education, Institute of Education
Sciences (2009), *The Condition of Education 2009* (NCES 2009-081), 118.
Retrieved from National Center for Education Statistics: http://nces.
ed.gov/pubs2009/2009081.pdf.

3 Livingston, G. (2014, June 5), *Growing Number of Dads Home with the
Kids*. Retrieved June 7, 2014, from Pew Research Center: http://www.
pewsocialtrends.org/2014/06/05/
growing-number-of-dads-home-with-the-kids/.

4 Planty, M., et al., US Department of Education, Institute of Education
Sciences (2009), *The Condition of Education 2009* (NCES 2009-081), 99,

101. Retrieved from National Center for Education Statistics: http://nces.ed.gov/pubs2009/2009081.pdf.

5 'GCSE Results 2013: The Complete Breakdown' (2013, August 22). Retrieved October 10, 2014, from the *Guardian*: http://www.theguardian.com/news/datablog/2013/aug/22/gcse-results-2013-the-complete-breakdown.

6 Farrell, W. (2001), *The Myth of Male Power: Why Men are the Disposable Sex* (p. 34). New York: Berkeley Books.

7 Retrieved May 20, 2014, from Scholarships.com: https://www.scholarships.com.

8 Kornrich, S. and Furstenberg, F. (2013), 'Investing in Children: Changes in Parental Spending on Children, 1972–2007' (pp.19–20), *Demography*, 50(1). Retrieved June 7, 2014, from http://www.ncbi.nlm.nih.gov/pubmed/22987208.

9 Kitroeff, N. (2014, February 7), 'Investing (More) in Daughters'. Retrieved June 5, 2014, from *New York Times*: http://www.nytimes.com/2014/02/09/education/edlife/investing-more-in-daughters.html?_r=0.

10 Hartmann, H. (1976), 'Capitalism, Patriarchy, and Job Segregation by Sex', *Women and the Workplace: The Implications of Occupational Segregation*, 1(3). Retrieved May 22, 2014, from http://www.jstor.org/discover/10.2307/3173001?uid=3739632&uid=2&uid=4&uid=3739256&sid=21104059578957; and Reilly, K. (1995), *Readings in World Civilizations*. New York, NY: St Martin's Press. See Elise Boulding's essay, 'Women and the Agricultural Revolution', pp. 21–5.

11 *Life Expectancy: Life Expectancy Data by World Bank Income Group* (n.d.). Retrieved May 6, 2014, from Global Health Observatory Data Repository, World Health Organization: http://apps.who.int/gho/data/view.main.700?lang=en.

12 Note: Poor women will live an average of 2.6 years (5 per cent) longer than poor men, and wealthy women will live an average of 7 years (10 per cent) longer than wealthy men.

   See: Kincel, B. (2010, April), *The Centenarian Population: 2007–2011*. From American Community Survey Briefs, US Census Bureau (ACSBR/12-18).

13 Arnst, C. (2007, June 13), 'A Gender Gap in Cancer'. Retrieved May 7, 2014, from *BusinessWeek*: http://www.businessweek.com/stories/2007-06-13/a-gender-gap-in-cancerbusinessweek-business-news-stock-market-and-financial-advice; and Parker-Pope, T. (2008, March 6), 'Cancer Funding: Does It Add Up?' Retrieved May 7, 2014, from the *New York Times*: http://well.blogs.nytimes.com/2008/03/06/cancer-funding-does-it-add-up/?_php=true&_type=blogs&_r=0.

14 Murphy, S.L., Xu, J., and Kochanek, K.D. (2013, May 8), *Deaths: Final Data for 2010*. Retrieved May 22, 2014, from National Vital Statistics

Reports, Centers for Disease Control and Prevention: http://www.cdc.
gov/nchs/data/nvsr/nvsr61/nvsr61_04.pdf.

15 *Suicide: Facts at a Glance* (2012). Retrieved June 20, 2014, from National
Center for Injury Prevention and Control, Division of Violence
Prevention, Centers for Disease Control and Prevention: http://www.
cdc.gov/violenceprevention/pdf/suicide_datasheet-a.pdf.

16 Siddique, H. (2014, February 18), 'Male Suicide Rate in UK Discovered
to be 3½ Times That of Women'. Retrieved October 13, 2014, from the
Guardian: http://www.theguardian.com/society/2014/feb/18/
male-suicides-three-times-women-samaritans-bristol.

17 *Census of Fatal Occupational Injuries Summary, 2012* (2013, August 22).
Retrieved May 6, 2014, from Bureau of Labor Statistics, US Department
of Labor (USDL-13-1699): http://www.bls.gov/news.release/cfoi.nr0.htm.

18 *Reported Injuries to Men Employees in Great Britain by Age of Injured Person
and Severity of Injury* (2013, October). Retrieved October 13, 2014, from
Health and Safety Executive: http://www.hse.gov.uk/Statistics/tables/
index.htm; and *Reported Injuries to Women Employees in Great Britain by
Age of Injured Person and Severity of Injury* (2013, October). Retrieved
October 13, 2014, from Health and Safety Executive: http://www.hse.
gov.uk/Statistics/tables/index.htm.

19 *Who is Homeless?* (2009, July). Retrieved May 7, 2014, from National
Coalition for the Homeless: http://www.nationalhomeless.org/
factsheets/who.html.

20 'Support for Single Homeless People in England, 2014' (2014, April 24)
(p. 9). Retrieved October 13, 2014, from Homeless Link: http://www.
homeless.org.uk/sites/default/files/site-attachments/Support%20
for%20Single%20Homeless%20People.pdf.

21 Knox, B. (2014, February 21), 'I'm the Duke University Freshman Porn
Star and for the First Time I'm Telling the Story in my Words'.
Retrieved April 26, 2014, from xojane: http://www.xojane.com/sex/
duke-university-freshman-porn-star.

22 *Statistics on Women and the Criminal Justice System* (p. 16) (2010,
November). Retrieved October 14, 2014, from Ministry of Justice, Gov.
uk: https://www.gov.uk/government/uploads/system/uploads/
attachment_data/file/217824/statistics-women-cjs-2010.pdf.

23 Rutherford, T. (2014, September 26), *Defence personnel statistics* (p. 9).
Retrieved October 14, 2014, from Parliament.uk.

24 Daniels, N. (2014, January 6), 'An Open Letter to Bearded Hipsters'.
Retrieved April 26, 2014, from the Nicki Daniels Interview: http://
nickidaniels.com/2014/01/06/beardedhipsters/.

25 McCarthy, A. (2011, August 4), 'Dealbreaker: He Won't Go Down on
Me'. Retrieved April 26, 2014, from *Good: Creative Solutions for Living Well
+ Doing Good*: http://magazine.good.is/articles/

dealbreaker-he-won-t-go-down-on-me; and Michael, D., 'Dating Younger Men can be Exciting for Women in their 40's & Up' (n.d.). Retrieved April 26, 2014, from YourTango: http://www.yourtango.com/experts/dawn-michael/dating-younger-men-can-be-exciting-women-her-40-s; and (2014, September 27–October 3), 'Fare Ladies', the *Economist*, 412(8906), 33; also see: http://www.economist.com/news/united-states/21620229-new-car-service-offers-lifts-women-women-fare-ladies; and Barreca, R. (2011, November 8), 'Why Women Should Pay Lower Taxes'. Retrieved April 26, 2014, from *Psychology Today*: http://www.psychologytoday.com/blog/snow-White-doesnt-live-here-anymore/201111/why-women-should-pay-lower-taxes.

26 *Who Must Register* (n.d.). Retrieved April 26, 2014, from Selective Service System: https://www.sss.gov/FSwho.htm.

27 Cryer, P., *The Start of Peace-Time National Service in Britain* (n.d.). Retrieved October 14, 2014, from 1900s.org.uk: http://www.1900s.org.uk/1949-1960-national-service.htm.

28 Beck, A.J., Berzofsky, M., Caspar, R., and Krebs, C. (2013, May), *Sexual Victimization in Prisons and Jails Reported by Inmates, 2011–12*. Retrieved April 26, 2014, from Bureau of Justice Statistics, US Department of Justice (NCJ 241399): http://www.bjs.gov/content/pub/pdf/svpjri1112.pdf; and Berzofsky, M., Krebs, C., Langton, L., Planty, M., and Smiley-McDonald, H. (2013, March 7), *Female Victims of Sexual Violence, 1994–2010*. Retrieved April 26, 2014, from Bureau of Justice Statistics, Office of Justice Programmes, US Department of Justice (NCJ 240655): http://www.bjs.gov/index.cfm?ty=pbdetail&iid=4594.

29 Walsh, A. (2004), *Race and Crime: A Biosocial Analysis* (pp. 23–5). Hauppauge, NY: Nova Biomedical.

30 *Forcible Rape* (2011). Retrieved April 26, 2014, from Federal Bureau of Investigation: http://www.fbi.gov/about-us/cjis/ucr/crime-in-the-u.s/2011/crime-in-the-u.s.-2011/violent-crime/forcible-rape.

31 *Sexual Violence: Facts at a Glance 2012* (n.d.). Retrieved April 26, 2014, from National Center for Injury Prevention and Control, Division of Violence Prevention, Centers for Disease Control and Prevention (CDC): http://www.cdc.gov/violenceprevention/pdf/sv-datasheet-a.pdf.

32 *Male Victims of Domestic and Partner Abuse 25 Key Facts* (2014, February). Retrieved May 27, 2014, from ManKind Initiative: http://www.mankind.org.uk/pdfs/25%20Key%20Facts_Feb%202014%20(final).pdf.

33 *United Kingdom* (n.d.). Retrieved September 23, 2014, from OECD Better Life Index: http://www.oecdbetterlifeindex.org/countries/united-kingdom/.

34 *Male Victims of Violence* (n.d.). Retrieved April 26, 2014, from National Coalition Against Domestic Violence: http://www.ncadv.org/files/MaleVictims.pdf.

35 VenerableB, (2014, March 26), 'Why Rape Is Sincerely Hilarious'. Retrieved May 27, 2014, from YouTube: https://www.youtube.com/watch?v=Ikd0ZYQoDko.

36 'Attorney General Eric Holder Delivers Remarks at the Annual Meeting of the American Bar Association's House of Delegates' (2013, August 12). Retrieved April 26, 2014, from Justice News, US Department of Justice: http://www.justice.gov/iso/opa/ag/speeches/2013/ag-speech-130812.html.

37 Gold, A.R. (1989, July 2), 'Sex Bias Is Found Pervading Courts'. Retrieved April 26, 2014, from the *New York Times*: http://www.nytimes.com/1989/07/02/us/sex-bias-is-found-pervading-courts.html.

38 'Men Sentenced To Longer Prison Terms Than Women For Same Crimes, Study Says' (2012, September 11). Retrieved April 26, 2014, from Huffington Post: http://www.huffingtonpost.com/2012/09/11/men-women-prison-sentence-length-gender-gap_n_1874742.html.

39 Farrell, W. (2001), *The Myth of Male Power: Why Men are the Disposable Sex* (p. 244). New York: Berkeley Books.

40 *Female Offender Programs and Services* (n.d.). Retrieved April 26, 2014, from California Department of Corrections & Rehabilitation: http://www.cdcr.ca.gov/Adult_operations/FOPS/index.html.

41 *Prison: The Facts* (pp. 3–5) (2013). Retrieved October 14, 2014, from Prison Reform Trust: http://www.prisonreformtrust.org.uk/Portals/0/Documents/Prisonthefacts.pdf.

42 *Daily Hansard – Westminster Hall*. Retrieved April 26, 2014, from House of Commons Hansard Debates for October 16, 2012 (pt 0002), United Kingdom Parliament: http://www.publications.parliament.uk/pa/cm201213/cmhansrd/cm121016/halltext/121016h0002.htm.

43 *Prison: The Facts* (pp. 1, 5, 8, 9) (2013). Retrieved October 14, 2014, from Prison Reform Trust: http://www.prisonreformtrust.org.uk/Portals/0/Documents/Prisonthefacts.pdf.

44 Sylla, M., Harawa, N., and Reznick, O.G. (2010), 'The First Condom Machine in a US Jail: The Challenge of Harm Reduction in a Law and Order Environment', *American Journal of Public Health*, 100(6). Retrieved April 26, 2014, from http://www.ncbi.nlm.nih.gov/pmc/articles/PMC2866591/.

45 Farrell, W. (2001), *The Myth of Male Power: Why Men are the Disposable Sex* (p. 107). New York: Berkeley Books.

46 Crooke, C. (2013, June), 'Women in Law Enforcement'. Retrieved April 10, 2014, from COPS e-newsletter, US Department of Justice: http://cops.usdoj.gov/html/dispatch/07-2013/women_in_law_enforcement.asp; and *Preventing Law Enforcement Officer Suicide*. Retrieved April 10, 2014, from International Association of Chiefs of Police: http://www.theiacp.org/Preventing-law-Enforcement-officer-suicide.

47 Christakis, E. (2012, October 4), 'Why Are Women Biased Against Other Women?' Retrieved April 10, 2014, from *Time*: http://ideas.time.com/2012/10/04/womens-inhumanity-to-women/; and Pollack, E. (2013, October 3), 'Why Are There Still So Few Women in Science?' Retrieved April 10, 2014, from the *New York Times*: http://www.nytimes.com/2013/10/06/magazine/why-are-there-still-so-few-women-in-science.html?pagewanted=1&_r=5&.

48 *The Myth of the 'Queen Bee': Work and Sexism* (2011, June 20). Retrieved December 4, 2014, from Association for Psychological Science: http://www.psychologicalscience.org/index.php/news/releases/the-myth-of-the-queen-bee-work-and-sexism.html.

49 Farrell, W. (2001), *The Myth of Male Power: Why Men are the Disposable Sex* (p. 131). New York: Berkeley Books.

50 Groysberg, B. and Abrahams, R. (2014, March), 'Manage Your Work, Manage Your Life'. Retrieved April 28, 2014, from *Harvard Business Review*: http://hbr.org/2014/03/manage-your-work-manage-your-life/ar/5.

51 Gottlieb, L. (2014, February 6), 'Does a More Equal Marriage Mean Less Sex?'. Retrieved April 28, 2014, from the *New York Times*: http://www.nytimes.com/2014/02/09/magazine/does-a-more-equal-marriage-mean-less-sex.html?_r=1.

52 Moore, T. (2014, February 9), 'What if Equality Is the Biggest Bonerkiller of All?'. Retrieved April 28, 2014, from Jezebel: http://jezebel.com/what-if-equality-is-the-biggest-bonerkiller-of-all-1518482932?utm_campaign=socialflow_jezebel_facebook&utm_source=jezebel_facebook&utm_medium=socialflow.

53 O'Keefe, V. (2014, August 12), 'A Stay-at-Home Dad Reports on the Mommy Wars'. Retrieved September 23, 2014, from *Time*: http://time.com/3104852/working-moms-stay-at-home-fathers/.

15. Economic Downturn

1 'Cost of Living in the U.S. Hits Record Highs Not Seen Since Financial Crisis' (2011, March 18). Retrieved January 10, 2012, from *Daily Mail*: http://www.dailymail.co.uk/news/article-1367705/Cost-living-America-hits-record-high-according-Consumer-Price-Index.html.

2 Note: Whites are much more uncertain than minorities about what the future holds for them.

   See: Brownstein, R. (2012, January 7), 'What the Great Recession Wrought: The State of the U.S. in 3 Years of Polls'. Retrieved January 10, 2012, from the *Atlantic*: http://www.theatlantic.com/business/archive/2012/01/what-the-great-recession-wrought-the-state-of-the-us-in-3-years-of-polls/251010/.

3 McLaughlin, M.A. (1988, December), *Trends in College Tuition And Student Aid Since 1970* (p. 3), Human Resources and Community Development Division, Congressional Budget Office; and Coder, J.F. and Cleveland, R.W. (1971, July 27), *Household Income in 1970 And Selected Social And Economic Characteristics of Households* (p. 1), US Department of Commerce, Consumer Income Statistics Branch, Population Division, US Census Bureau (P60-79); and *Median and Average Sales Prices of New Homes Sold in United States* (n.d.). Retrieved April 28, 2014, from US Census Bureau: http://www.census.gov/const/uspriceann.pdf.

4 Symonds, W.C., Schwartz, R.B., and Ferguson, R. (2011, February), 'Pathways to Prosperity: Meeting the Challenge of Preparing Young Americans for the 21st Century' (p. 2). Retrieved May 30, 2014, from Report issued by the Pathways to Prosperity Project, Harvard Graduate School of Education: http://www.gse.harvard.edu/news_events/features/2011/Pathways_to_Prosperity_Feb2011.pdf.

5 Hill, A. (2011, June 17), 'The Cost of Living: 1971 v Today'. Retrieved October 14, 2014, from the *Guardian*: http://www.theguardian.com/worklifeuk/cost-of-living-1971-today.

6 *UK Labour Market, September 2014* (p. 17) (2014, September 17). Retrieved October 10, 2014, from Office for National Statistics: http://www.ons.gov.uk/ons/dcp171778_374770.pdf.

7 *UK Wages Over the Past Four Decades – 2014* (p. 11) (2014, July). Retrieved October 10, 2014, from Office for National Statistics: http://www.ons.gov.uk/ons/dcp171776_368928.pdf.

8 *Tuition Costs of Colleges and Universities, Digest of Education Statistics, 2012* (2013). Retrieved April 28, 2014, from US Department of Education, National Center for Education Statistics (NCES 2014-015): http://nces.ed.gov/fastfacts/display.asp?id=76; and *Money Income of Households, Families, and Persons in the United States* (1991, August) (p. 1), US Department of Commerce, Economics and Statistics Administration, US Census Bureau (P60-174); and *Median and Average Sales Prices of New Homes Sold in United States* (n.d.). Retrieved April 28, 2014, from US Census Bureau: http://www.census.gov/const/uspriceann.pdf.

9 Symonds, W.C., Schwartz, R.B., and Ferguson, R. (2011, February), 'Pathways to Prosperity: Meeting the Challenge of Preparing Young Americans for the 21st Century' (p. 2). Retrieved May 30, 2014, from Report issued by the Pathways to Prosperity Project, Harvard Graduate School of Education: http://www.gse.harvard.edu/news_events/features/2011/Pathways_to_Prosperity_Feb2011.pdf.

10 Ibid.

11 Greenstone, M. and Looney, A. (2011), *Trends* (p. 11). Retrieved June 8, 2014, from The Milken Institute: http://www.milkeninstitute.org/publications/review/2011_7/08-16MR51.pdf.

12 Ibid.

13 *Tuition Costs of Colleges and Universities, Digest of Education Statistics, 2012* (2013). Retrieved April 28, 2014, from US Department of Education, National Center for Education Statistics (NCES 2014-015): http://nces. ed.gov/fastfacts/display.asp?id=76; and *Median and Average Sales Prices of New Homes Sold in United States* (n.d.). Retrieved April 28, 2014, from US Census Bureau: http://www.census.gov/const/uspriceann.pdf; and DeNavas-Walt, C., Proctor, B.D., and Smith, J.C. (2011, September), *Income, Poverty, and Health Insurance Coverage in the United States: 2010* (p. 5). US Department of Commerce, Economics and Statistics Administration, US Census Bureau (P60-239).

14 *Table 47a Average Regional House Prices* (n.d.). Retrieved October 14, 2014, from University of York: http://www.york.ac.uk/res/ukhr/ukhr1011/ updates/pdf/11-047ab.pdf.

15 *Figure 1: Median Full-time Gross Weekly Earnings in Current and Constant (2012) Prices, UK, April 1997 to 2012* (n.d.). Retrieved October 14, 2014, from Office for National Statistics: http://www.ons.gov.uk/ons/rel/ ashe/patterns-of-pay/1997-to-2012-ashe-results/patterns-of-pay-2012. html#tab-Trends-in-weekly-earnings.

16 *United Kingdom* (n.d.). Retrieved September 23, 2014, from OECD Better Life Index: http://www.oecdbetterlifeindex.org/countries/ united-kingdom/.

17 Maguire, K. (2014, January 9), 'Where Do You Rank in the Official Earnings List? Figures Reveal Huge Pay Gap between Rich and Poor'. Retrieved October 14, 2014, from *Mirror*: http://www.mirror.co.uk/ news/uk-news/uk-average-salary-26500-figures-3002995.

18 Osborne, H. (2014, August 19), 'UK House Prices in June Reach New Record High'. Retrieved October 14, 2014, from the *Guardian*: http:// www.theguardian.com/money/2014/aug/19/ uk-house-prices-record-high.

19 Matthews, D. (2013, August 8), 'International and Postgraduate Student Fees Survey, 2013'. Retrieved October 14, 2014, from *Times Higher Education*: http://www.timeshighereducation.co.uk/features/ international-and-postgraduate-student-fees-survey-2013/2006262. fullarticle.

20 Hymowitz, C. (2012, January 4), 'Behind Every Great Woman'. Retrieved January 7, 2012, from *BusinessWeek*: http://www.businessweek.com/ magazine/behind-every-great-woman-01042012.html.

21 Mount, F. (2012), *Mind the Gap: The New Class Divide in Britain* (pp. 58–9, 237). Croydon: Short Books (UK) Ltd.

22 Ibid. (p. 238).

23 Ragan, M. (2011, August 1), 'Mid-Life: Change, Transition and Re-Definition'. Retrieved October 16, 2014, from Psychotherapy &

Spirituality Institute: http://mindspirit.org/articles/
mid-life-change-transition-and-re-definition/.

24 Mount, F. (2012), *Mind the Gap: The New Class Divide in Britain* (p. 52).
Croydon: Short Books (UK) Ltd.

25 Adams, R. (2014, October 5), 'Too Many Schools Fail Pupils from
Disadvantaged Backgrounds, Says Report'. Retrieved October 14, 2014,
from the *Guardian*: http://www.theguardian.com/education/2014/
oct/06/schools-fail-pupils-disadvantaged-backgrounds.

Part III

16. What the Government Can Do

1 Bush, M. (2014, January 19), 'Trust in Government Plunges to Historic
Low'. Retrieved November 24, 2014, from Edelman: http://www.
edelman.com/news/trust-in-government-plunges-to-historic-low/.

2 Retrieved November 24, 2014, from Twitter: https://twitter.com.

3 'Postsecondary Success' (n.d.). Retrieved November 24, 2014, from Bill
& Melinda Gates Foundation: http://www.gatesfoundation.org/
What-We-Do/US-Programme/Postsecondary-Success.

4 'Fractured Families: Why Stability Matters' (p. 23) (2013, June).
Retrieved October 10, 2014, from the Centre for Social Justice: http://
www.centreforsocialjustice.org.uk/UserStorage/pdf/Pdf%20reports/
CSJ_Fractured_Families_Report_WEB_13.06.13.pdf.

5 Martin, D. (2014, January 16), 'A Quarter of British Children are
being Raised by a Single Parent, New Figures Reveal'. Retrieved
October 10, 2014, from Mail Online: http://www.dailymail.co.uk/
news/article-2540974/Britain-fourth-highest-number-single-
parents-EU.html.

6 *Bisphenol-A (BPA) Frequently Asked Questions* (n.d.). Retrieved November
24, 2014, from Food Standards Agency: https://www.food.gov.uk/
science/bpa/foodcontactmaterialsbpafaq.

7 *Bisphenol A* (2014, October 27). Retrieved November 24, 2014, from
European Food Safety Authority: http://www.efsa.europa.eu/en/
topics/topic/bisphenol.htm.

8 'SF Bans Water Bottles' (2014, March 11). Retrieved November 24, 2014,
from *San Francisco Bay Guardian*: http://www.sfbg.com/2014/03/11/
sf-bans-water-bottles.

9 'Record Numbers of Men Teaching in Primary Schools – But More Still
Needed' (2012, July 6). Retrieved October 10, 2014, from Gov.uk:
https://www.gov.uk/government/news/
record-numbers-of-men-teaching-in-primary-schools-but-more-still-
needed.

10 *Overweight and Obese* (n.d.). Retrieved May 16, 2014, from Centers for Disease Control and Prevention: http://www.cdc.gov/obesity/data/adult.html.

11 'School Ditches Junk Food' (2014, September 7). Retrieved October 10, 2014, from Mail Online: http://www.dailymail.co.uk/health/article-207286/School-ditches-junk-food.html.

12 Heckman, J.J. (2011), *The Economics of Inequality: The Value of Early Childhood Education*. Retrieved June 8, 2014, from American Federation of Teachers: http://www.aft.org/pdfs/americaneducator/spring2011/Heckman.pdf.

13 OECD (2012), *Equity and Quality in Education: Supporting Disadvantaged Students and Schools* (p. 14). Retrieved June 8, 2014, from OECD Publishing: http://dx.doi.org/10.1787/9789264130852-en.

14 *PISA 2012 Results in Focus: What 15-year olds Know and What They can do with What They Know* (p. 26) (2013). Retrieved June 8, 2014, from Organisation for Economic Co-operation and Development: http://www.oecd.org/pisa/keyfindings/pisa-2012-results-overview.pdf.

15 Symonds, W.C., Schwartz, R.B., and Ferguson, R. (2011, February), 'Pathways to Prosperity: Meeting the Challenge of Preparing Young Americans for the 21st Century' (p. 26). Retrieved May 30, 2014, from Report issued by the Pathways to Prosperity Project, Harvard Graduate School of Education: http://www.gse.harvard.edu/news_events/features/2011/Pathways_to_Prosperity_Feb2011.pdf.

16 Paglia, C. (2014, March 13), 'Put the Sex Back in Sex Ed'. Retrieved September 30, 2014, from *Time*: http://time.com/23054/camille-paglia-put-the-sex-back-in-sex-ed/.

17 *What a Small Town's Teen Pregnancy Turnaround Can Teach the U.S.* (2014, March 30). Retrieved June 5, 2014, from National Public Radio: http://www.npr.org/2014/03/30/296441067/what-a-small-towns-teen-pregnancy-turnaround-can-teach-the-u-s.

18 Segal, D. (2014, March 28), 'Does Porn Hurt Children?'. Retrieved October 9, 2014, from the *New York Times*: http://www.nytimes.com/2014/03/29/sunday-review/does-porn-hurt-children.html?_r=0.

19 *A Framework for Sexual Health Improvement in England* (2013, March 15). Retrieved October 13, 2014, from Department of Health: https://www.gov.uk/government/uploads/system/uploads/attachment_data/file/142592/9287-2900714-TSO-SexualHealthPolicyNW_ACCESSIBLE.pdf.

20 Martin, D. (2014, January 16), 'A Quarter of British Children are being Raised by a Single Parent, New Figures Reveal'. Retrieved October 10, 2014, from Mail Online: http://www.dailymail.co.uk/news/article-2540974/Britain-fourth-highest-number-single-parents-EU.html.

17. What Schools Can Do

1 Symonds, W.C., Schwartz, R.B., and Ferguson, R. (2011, February), 'Pathways to Prosperity: Meeting the Challenge of Preparing Young Americans for the 21st Century', (pp. 15, 38). Retrieved May 30, 2014, from Report issued by the Pathways to Prosperity Project, Harvard Graduate School of Education: http://www.gse.harvard.edu/news_events/features/2011/Pathways_to_Prosperity_Feb2011.pdf.

2 Ibid.

3 *Single-Sex vs. Coed: The Evidence* (n.d.). Retrieved June 8, 2014, from National Association for Single Sex Public Education: http://www.singlesexschools.org/research-singlesexvscoed.htm; also see Kessels, U. and Hannover, B. (2008), 'When being a Girl Matters Less: Accessibility of Gender-related Self-knowledge in Single-sex and Coeducational Classes and its Impact on Students' Physics-related Self-concept of Ability', *British Journal of Educational Psychology*, 78 (Pt. 2). Retrieved June 8, 2014, from http://www.ncbi.nlm.nih.gov/pubmed/17535522.

4 Barsheghian, T. (2011, July 20), 'Mobile Learning: Are We on the Cusp of Something Big?'. Retrieved January 4, 2012, from KQED: http://mindshift.kqed.org/2011/07/mobile-learning-are-we-on-the-cusp-of-something-big/#more-13850.

5 Twenge, J.M. and Campbell, W.K. (2009), *The Narcissism Epidemic: Living in the Age of Entitlement* (p. 48). New York, NY: Free Press.

18. What Parents Can Do

1 Vaillant, G.E. (2012), *Triumphs of Experience: The Men of the Harvard Grant Study* (p. 126). Cambridge, MA: Belknap Press.

2 Rosin, H. (2014, March 19), 'The Overprotected Kid'. Retrieved June 25, 2014, from the *Atlantic*: http://www.theatlantic.com/features/archive/2014/03/hey-parents-leave-those-kids-alone/358631/#disqus_thread.

3 Dweck, C.S. (2006), *Mindset: The New Psychology of Success*. New York, NY: Ballantine Books.

4 Gates, R.M. (2014), *Duty: Memoirs of a Secretary at War* (pp. 14–15). New York, NY: Knopf.

5 Symonds, W.C., Schwartz, R.B., and Ferguson, R. (2011, February), 'Pathways to Prosperity: Meeting the Challenge of Preparing Young Americans for the 21st Century' (p. 3). Retrieved May 30, 2014, from Report issued by the Pathways to Prosperity Project, Harvard Graduate School of Education: http://www.gse.harvard.edu/news_events/features/2011/Pathways_to_Prosperity_Feb2011.pdf.

6 *The Good, the Bad and the Dirty: The iVillage 2013 Married Sex Survey Results* (2013, February 11). Retrieved November 24, 2014, from iVillage: http://www.ivillage.com/ married-sex-survey-results-sex-week/6-b-520245#521337.

7 Vaillant, G.E. (2012), *Triumphs of Experience: The Men of the Harvard Grant Study* (p. 218). Cambridge, MA: Belknap Press.

8 Lenhart, A., Ling, R., Campbell, S., and Purcell, K. (2010, April 20), *Teens and Mobile Phones*. Retrieved June 7, 2014, from Pew Research Center: http://www.pewinternet.org/2010/04/20/ teens-and-mobile-phones/.

9 'National Sleep Foundation 2014 Sleep In America Poll Finds Children Sleep Better When Parents Establish Rules, Limit Technology and Set a Good Example' (2014, March 3). Retrieved June 17, 2014, from National Sleep Foundation: http://sleepfoundation.org/media-center/press-release/ national-sleep-foundation-2014-sleep-america-poll-finds-children-sleep.

10 Clark, N. and Scott, P.S. (2009), *Game Addiction: The Experience and the Effects* (p. 105). Jefferson, North Carolina: McFarland & Company.

11 Wright, B. (2014, November 24), 'London is Losing Ground to New York in Battle of the Finance Centres'. Retrieved November 24, 2014, from the *Telegraph*: http://www.telegraph.co.uk/finance/11249562/London-is-losing-ground-to-New-York-in-battle-of-the-finance-centres.html.

19. What Men Can Do

1 Deem, G., personal communication, April 13, 2014.

2 Monet, V., personal communication, June 30, 2014.

3 Pavlina, S. (2007, April 9), 'Sex Energy'. Retrieved April 14, 2014, from Steve Pavlina: http://www.stevepavlina.com/blog/2007/04/sex-energy/.

4 Note: Time Bandit Calculations:

   Annual average time a teen male plays video games: Calculation is based on 13 hours per week. (Gentile, D.A., et al., 'The Effects of Violent Video Game Habits on Adolescent Hostility, Aggressive Behaviours, and School Performance,' *Journal of Adolescence*, 27 (2004): 6.)

   Learning the foundations of a new language: Per Rosetta Stone, it takes about 40 to 50 hours to complete the content in each level; there are four or five levels per language. Calculation is the average between 160 and 250 hours.

   Learning to play guitar with regular practice: According to TheGuitarLesson.com, it takes six months of regular practice to achieve an intermediate level of mastery. Calculation is based on practising 10 hours a week for six months.

Playing a sport during an intramural season: Calculation is based on 4 hours of practice and competition time per week for eight weeks.

Learning to salsa dance: According to DanceSF.com it takes about two four-week beginner courses to be good enough to dance socially. This calculation is based on 2.5 hours per class plus 2.5 hours of practice per week.

5 '10 Life Lessons From Navy SEAL Admiral McRaven's Amazing Commencement Speech' (2014, May 27). Retrieved May 31, 2014, from *Business Insider*: http://www.businessinsider.com/10-life-lessons-from-navy-seal-2014-5.

6 Kremer, W. (2013, January 3). 'Does Confidence Really Breed Success?' Retrieved June 12, 2014, from BBC News: http://www.bbc.com/news/magazine-20756247.

7 Erikson, E.H. (1994), *Identity: Youth and Crisis* (p. 19). New York, NY: W.W. Norton & Company.

8 Cameron, J. (1992), *The Artist's Way: A Spiritual Path to Higher Creativity* (pp. 9–14). New York, NY: Tarcher/Putnam.

9 Carr, N.G. (2010), *The Shallows: What the Internet Is doing to Our Brains* (p. 179). New York: W.W. Norton.

10 Vrangalova, Z. (2014, April 16), 'Bros, This Is How Your Slut-Shaming Is Backfiring. A Sex Researcher Explains'. Retrieved May 9, 2014, from Playboy: http://playboysfw.kinja.com/bros-this-is-how-your-slut-shaming-is-backfiring-a-se-1563665480.

11 *Gender Differences in Voter Turnout* (2011). Retrieved April 28, 2014, from the Center for American Women and Politics, Eagleton Institute of Politics, Rutgers University: http://www.cawp.rutgers.edu/fast_facts/voters/documents/genderdiff.pdf.

12 *United Kingdom* (n.d.). Retrieved September 23, 2014, from OECD Better Life Index: http://www.oecdbetterlifeindex.org/countries/united-kingdom/.

20. What Women Can Do

1 Sommers, C.H. (2013), *The War Against Boys: How Misguided Policies Are Harming Our Young Men* (p. 3). New York, NY: Simon & Schuster.

2 Argintar, L. (2013, November 15), 'The 50 Truths About Love And Sex Every Gen-Y Girl Must Realize'. Retrieved April 14 2014, from Elite Daily: http://elitedaily.com/women/50-truths-love-sex-every-gen-y-girl-must-realize/.

3 Rudder, C. (2014, July 28), 'We Experiment On Human Beings!'. Retrieved July 29, 2014, from OkCupid: http://blog.okcupid.com/index.php/we-experiment-on-human-beings/.

21. What the Media Can Do

1 'The Female/Male Digital Divide' (2014, March 5). Retrieved April 28, 2014, from Nielsen: http://www.nielsen.com/us/en/newswire/2014/the-female-male-digital-divide.html.

2 Smith, A. and Duggan, M. (2013, October 21), *Online Dating & Relationships*. Retrieved April 14, 2014, from Pew Research Center: http://www.pewinternet.org/2013/10/21/online-dating-relationships/.

3 Parthasarathy, N., personal communication, August 4, 2014.

4 Gallop, C. (2013, December 4), 'The Difference between Porn and #Realworldsex: an Ongoing Discussion'. Retrieved January 10, 2014, from MakeLoveNotPorn: http://talkabout.makelovenotporn.tv/2013/12/04/the-difference-between-porn-and-realworldsex-an-ongoing-discussion/.

5 Madamcurator (2013, December 5), 'I'm a Typical 24 year old guy and I Think your Site is Great'. Retrieved January 10, 2014, from MakeLoveNotPorn: http://talkabout.makelovenotporn.tv/2013/12/05/im-a-typical-24-year old-guy-and-i-think-your-site-is-great/.

6 'Gates Foundation Awards Grants to Test Ideas Ranging from using Big Data for Social Good to Inventing the Next Generation of Condoms' (2013, November 20). Retrieved August 4, 2014, from Bill & Melinda Gates Foundation: http://www.gatesfoundation.org/Media-Center/Press-Releases/2013/11/Gates-Foundation-Awards-Grants-to-Test-Ideas.

7 Bavelier, D. (2012, June), 'Your Brain on Video Games'. Retrieved June 20, 2014, from TED: http://www.ted.com/talks/daphne_bavelier_your_brain_on_video_games.

8 McGonigal, J. (2011), *Reality Is Broken: Why Games Make Us Better and How They Can Change The World* (Inside cover, pp. 219–32). New York, NY: Penguin Press.

Conclusion

1 Sedgwick, W. (1888, July), *Studies From the Biological Laboratory* (pp. 396–9), Baltimore, Maryland: N. Murray, Johns Hopkins University. Retrieved April 21, 2014, from Internet Archive: https://archive.org/details/studiesfrombiol00martgoog.

2 Turkle, S. (2012, February), 'Connected, But Alone?' Retrieved April 21, 2014, from TED: http://www.ted.com/talks/sherry_turkle_alone_together.

Recommended Resources

Books

Carr, Nicholas, *The Shallows: What the Internet Is Doing to Our Brains*, W.W. Norton & Co., 2010. theshallowsbook.com

Farrell, Warren, *The Myth of Male Power: Why Men Are the Disposable Sex*, Berkley Trade, 2001. warrenfarrell.org

McGonigal, Jane, *Reality Is Broken: Why Games Make Us Better and How They Can Change the World*, Penguin Press, 2011. realityisbroken.org

Sax, Leonard, *Boys Adrift: The Five Factors Driving the Growing Epidemic of Unmotivated Boys and Underachieving Young Men*, Basic Books, 2009. boysadrift.com

Sommers, Christina Hoff, *The War Against Boys: How Misguided Policies Are Harming Our Young Men*, Simon & Schuster, 2013.

Szalavitz, Maia and Perry, Bruce D., *Born for Love: Why Empathy Is Essential – and Endangered*, William Morrow Paperbacks, 2011.

Turkle, Sherry, *Alone Together: Why We Expect More from Technology and Less from Each Other*, Basic Books, 2011. alonetogetherbook.com

Vaillant, George E., *Triumphs of Experience: The Men of the Harvard Grant Study*, Belknap Press, 2012.

Wilson, Gary, *Your Brain on Porn: Internet Pornography and the Emerging Science of Addiction*, Commonwealth Publishing, 2014. yourbrainonporn.com

Films

Digital Nation: Life on the Virtual Frontier, directed by Rachel Dretzin. PBS Films (Frontline), 2010. pbs.org/wgbh/pages/frontline/digitalnation/

Journeyman, directed by Charlie Borden and Kevin Obsatz. MirrorMan Films, 2007. mirrormanfilms.org/film.html

The Medicated Child, directed by Marcela Gaviria. PBS Films (Frontline), 2008. pbs.org/wgbh/pages/frontline/medicatedchild/

Raising Cain: Boys in Focus, directed by Paul Stern. PBS Films, 2006. pbs.org/opb/raisingcain/

Support groups

Action on Addiction: actiononaddiction.org.uk

Computer Gaming Addicts Anonymous: cgaa.info

'No Fap' forum on Reddit: reddit.com/r/nofap/

On-Line Gamers Anonymous: olganon.org

Sex Addicts Anonymous: saa-recovery.org

Acknowledgements

With special thanks to TED Inc., Jeremy Bailenson, Roy Baumeister, Charlie Borden of MirrorMan Films, Bernardo Carducci, Geoffrey Cohen, Nick Cohen, Phil Davies, Gabe Deem, Larry F. Dillard Jr., Andrew Doan, Warren Farrell, Robert M. Gates, Cindy Gallop, Celeste Hirschman, Miranda Horvath, Ariel Levy, Jane McGonigal, Tucker Max, Ogi Ogas and Sai Gaddam, Namisha Parthasarathy, Steve Pavlina, Jeff Perera, Robert M. Putnam, Keeley Rankin, Katie Salen, Leonard Sax, P.W. Singer, Joel Stein, Sherry Turkle, Zhana Vrangalova, Mark D. White, Gary and Marnia Wilson (creators of YourBrainOnPorn.com), Paul Zak, and everyone who participated in our surveys.

The author and publishers would also like to thank the following for permission to reprint copyright material: Basic Books, a member of The Perseus Books Group, for quotations from *Boys Adrift: The Five Factors Driving the Growing Epidemic of Unmotivated Boys and Underachieving Young Men*. Copyright © 2009 by Leonard Sax; The Belknap Press of Harvard University Press for material from *Triumphs of Experience: The Men of the Harvard Grant Study*. Copyright © 2012 by George E. Vaillant; The Free Press, a Division of Simon & Schuster, Inc., for material from *Female Chauvinist Pigs: Women and the Rise of Raunch Culture*. Copyright © 2005 by Ariel Levy. All rights reserved; McFarland & Company, Inc. for material from *Game Addiction: The Experience and the Effects*. Copyright © 2009 by Neils Clark and P. Shavaun Scott, McFarland & Company, Box 611, Jefferson, NC 28640 (mcfarlandpub.com); the Penguin Random House Group Inc for material from *A Billion Wicked Thoughts: What the world's largest experiment reveals about Human Desire*. Copyright © 2012 Ogi Ogas and Sai Gaddam; the Penguin Random House Group Ltd for material from *Duty: Memoirs of a Secretary at War*. Copyright © 2014 Robert M. Gates; Simon & Schuster, Inc. for material from *The War Against Boys*. Copyright © by Christina Hoff Sommers; Short Books for material from *Mind the Gap: The New Class Divide in Britain*. Copyright © 2012 Ferdinand Mount; WGBH Educational Foundation for material from 'Digital Nation'. *Frontline*. WGBH-TV Boston, February 2, 2010. Copyright © 2010 – 2015 WGBH Educational Foundation.

Index